THE CRITICAL LEGAL POCKETBOOK

The Critical Legal Pocketbook

Edited by

Illan rua Wall, Freya Middleton, Sahar Shah and CLAW

CLAW includes

Charlotte Green
Chanel Williams
Zahra Abdul-Malik
Sukhi Ruparelia
Jemimah Geragory
Kiara McElland
Raghav Shroff
Lia Lehto
Minnona Williams

COUNTERPRESS
OXFORD

First published 2021
Counterpress, Oxford
http://counterpress.org.uk

© 2021 Illan rua Wall, Freya Middleton, Sahar Shah

Contributing authors retain copyright in their individual contributions to this book. Rights to publish and sell the book in print, electronic and all other forms and media are exclusively licensed to Counterpress Limited. An electronic version of this book is available under Creative Commons Attribution-Non-Commercial (CC-BY-NC 4.0) license. International license via Counterpress website: http://counterpress.org.uk.

ISBN: 978-1-910761-11-3 (Paperback)
ISBN: 978-1-910761-08-3 (ePDF)

Typeset in 10.5 on 12pt Sabon

Global print and distribution by Ingram

Erratum: Chapter 34 is an early draft that was printed in error. Please refer to the ebook (ISBN: 978-1-910761-08-3) for the correct and updated version of this chapter.

Contents

1. Introduction: Critical Attractions 1
   Illan rua Wall, Sahar Shah, Freya Middleton

2. Mooting 11
   ADVOCACY, LITIGATION, STRATEGY
   Christine Schwöbel-Patel

3. Thinking about Descriptions 18
   LAW & LITERATURE, LEGAL WRITING
   Marco Wan

4. On What Passes for Legal Theory 23
   LEGAL THEORY, JURISPRUDENCE
   Illan rua Wall

5. The Radical Lawyer 31
   LEGAL PRACTICE, THE BAR, ACTIVISM
   Zeenat Islam

6. Concept: A Deviant Student 52
   Stephen Connelly

7. Concept: Positivism 54
   Ben Golder

8. How to Run an Empire (Lawfully) 56
   PUBLIC INTERNATIONAL LAW, INTERNATIONAL ECONOMIC LAW
   Ntina Tzouvala

9. Law In The Anthropocene 63
   CLIMATE CHANGE, ENVIRONMENTAL ACTIVISM & LAW
   Daniel Matthews

10. Concept: Neoliberalism 70
    Jessica Whyte

11. Concept: Hegemony 72
    Henrique Carvalho

12. Controlling Refugees 74
    REFUGEE LAW, MIGRATION, INTERNAL DISPLACEMENT
    Simon Behrman

13. Law in the Climate Crisis 80
    INTERNATIONAL ENVIRONMENTAL LAW
    Sam Adelman

14. Concept: Colonialism & Imperialism 86
    Christine Schwöbel-Patel

15. Concept: Third World Approaches to International Law 88
    Rohini Sen

16. Contract Law and Empire 90
    CONTRACT LAW, LEGAL HISTORY
    Máiréad Enright

17. Unreasonable Expectations 102
    CONTRACT LAW
    Sahar Shah

18. Decentering Property Norms 118
    PROPERTY LAW, LAND LAW
    Smith Ouma

19. The Radical Fringes of Tort Law 125
    TORT LAW, LITIGATION
    Colin Murray

20. Concept: Colonial Modernity 139
    Sahar Shah

21. Concept: Power 142
    Alex Sharpe

22. The Biopolitics of Environmental Law 145
    ENVIRONMENTAL LAW, LEGAL THEORY
    Vito De Lucia

23. Law at the Intersection 151
    FEMINIST LEGAL THEORY, CRITICAL RACE THEORY
    Carolina Alonso Bejarano

24. Concept: Care and Vulnerability 160
    Vanessa Munro

25. Concept: Social Reproduction 162
    Serena Natile

26. Criminal Injustice 165
    CRIMINAL LAW, CRIMINOLOGY
    Yvette Russell

27. Making and Br(e)aking Power 179
    CONSTITUTIONAL LAW
    Angus McDonald

28. Constitutional Justice 187
    PUBLIC LAW, POVERTY LAW
    Karen Ashton

29. Concept: The State 194
    Illan rua Wall

30. Concept: Ideology 196
    Tor Krever

31. Witnessing Health Law 198
    MEDICAL LAW, HEALTH LAW
    Ruth Fletcher

32. A Living Labour of Law 206
    EMPLOYMENT LAW, LABOUR LAW
    Anastasia Tataryn

33. Human Rights as a Contested Terrain 213
    INTERNATIONAL HUMAN RIGHTS LAW
    Raza Saeed

34. Thinking Rights as Relations 223
    HUMAN RIGHTS, LEGAL THEORY
    Bal Sokhi-Bulley

35. Concept: Space 230
    Andreas Philippopoulos-Mihalopoulos

36. Concept: Strategy 232
    Stacy Douglas

37. Trusts and Kleptocracy 234
    EQUITY AND TRUSTS LAW
    Adam Gearey

38. Intellectual Property 245
    INTELLECTUAL PROPERTY LAW
    Ben Farrand

39. Money 253
    BANKING AND FINANCE LAW, LAW & ECONOMICS
    Stephen Connelly

40. Technology with Legal Education 267
    LEGAL EDUCATION, BLOCKCHAIN, LEGAL THEORY
    Robert Herian

1

Introduction: Critical Attractions

Illan rua Wall, Sahar Shah, Freya Middleton

This started as a pocketbook, we promise it did. It was going to be a little collection of ideas that could be tucked away neatly. We hoped it could be pulled out when confronted by the wall of ideology that most law schools peddle. We hoped you would look to it for different perspectives on a module you might be finding hard to grasp, or a course that felt claustrophobic. Since that initial idea, the project has expanded and now we are sure that no one is ever going to want to (or be able to) put it anywhere near their pockets. But the name has stuck because we still think it should be used as a pocketbook. This is a book that you might keep with you, that you might come back to over and again as you are confronted with new legal myths, new modes of domination or ingrained privilege. This is a pocketbook in spirit, despite its size. The editors of this book are all part of CLAW (Critical Lawyers at Warwick), we are a group of students and academics within the Centre for Critical Legal Studies at Warwick Law School in the UK and we have been working on this book project for the past couple of years. The aim of the book is to reflect the core parts of your curriculum back to you in a way that renders them different.

We hope to put your modules through a dark mirror that punctures the dull technicality, conservative dogma, and pervasive neoliberalism of legal education. So some of the chapters may seem strange or uncomfortable, to a conventional legal view. This discomfort is important to recognise and understand. We often feel frustrated when we do not see what we expect re-presented back to us. For instance, being asked to think about contemporary contract law by exploring cases around slavery or the Irish famine; or being invited to breach the rules of decorum and politeness in a moot and challenge the positionality of the judge may not be what your professors expect. But it is important to bare with this discomfort and grasp the way that these historic cases show us something essential about the way that contract law functions. To stay in the frustration and try to understand what that feeling is telling you about how you approach the world. Perhaps you will end up disagreeing, but to jump directly to antagonism without self-analysis is a problem.

The 'critical' in the title should be understood as gathering a wide variety of different types of 'critical approaches' to law. By this, we do not just mean the usual critical theories of law—Marxism, feminism, post-structuralism, post-colonialism and critical race theory, but also the critical fringes of law and literature, law and film, socio-legal studies, legal ethnography and legal geography. This pocketbook aims to give you tastes of these different forms of critical legal thinking, presenting a plurality of critical legal work. So, you might ask, what exactly unites and classifies these diverse areas or modes of enquiry as *critical*? Before we hazard any comment on this, it is important to see the danger within the question. It implies that there is some core analysis beneath feminism, Marxism, critical race theory and socio-legal theory (for instance) and this secret essence is what we call 'critical'. Instead of such a reductive view, this book suggests that it is far more productive to celebrate the plurality and variety of all of these critical approaches to law. In other words, the disunity (dissensus or non-identity) of critical legal thinking is key to its insights.

The dangers of reducing critical legal studies to a singular, essential set of ideas can be seen in the old 'critical legal studies' that was popularised in the US in the 1980s, and associated with names like Duncan Kennedy, Karl Clare, Drucilla Cornell, David Kennedy, Roberto Unger amongst others. Very quickly, and perhaps against the wishes of the primary theorists, a reductive dogma was established. Law is politics, statutes and judgments are indeterminate, and the critic should thrash juridical texts to underline their politics. These central analyses were fixed, making them easy to grasp and enticing initially. But they quickly grew stale as the limits of their analyses became apparent.[1] Sometimes your lecturers may refer to this form of critical legal studies as *everything* you need to know about critical legal thinking. In this,

---

1. Corinne Blalock, 'Neoliberalism and the Crisis of Legal Theory' 77 *Law and Contemporary Problems* (2015), 71; James Gilchrist Stewart, 'Panic at the Law School! A Critical Case for Legal Subcultures,' *Law and Critique* (2021); Peter Goodrich, 'Sleeping with the Enemy: An Essay on the Politics of Critical Legal Studies in America' 68 New York University Law Review (1993) 389.

they are performing an imperial move, essentially silencing the very different critical traditions that are found around the world. While it is much more messy to think about all these different modes and forms of critique, we want to suggest that this plurality is really important. As Connal Parsley points out, this plurality itself emerges from the radically different nature of people's experiences as they appear before the law.[2] On this, we draw inspiration from decolonial thinkers such as Walter Mignolo and Catherine Walsh,[3] who caution against texts which deploy a singular authoritative voice to define (and appropriate) the subject under consideration. We aim not to *constitute* 'Critical Legal Studies', but rather to contribute to a range of conversations that we feel can be productively thought of as *critical*. Critical legal thinking can take any of the forms you see in this book, but this is not to say that any of these perspectives are fundamentally or only 'Critical Legal Studies'.

So let us return to that question of what connects the analyses within the book as critical? Instead of identifying some core set of ideas which could be used to draw the boundary between what is authentically critical and what is not, we want to suggest that it is useful to think of a series of gravitational attractions, that draw critical (legal) thinking. In 'Critical Theory and Law' Emilios Christodoulidis points to the classical grounding of critical theory as a 'thinking that locates itself in history'.[4] This pithy diagnosis holds two connected meanings. Firstly, and most obviously, it means that whatever problem is under consideration, it will need to be historicised to be understood. So for instance, if you needed to grasp the way that human rights became the hegemonic langauge of progressive politics in the 1990s and early 2000s, you might investigate the way that it was important for the emerging neoliberal project which came to a position of hegemony in the 1990s.[5] Or if you wanted to understand how police try to contain and limit Black Lives Matter protests, you might explore the gradual development of techniques for supressing and subjugating colonised peoples and how these 'boomerang' back to the metropolitan states

---

2. Connal Parsley, 'Legal Critique in the Age of Neoliberalism' 27.4 Griffith Law Review, (2018) 386
3. Walter Mignolo and Catherine *Walsh On Decoloniality* (Duke University Press, 2018)
4. Emilios Christodoulidis, 'Critical Theory and the Law: Reflections on Origins, Trajectories and Conjunctures' in Christodoulidis, *Research Handbook in Critical Legal Studies* (2019) 5
5. See Jessica Whyte, *The Morals of the Market* (Verso, 2019), Costas Douzinas, *The End of Human Rights* (Hart, 2000)

as 'public order management'.[6] Within this historicisation, is also the importance of theorisation. Without theory, history really is 'just one fucking thing after another' as Alan Bennett paraphrases in The History Boys. But theoretical paradigms become more or less important as times change. Critical approaches to law tend to see their own thinking as historically situated—with a genealogy or intellectual history of their own. They respond to particular events with particular ideas. Some would go so far as to say that there is a limit of what is thinkable at any time. Some thinkers (like Nietzsche) might have sought to produce 'untimely' ideas, meditations that were out of their time, addressing a future that has not yet arrived. But most of the time we are stuck thinking within the bounds of our time. Jacques Rancière argues that there are limits of the sayable and the thinkable at any given moment.[7] But this does not lead to stasis. Instead, at particular ruptural moments, 'the new' can enter the scene. Rancière is interested in particular in moments of revolt or protest, but we could go much further than that and think of moments of crisis or catastrophe which often seem to reconfigure social and political relations (usually not for the better). Ultimately, the entry of the new reconfigures the world and what is thinkable and sayable. This means we require new concepts and new theories which can help make sense of it afresh. And it means that we need new histories of the present to understand what nascent aspects of the past got us into this new position.

A second site of attraction in the book is the language of 'surface' and 'depth' in thinking about political, economic, social and legal relations. On the surface of law, everything seems rosy. Lawyers are a force for good, judges are fair and unbiased, everyone gets a fair hearing, norms are neutral and can be applied in a predictable manner, the state is democratic and responsive to the demands of the populace, law restrains those who abuse their power. But beneath this calm surface, law has its monsters, and they are many; the leviathan of the state, the golems of racism and mysogyny, the hydra of coloniality, the vampire of capitalism. These are part of law, not disassociatable from it. Because, to a large extent 'Law' means 'Western law'. It need not be, but with a few fairly major exceptions, British and French law have been violently and coercively imposed on regions through colonial

---

6. See Illan rua Wall, *Law and Disorder* (Routledge, 2021), James Trafford, *The Empire at Home* (Pluto, 2020), Patricia Owens *Economy of Force* (Cambridge University Press, 2015), Stuart Schraeder *Badges without Borders* (University of California Press, 2019)
7. Jacques Rancière, 'Ten Theses on Politics', 5.3 *Theory & Event* (2001).

and neo-colonial apparatuses over the last four hundred years. In the chapters of this pocketbook, you will find these monsters lurking in the hidden patterns beneath law's rational surface: from analytics of capitalism, gender or race to the 'slow violence' of climate change or long establishment of the coloniality of western law. It is important to remember that surface/depth is a metaphor that helps you to conceptualise critical analysis of law.[8] It suggests that you will need to pay very close attention to structural patterns that become significant only when you look systemically at the way a social system emerges and functions. Many of these monsters hide in plain sight, the challenge is to look beyond their self-agrandising and pacifying explainations, and to glimpse the monstrous beneath. Your law lecturers may play the good policeman—'move along folks, nothing to see here'—but it is essential to grasp the horror.

There are lots of different ways of approaching these structures of subjection and domination. To take just three different approaches, ideology critique is one of the key traditional ways of thinking about surface and depth, legal aesthetics pays particular attention to the way law appears and how that affects its audience, and there is a growing interest in different epistemologies—particularly epistemologies of the south.[9] This latter approach is 'an engagement with the ways of knowing from the perspectives of those who have systematically suffered the injustices, dominations and oppressions caused by colonialism, capitalism, and patriarchy.'[10] Crucially, while the surface/depth metaphor is a useful place to begin with some of these approaches, the further you go with them the greater they will complicate such easy binaries.

A third centre of gravity emerges once a critical anlysis has established some structural forces at play in large scale injustice. By historicising these structures, the aim is to understand how and why they emerged. This can help us see the ways in which what appears to be an immovable (necessary) or that it could be different (contingent). The word 'contingency' is very important here. It means that something is the way that is, by virtue of countless social, epistemological,

---

8. See Luis Eslava, 'The Teaching of (Another) International Law: Critical Realism and the Question of Agency and Structure' 54.3 *The Law Teacher*, 368
9. Boaventura de Sousa Santos, *Epistemologies of the South. Justice against Epistemicide* (Paradigm Publishers, 2014).
10. Boaventura de Sousa Santos 'Epistemologies of the South and the Future' 1 *From the European South* (2016) http://europeansouth.postcolonialitalia.it (accessed 18/06/2021)

ideological, political, historic, spiritual, and affective factors—rather than any sort of logical or inherent necessity. Unpacking the elements that make something appear necessary when it is actually contingent, helps to show how the world could be different. This is particularly important in law, where the entire edifice is designed to convey a longstanding authority: the judge embodies the majesty of the state, the principle is well-established, the proceedure is habitual. Even as law changes (every decision in common law alters the fabric of the system, it adds, subtracts, intensifies or undermines), its immovable authority is apparently maintained. So establishing the conditions under which something emerged, helps to dispell the aura of necessity that law is shrouded within. However, we must also be cautious with contingency.

Just because something need not be a certain way, does not mean that it will necessarily change.[11] For instance, for centuries critics have remarked on the way that Western property law establishes a possessive individualism. As Smith Ouma shows clearly in this pocketbook, this Western imagination of property can be challenged by turning to the commons. However, this is only the first step. We must not forget (how could we) the massive global institutions founded upon a defense of private property rights. Entire legal systems have been redrawn in order to mainline this possessive individualism. In this way, contingency is deployed not to produce a better world, but to destroy legal systems which are percieved to be less efficient or downright hostile to global capitalism.[12] As Fleur Johns points out: 'Many mechanisms of power that prevail on the global plane thrive on contingency, rather than negate it.'[13] Thus the critical utility of contingency now that neoliberalism has achieved a hegemonic status is at least open to question. Neolberalism is like a termite, Wendy Brown insists.[14] It burrows

---

11. Susan Marks, 'False Contingency' 62.1 *Current Legal Problems* (2009) 1
12. Celine Tan, 'Reviving the Emperor's Old Clothes: The Good Governance Agenda, Development and International Investment Law', in Stephen Schill, Christian Tams, and Rainer Hofmann (eds.) *International investment law and development : bridging the gap* (Edward Elgar, 2015) 147; Tor Krever, 'The Legal Turn in Late Development Theory: The Rule of Law and the World Bank's Development Model,' 52.1 *Harvard International Law Journal* (2011), 287
13. Fleur Johns, 'On Dead Circuits and Non-Events' in Ingo Venzke and Kevin John Heller, *Contingency in International Law* Oxford University Press, 2021) 42. See also Ntina Tzouvala, 'Contingency in the History of International Law?', *Völkerrechtsblog*, 15.06.2021.
14. Wendy Brown, *Undoing the Demos: Neoliberalism's Stealth Revolution* (MIT Press, 2015) 161. For an even bleaker account of the relation between human rights and neoliberalism, see Jess Whyte, *The Morals of the Market* (Verso, 2019)

into liberal normative structures like human rights or the rule of law, consuming their interior moral and political content. Instead of ways of holding the state to account, these erstwhile liberal forms become vehicles for further marketisation. Human rights discourse is used to ensure that the free speech of corporations is protected or the rule of law become a way for multinationals to save themselves from national attempts to tax or nationalise their operations.[15]

A fourth centre of gravity around which certain critical approaches gather, is the understanding of the way law operates in and through 'culture'. To begin with, we might observe that law is a textual form of reasoning, and as such, it deploys various narrative devices in order to work as law. Law is a form of literature.[16] It just takes place in the field of pain and death as Robert Cover famously insisted.[17] We can also identify the way that law, legal actors, proceedures and problems can be represented in particular literature, theatre, TV or film. These representations can tell us about popular understandings of law, either in a straightforward narrative sense or in much more sophisticated and dynamic ways, they can grant access to socio-cultural norms and subconcsious structures.[18] But we can go further than this as well, and begin to think about the ways that law is mediated and sensed.

Consider, for instance, the role that law has played in popular discourse in the past year (2020-21). It has made conspicuous appearances in popular consciousness: the election of US president Joe Biden and ousting of Donald Trump, the way powerful investors are set to profit from the COVID-19 pandemic at the expense of communities in the Global South, the massive popular unrest in Colombia in May and June, the treatment of US pop singer Britney Spears at the hands of her father, the scandal that the Amazon rainforrest is now emitting more carbon then it absorbs, and the racially-characterised treatment of Meghan Markle by the UK media. These are not simply legal cases

---

15. Illan rua Wall, 'Neoliberal Termites and Zombie Human Rights' in Bethania Assy, *Human Rights: Between capture and emancipation* (PUC Press, 2021) (in Portuguese: 'Cupnis Neoliberalais e Direitos Humanos Zumbis' in Assay, *Direitos Humanos entre Captura e Emancipação*)
16. Costas Douzinas and Adam Geary, *Critical Jurisprudence* (Hart, 2005)
17. Robert Cover, 'Violence and the Word' 95 *Yale Law Journal* (1986) 1601
18. William MacNeil *Lex Populi: The Jurisprudence of Popular Culture* (Stanford University Press, 2007); Cassandra Sharp and Marett Leiboff *Cultural Legal Studies* (Routledge, 2016); Mónica López Lerma *Sensing Justice Through Contemporary Spanish Cinema* (Edinburgh University Press, 2020); Marco Wan, *Film and Constitutional Controversy* (Cambridge University Press, 2021)

that are neutrally reported in the media. Instead the way that these cases are taken up and deployed in the media (the way they are 'mediatised') is part of the legal phenomenon itself. In other words, we can think of law as more than an isolated case or event. Instead we must see that law also encompasses the ways it is communicated, received, reacted to and ultimately entered into a broad cultural repretoire. In this way, law is not just some abstract force, it is also sensed.[19] It is grasped by an audience through ideological forms and cultural scripts that are vaguely familiar to all within a particular culture. Effective legal stories have expectations about baddies getting their dues, and goodies getting justice. There will be heros and villains. One of the most original accounts of this is in Elisabeth Anker's *Orgies of Feeling*. There Anker argued that we could understand major politico-legal events like the US 'war on terror', by analysing the genre in which they were cast.[20] She insisted that melodrama typified the genre expectations and character types that were created and intensified by political and legal actors. And these aesthetic forms helped to shape the public reaction and understanding of that apparently never-ending war.

This broader understanding of cultural legal studies is not just some elite aesthete form of analysis. Cultural understandings of the role of law, of what can be achieved or how it can destroy are essential if we are ever to understand the dynamics of social and political change.[21] A particularly clear example of this is the murder of George Floyd, the Black Lives Matter protests that it sparked and the subsequent successful prosecution of his murderer—the police officer Derek Chauvin. As Matt Tabbi shows in *I Can't Breathe* the cultural scripts are well established for minimising and invisibilising the death of black people in the US .[22] He shows how Eric Garner's death in 2014 was minimised

---

19. See Andrea Pavoni et al, *Taste* (University of Westminster Press, 2018). See also the collection of papers on law and sense: Mairead Enright and Tina Kinsella, 'Legal Aesthetics in the Touching Contract' *Law Culture and the Humanities* (Forthcoming), Alison Young, 'Arrested Mobilities' *Law Culture and the Humanities* (forthcoming), Olivia Barr, 'How to Notice Kaleidoscopic Legal Places', *Law Culture and the Humanities* (forthcoming), Illan rua Wall, 'The Ordinary Affects of Law' *Law Culture and the Humanities* (forthcoming), and Daniel Matthews, 'Law and Aesthetics in the Anthropocene' *Law Culture and the Humanities* (forthcoming).
20. Elisabeth Anker, *Orgies of Feeling* (Duke University Press, 2014)
21. It is worth your time exploring the work of Stuart Hall on these questions. In particular, for cultural legal studies, the extraordinary book: Stuart Hall, Brian Roberts, John Clark, Tony Jefferson, Chas Critcher *Policing the Crisis: Mugging the State, and Law and Order* (Macmillan 1978)
22. Matt Tabbi, *I Can't Breathe: The Killing that Started a Movement* (W. H. Allen,

by emphasising his petty criminality, complex familial situation and longstanding issues with the authorities. At the same time, there were cultural scripts at play that rendered the complaints against the police officer who killed Garner invisible and deemed the system of racialised overpolicing as irrelevant. That minimization and invisibilisation of the state killing of black people is precisely a problem of popular legal culture. And that field of analysis can therefore also help us grasp the ways that new cultural formations emerge in which police killings might not be left to disappear (at least not without a fight). The growing sense of a movement for racial justice and against police brutality, led by the black community, began to disrupt these scripts by making visible their fabrications, their silences and innuendos. The anger, mourning and solidarity that were staged through the protests began to create different expectations about policing racialised communities. The stories George Floyd, Eric Garner, Breonna Taylor and Trayvon Martin, are not isolated events. They are connected together through an understanding of structural racism. The ways in which this culture of anti-racism takes hold and challenges the invisibilisation of black life and death forms a new part of the legal story. And thereby it changes the course of the events themselves.

A final gravitational site pulls at many of the pieces in this pocketbook is how to use law to resist modes of domination, discipline and impoverishment. In a sense, it is only possible to get to this strategic question—the *how to* rather than the *against what* of resistance—by first having a solid understanding of the state of the partiular situation. Understanding the situation (how it emerged, how it can be conceptualised and why it is significant) is key to identifying the ways that it might be changed. Strategy is the name for the overarching analysis of the nature of the change, and tactics are the different ways in which it might be possible to effect that change.[23] Ultimately, strategy is future-looking in the sense that it seeks to grasp what is possible in the future and work towards it in the present.

~~~~~~~~~~~~

Before you begin the book, let us briefly say something about the way it is structured. We have primarily focused on the undergraduate

---

2017)
23. Rob Knox 'Strategy and Tactics' 21 *Finnish Yearbook of International Law* (2012), 193

curriculum. We have not separated out or specifically labelled feminist, post-structural, Marxist, post-colonial or anarchist legal critique. Instead we have grouped together chapters that speak to one another, sharing concerns and ideas. We might call this an immanent (rather than transcendent) structure. That means that the structure comes from within the chapters and from the shared concerns amongst them. To try to amplify this structure we have identified a number of important concepts and phenomena. These range from particular theoretical analyses (vulnerability, social reproduction, third world approaches to international law) to analyses of particular phenomena (the state, imperialism, neoliberalism, modernity). We will also connect these concepts and phenomena to particular chapters. We have asked our comrades and collaborators to write their contributions in ways that might help undergraduates and curious secondary school students. Some are clearly aimed at first year students, others are for those who are coming to the end of their time as an undergraduate. Wherever you are in your studies, we hope you get something out of this pocketbook.

2

Mooting

ADVOCACY, LITIGATION, STRATEGY

Christine Schwöbel-Patel

Mooting is a key part of legal education, particularly for those interested in pursuing a career in litigation. The vast majority of personal reflections on mooting exercises and competitions are decidedly positive. Typically, such reflections stress how mooting can help 'build confidence in public speaking, general research, and presentation skills'.[1] Reflections also often praise the camaraderie between team mates.[2] This may be true, but what is not problematised, particularly for students sensitive to critiques of law in its social, economic, and cultural context, is that mooting is also the *play-acting of integration into the institutionalised inequalities of the law*. Viewed primarily as a space in which oratory is practiced, the moot court as a space of reproduction of privilege remains untested. A critical take on mooting therefore not only necessitates the making explicit of this reproduction in the context of the neoliberal order, it must also consider forms of disrupting it.

Although there are different mooting models, all moots share common features: Mooting involves the arguing over points of law only; the participants work in teams; the 'judges' have a dual role of

---

1. 'What is Mooting', *Oxford University Press,* accessed 13 August 2020, https://global.oup.com/ukhe/mooting/whatismooting/?cc=gb&lang=en&.
2. Sarah Baksh, Kara John and Matthew Chin Barnes, 'A Caribbean Perspective About Participating in the 2020 John H. Jackson Moot Court North American Round in the Middle of the COVID-19 Pandemic' *Afronomicslaw.org,* 26 April 2020, accessed 13 August 2020, https://www.afronomicslaw.org/2020/04/26/a-caribbean-perspective-about-participating-in-the-2020-john-h-jackson-moot-court-north-american-round-in-the-middle-of-the-covid-19-pandemic/

participating in the play-acting and as observers and scorers of the teams; mooting is a competition with winners and losers; and it is immersive play-acting. Apart from these constitutive features of a moot, there are other common features, 'softer' ones. These 'softer' features include expectations around intonation and posture, smart dress and solemnity—the imitation of an ideal-type advocate. 'Softer' features of a moot are not simply 'decorative' alongside the points of law presented by mooters; they have a structuring function in the reproduction of privilege.

The Fictitious Neutrality of Law

Before turning to a closer analysis of the ideal-type advocate, let us begin with the approach to *law* favoured in moots. In mooting competitions, points of law are argued from a positivist perspective, meaning first and foremost that the law- and norm-making process is left out of the picture. Questions of who makes laws, whose voices are typically amplified, and whose interests are commonly favoured are deemed irrelevant. The adherence to legal positivism reproduces the myth of the neutrality of the law. Commitments to a supposed neutrality of law produce a fictitious binary between politics and law—whereby this often takes the form of law being utilised to 'tame' excesses of politics. The very first lessons drawn from critical theory (as will be evident in many chapters in this Handbook) question the purported neutrality of law. Mooters must ignore the rich traditions of critiquing inequalities hidden through law's supposed neutrality. As Wouter Werner observes in his reflection on moot courts, mooting mostly means 'leaving behind many of the critical skills that should make up academia', and, one might add, a legal practice too.[3] This creates a problematic binary between 'law for practice' and 'law for academia'. For sure, strategic litigation relies in large part on playing along with the myth of law's neutrality and adhering to court decorum in order to achieve the legal outcome that may prove tactically beneficial for the marginalised party. But the reproduction of law's neutrality and the imitation performed at the moot has arguably more far-reaching effects of exclusion, unsettling some of the assumptions around strategic litigation.

---

3. Wouter Werner, 'Moot Courts, Theatre and Rehearsal Practices', in *Backstage Practices of Transnational Law*, ed. Lianne Boer and Sofia Stolk (Routledge, 2019), 157.

Mooting Decorum, or 'Aesthetic Expressions of Respect for The Established Order'

From the unspoken, and yet central, positivist approach to law adopted in moots, we turn to the 'rules of decorum'. These rules are passed down from one mooting generation to another and are mentioned explicitly in mooting handbooks and guidelines. Whilst described above as 'softer' features, they are by no means secondary. The formality of addressing the judge and the opponent are elevated to criteria which can impact the scores of a mooting contestant in the same way as points of law. Some mooting guidelines begin with decorum, and many go into great detail, including the length of skirts and heels permitted for female contestants. 'Neutral colours' and 'plain' clothes are frequently referenced as preferable.[4] Such rules on appropriate dress and behaviour represent the emulation of an imagined ideal-type advocate: This ideal-type is usually male, white, with an expensive education—someone who has long learned to command the attention of others. Authority is expressed through language, mannerisms and dress. An air of vanity and conceit, whilst maintaining solemn deference to the judge at all times, is common. Indeed, solemnity is a key part of the performance of an ideal-type advocate (and hence moot court participant). From the prime position of the judge, to the dark robes, to the speech inflections, the rituals of solemnity create an atmosphere of a grave situation. Politically, the idea of law as the solemn upholding of state power has been accompanied by a campaign for positive associations of 'law and order', routinising and naturalising the coercive power of the state.[5] The speaking on behalf of the law on the one hand and the 'softer' aspects of imitation on the other hand culminate in what anti-imperialist thinker Franz Fanon described as 'aesthetic expressions of respect for the established order'.[6] The biases of class, race and gender are consequently expressed and reproduced not only through a fictitious neutrality of the law but also through 'decorum'.

---

4. For example: 'Mooting' in *The English Legal System*, 17th ed. (Routledge, 2016-2017), Online website which supports book: accessed 7 September 2020, https://routledgetextbooks.com/textbooks/9781138944459/mooting.php
5. On the political origins of law as the solemn upholding of the coercive state in the UK, see Stuart Hall, '1970: Birth of the Law and Order Society' in *Stuart Hall: Selected Political Writings*', ed. Sally Davison, David Featherstone, Michael Rustin and Bill Schwarz (Lawrence and Wishart, 2017), 158-171, particularly 165.
6. Franz Fanon, *The Wretched of the Earth* (Penguin Classics, 2001, originally published 1961), 29.

Exclusions in Action

Expectations on law students to imitate an ideal-type advocate create biases in favour of students who demonstrate a willingness to submit to and reproduce existing privileges. Necessarily, expectations place a higher burden on students who may not feel comfortable wearing a suit, who speak with a dialect from the 'periphery', or who have learned to question the authority of judges due to structural inequalities they have experienced. Bias not only works backwards (based on what a student brings to the moot); it also works forwards in terms of conditioning a young generation of lawyers in how to approach the law. With the appropriate dress, mannerisms, and deference to legal authority, the aspiring lawyer slips onto the side of the powerful. If they had intended to defend the interests of a marginalised group in the legal forum, they are already undergoing a process of distancing from said group.

These biases can be illustrated through the dynamics of *international* mooting competitions in particular. International legal institutions that are fora for international mooting competitions (such as the International Court of Justice and the International Criminal Court) often understand themselves as adopting a stance of legal humanitarianism. But the emulation of the ideal-type advocate and the pretence of law's neutrality creates of fiction of the equity of positions: The interests of Western powerful states are placed vis-a-vis the interests of states in the Global South as though these were two equal positions. The moot, like the 'real thing', therefore renders the unequal power and negotiating positions of Global South states invisible through the fiction of equal legal opponents. Its significance not only lies in the mimicking of unequal positions; it also *reproduces* these for younger generations. In mooting competitions, Western standards of courtroom decorum are expected of all participants. When lawyers from the Global South emulate the established order, the exploited are placed on the side of the Other, of dissent; and at worst on the side of illegality. Not only does the moot normalise the rendering invisible of the inequality of arms between states, it also depoliticises it. In the 21st century, the politics of the depoliticisation of law has been solidified for law students under the term of 'professionalism'. To enact the solemnity of law and to invoke law and order is for today's mooters to act, not politically, but *professionally*.

The Competition

Closely related to 'professionalism' is the notion of being 'competitive'. And it is here that we encounter what makes mooting distinct within the contemporary neoliberal order. One might consider the moot as a theatre of law to be a century-old tradition around story-telling and morality—as many scholars of law and literature do. However, there is something specific about the abundance of mooting competitions in the 21st century. The growth in new competitions and the growth in importance of existing competitions speaks to the centering of *competitiveness* as the organising structure of the neoliberal order. Competitions are about gaining superiority over a similar good or service in an open market system. Once dominant in the sphere of the market of exchangeable goods, competition has since become normalised in areas previously reserved for the public sphere such as education, healthcare, and provision of essential goods such as clean water or a secure environment.

The importance of mooting competitions is symptomatic of marketised higher education. Mooting requires teams from different universities to compete against one-another. Generally, only one team per university is permitted to take part. A 'win' is also considered a win for the reputation of the university, and therefore a win for marketing the law school to prospective fee-payers. Not only the 'win' of the competition itself is important; all skills are placed within this competitive frame: Prizes for 'best oralist' and 'best memorials' are commonly awarded. 'Best dressed' not yet. The commodification of these skills carries through to the individual candidate, who presents these 'wins' as distinguishing features on their CVs. Often, quite rightly so, as these competitions are tough. However, what is then made sellable is the ability to compete on the grounds set out above: How well can one maintain the pretence of the neutrality of law and how well can one emulate the ideal-type advocate?

A Strategy of Rupture

What would an advocacy exercise look like that is not an imitation of the existing hegemonic structures and that consequently does not reproduce privilege within the neoliberal order, instead unsettling existing privileges? Fanon famously declared: 'Humanity is waiting for something other from us than such an imitation, which would be almost an obscene caricature'.[7] We might, for example, take inspiration from the idea of the trial of rupture and translate this into mooting. The trial of rupture moot considers ways in which legal tools can be used to highlight structural inequalities.

A strategy of rupture has most successfully been pursued in criminal trials, incorporating the tactic of 'sacrificing' the defendant. Defence is no longer an objective here; instead the exposure of the political power behind the court is the objective. A famous lawyer who pursued a 'strategy of rupture' in the courtroom, was radical French lawyer Jacques Vergès.[8] Invariably called 'terror's advocate' or 'devil's advocate' because of his notorious defendants, Vergès believed that some trials must 'shift the events to outside the courtroom and win over public opinion for the defendants.'[9] Vergès relished the opportunity of holding a mirror to the powers constituting the court, unsettling impressions of the neutrality of the court, and the bench. Vergès was by no means the first to use the legal tactic of rupture in and outside of the courtroom for anti-imperial means.

Early 20th century revolutionary Rosa Luxemburg also used the public space of the courtroom and the attention of the media as a political opportunity, when she was accused of slandering the German army. Together with her lawyer Paul Levi, Luxemburg utilised the attention on the trial as a means to put the German Minister of War on the spot, calling over a thousand witnesses to speak on army brutality.[10] The attendant public attention, which Levi and Luxemburg courted and welcomed, allowed for the debate about anti-militarism and anti-imperialism to spill over into a broader domain. For Luxemburg, Levi and others in the Social Democrat Party (before it split precisely on the point of militarism), there was no neutrality of the law or procedural even-handedness in the courtroom. Historian Henning Grunwald, observes that for them trials did not present a level playing field—despite illusions of it—but presented a key arena of the class struggle, a political battlefield.[11]

---

7. Franz Fanon, *The Wretched of the Earth*, 254.
8. Jacques Vergès, *De la stratégie judiciaire*, [1968] (Les Éditions de Minuit,1981).
9. 'Interview with Notorious Lawyer Jacques Vergès: 'There Is No Such Thing as Absolute Evil'', *Spiegel Online*, 21 November 2008, accessed 13 August 2020, www.spiegel.de/international/world/interview-with-notorious-lawyer-jacques-verges-there-is-no-such-thing-as-absolute-evil-a-591943.html
10. Henning Grunwald, *Courtroom to Revolutionary Stage: Performance and Ideology in Weimar Political Trials* (Oxford University Press, 2012), 18.
11. Grunwald, *Courtroom to Revolutionary Stage*.

A strategy of rupture theatrically seeks to *unmask* the assumption of the separation of the political and the legal for the purposes of anti-imperialism.[12] Based on the two highlighted forces which reproduce hierarchies in mooting (neutrality of law and decorum), a strategy of rupture in a moot would seek to forcefully bring the political nature of positivist laws to the fore. As to decorum: Non-conformist, revolutionary, or indigenous dress, a range of emotions, and a diversity of linguistic inflections would no doubt disrupt the solemnity of the moot. These possibilities of rupture allow a broader profile of law students into the often exclusive sphere of mooting—notably those students who have no desire to imitate the ideal-type advocate of the elite, but intend wish to establish more radical trajectories for mooting, and ultimately for anti-imperial law in practice.

FURTHER READINGS

- Henning Grunwald, *Courtroom to Revolutionary Stage: Performance and Ideology in Weimar Political Trials* (Oxford University Press, 2012).
- Duncan Kennedy, 'Legal Education and the Reproduction of Hierarchy' (1982) 32(4) *Journal of Legal Education* 591-615.
- Ngugi Wa Thiong'o, *Decolonising the Mind: The Politics of Language in African Literature* (Heinemann Educational, 1986).
- Wouter Werner, 'Moot Courts, Theatre and Rehearsal Practices', in *Backstage Practices of Transnational Law*, ed. Lianne Boer and Sofia Stolk (Routledge, 2019) 157-173.

---

12. Christine Schwöbel-Patel, *Marketing Global Justice: The Political Economy of International Criminal Law* (Cambridge University Press, 2021), Chapter 8.

3

Thinking about Descriptions

LAW & LITERATURE, LEGAL WRITING

Marco Wan

Law is a form of language: statutes, legal arguments, and judicial opinions are unimaginable without language. This is an obvious, even banal, claim to make, but its implications are far reaching. If law is a form of language, then what might it mean to think about it in relation to other forms of linguistic and interpretative practices, such as history, philosophy, and, particularly for the purposes of this essay, literature? Some scholars have argued that lawyers, jurists, and law students should read literature because it can help us make more informed and more empathetic judgments. Other scholars have contended that law can be understood not only as a collection of rules and principles, but as a form of narrative. This latter group points out that legal advocacy has its origins in the study of rhetoric, that trials in the courtroom can be structured like dramatic performances, and that judicial reasoning is often underpinned by 'literary' figures and tropes like metaphors, similes, and repetition.

In this short essay, I want to probe the idea of law as narrative. What happens when we think about the language of law not only through the lens of legal analysis, but from the perspective of literary criticism? What if we read cases not only in light of concepts such as *stare decisis*, proportionality, or *mens rea*, but in terms of categories such as characterization, point of view, irony, or intertextuality? Would that show us something new about the way the law works, and about how legal language structures our relationship to reality?

Let us take one of these literary categories: description. Anyone who has ever picked up a nineteenth century novel will recognize that description is integral to fiction: think of the vivid portrait of the town of Verrières in the first chapter of Stendhal's *The Red and the Black*, or the memorable vision of London and the Court of Chancery in the first pages of Dickens's *Bleak House*. In part because of the importance of realist novels to literary studies, scholars of literature have spent much time reflecting on the kind of work descriptions do. Beyond English or comparative literature departments, however, description has received somewhat less attention. One reason seems to be that it is often regarded as intellectually unsophisticated: when we say that something is descriptive, we usually mean that it is the opposite of something else that is more worthy of our attention. In other words, to characterize something as 'description' is often to imply that it is *merely* description, and 'to contrast it to what it is *not*—not interpretation, not explanation, not prediction, not prescription'.[1] I have never heard a law lecturer say 'this paper is not well argued or analytical, but it is wonderfully descriptive, so I'll give it a First'. When it comes to legal judgments, too, descriptions of the facts of a case are often presented as secondary to the legal principles formulated in that case: case books typically summarize such descriptions, and include excerpts of only the 'substantive' sections of the judgment where the contours of an existing doctrine is clarified or where a change in an existing legal rule is put forward. Within legal studies, descriptions are usually taken as ancillary, as subordinate, and as the backdrop, however necessary, to the law which is the real point of our interest.

In light of the literary interest in description, let us re-open the question about why and how courts describe. Let us take an example: Lord Denning's dissent in *Miller v. Jackson*.[2] In that case, the Court of Appeal held that cricket balls flying over the boundaries of a cricket club and into the property of Mr. and Mrs. Miller constituted both negligence and nuisance. Though Lord Denning allows the appeal on the grounds that the club was willing to pay for the damage done, he disagrees with the majority's decision: he opines that 'the club were entitled to use this ground for cricket in the accustomed way. It was not a nuisance, nor was it negligent of them so to run it'. He begins his dissent with the following description of the facts:

> In summertime village cricket is the delight of everyone. Nearly every village has its own cricket field where the young men play and the old men watch. In the village of Lintz in County Durham they have their own

---

1. Sharon Marcus, Heather Love, and Stephen Best, 'Building a Better Description,' 135(1) *Representations* (2016), 1-21.
2. *Miller and another v. Jackson and Others* [1977] 3 All ER 338.

ground, where they have played these last seventy years. They tend it well. The wicket area is well rolled and mown. The outfield is kept short. It has a good club-house for the players and seats for the onlookers. The village team play there on Saturdays and Sundays. They belong to a league, competing with the neighbouring villages. On other evenings after work they practice while the light lasts. Yet now after these 70 years a Judge of the High Court has ordered that they must not play there anymore. He has issued an injunction to stop them. He has done it at the instance of a newcomer who is no lover of cricket. This newcomer has built, or has had built for him, a house on the edge of the cricket ground which four years ago was a field where cattle grazed. The animals did not mind the cricket. But now this adjoining field has been turned into a housing estate. The newcomer bought one of the houses on the edge of the cricket ground. No doubt the open space was a selling point. Now he complains that, when a batsman hits a six, the ball has been known to land in his garden or on or near his house. His wife has got so upset about it that they always go out at weekends. They do not go into the garden when cricket is being played. They say that this is intolerable. So they asked the Judge to stop the cricket being played. And the Judge, I am sorry to say, feels that the cricket must be stopped: with the consequences, I suppose, that the Lintz cricket-club will disappear. The cricket ground will be turned to some other use. I expect for more houses or a factory. The young men will turn to other things instead of cricket. The whole village will be much the poorer. And all this because of a newcomer who has just bought a house there next to the cricket ground.

The opinion is structured conventionally: it starts with the facts, before moving on to the application of the relevant legal principles to the facts. This is a passage much discussed by scholars interested in law and narrative: for instance, Bernard S. Jackson regards it as a moment in which judicial rhetoric becomes expressed in narrative form, and William Twining argues, more critically, that it is a linguistic performance 'spoiled by poor advocacy'.[3] What I want to foreground here is the work of description: far from providing a transparent window into the reality of dispute, the description frames the dispute as a scenario in which an idyllic English village comes under threat from the destructive forces of urbanization and industrialization. In this scenario, the cricket

---

3. Bernard S. Jackson, 'Narrative Theories and Legal Discourse', in *Narrative in Culture: The Uses of Storytelling in the Sciences, Philosophy, and Literature*, ed. by Christopher Nash (London: Routledge, 1990), pp.23-51 (24-26) and William Twining, *Rethinking Evidence: Exploratory Essays*, 2nd edn. (Cambridge: Cambridge University Press, 2006), p.304.

club is aligned with the peace and harmony of the village, whereas the Millers are presented as part of a commercial encroachment eradicating everything in its path. The description is not ideologically neutral but creates the factual matrix for the judge's conclusion. The boundary between the descriptive and the argumentative becomes blurred, and language fashions the world upon which the law is applied.

In the description, cricket is imagined as the backbone of the community: it is the 'delight of everyone' and brings together different generations—'the young men play and the old men watch'. The benefits of cricket are self-evident: 'nearly every village' has a cricket field. The repetition of '70 years' suggests that the sport is part of a tradition, a cultural heritage that should be protected from intrusion. The Romantic imagery further adds to the sense of the idyllic, of a world uncontaminated by the profit motive: notice the eternal 'summertime' which opens the opinion; the green fields that existed before houses were built over them; and the animals that once grazed serenely. The lazy summer is brought to an end by an abrupt temporal shift: 'Yet now ... a judge ... has issued an injunction to stop them'. What is the cause of this intrusion? The villain with no name, known only as the 'newcomer'—this word is repeated four times—'who is no lover of cricket'. This newcomer is powerful and knows how to use the law to achieve their own selfish ends, and so the judge, 'much against his will', has to stop the cricket. The description ends with the image of a dystopian future: the peace and harmony will 'disappear'; the village will be overtaken by 'more houses' or even 'a factory'; 'the young men will turn to other things' (presumably become factory workers?), and 'the whole village will be much poorer' as community, tradition, and history get edged out by greed and commercialism. This, then, is the beginning of the end: 'all this because of a newcomer who has just bought a house there next to the cricket ground'. Little wonder, then, that Lord Denning dissents from the majority.

Thinking about legal descriptions through a literary-critical lens foregrounds the role played by aspects of legal discourse that are often presented as secondary, and thereby encourages us to re-evaluate basic assumptions about the pedagogy, nature, and operation of law. Descriptions are not objective or ideologically neutral, and while they usually do not form part of the *ratio decidendi* of a case it would be a mistake to think of them as simple factual background. Descriptions, like much of law, are formed through a process of linguistic construction; they constitute part of a wider set of narratives which shape the courts', and also society's, views of guilt and innocence, liability and freedom, responsibility and irresponsibility, and, ultimately, justice and injustice. Thinking about law in light of the concepts, theories, and concerns of literary analysis can lead to a new understanding of how law structures our vision of the world.

FURTHER READINGS

- Peter Brooks and Paul Gewirtz (ed.), *Law's Stories: Narrative and Rhetoric in the Law* (New Haven: Yale University Press, 1996).
- Michael Hanne and Robert Weisberg (ed.), *Narrative and Metaphor in the Law* (Cambridge: Cambridge University Press, 2018)
- Martha C. Nussbaum, *Poetic Justice: The Literary Imagination and Public Life* (Boston: Beacon Press, 1995).
- Ravit Reichman, 'Narrative and Rhetoric', in *Law and the Humanities: An Introduction*, ed. by Austin Sarat, Matthew Anderson, and Cathrine O. Frank (Cambridge: Cambridge University Press, 2010), pp.377-398.
- Ian Ward, 'Legal Education and the Democratic Imagination,' 3(1) *Law and Humanities* (2009), 97-112.

4

On What Passes for Legal Theory

Legal Theory, Jurisprudence

Illan rua Wall

For some reason, law schools in the common law worlds (and beyond) are fixated on one strand of legal theory, and a particular question that lies at the heart of that tradition: 'What is Law?'. It might seem like a fairly straight-forward and important question—afterall (its defenders would say) how can you study law without first delineating what it is, and what it is not. But this question takes on the significance of a fetish for this strand of legal theory. And law schools fall into their trap. They build modules and degree courses around it. Students graduate thinking that this is what passes for legal theory. This essay will show you the unfortunate significance of this mistake.

'What is Law?'

If you take a Jurisprudence module you will certainly hear the 'What is Law?' question asked a great deal. It will be associated with the names Austin, Kelsen, Hart, Raz, Finnis, Dworkin, and perhaps a few more contemporary others as well. The question has proven extraordinarily important for legal philosophers coming from the 'positivist' schools of thought—those who tend to view law as a self-contained science. But it has also helped non-positivist theorists (largely from the 'analytic tradition' of Anglo-American legal philosophers) to explain their conception of legality. What unites these theorists is that they really want to be really *really* clear about what law really _really_ is… Once that question is answered (they would tell you), everyone can move on to other problems.

But, as most of these theorists also know, the exercise of reading and studying theories on 'What is Law?' rarely aims to answer how law matters in the world. Rather, the mainstream theories teach the law student a method, they discipline you into thinking of law in a particularly abstracted way. The message is that by understanding 'Law', you need to close out race, gender, sexuality, class, global inequality, and everything else that would make the exercise messy. You need to put the history of appropriation and subjection to the side, and isolate this one set of relations that we are calling 'the Law'. All the world's on pause, so that you can answer this one simple question. The problem, is that all of those histories, those inequalities, those injustices *constitute* actually existing law. If we exclude them from consideration when we think about law, we are no longer seeking to understand a social formation. Instead the 'What is Law?' theories generate a projection. It's what law might be… in the fantasies of your everyday Oxford/Harvard law professor (who is mostly male, white, and from a privileged educational background).

It is really important to note that for many people, these theories hold a certain attraction. They can be very diverting, requiring an intense effort of the mind. You have to think yourself inside them. And because they require little foreknowledge about law (its histories or the experiences of those most intensely subjected to it), it seems readily comprehensible and neat. 'The Law' seems to be a puzzle and if you can just fit all the pieces together, you might solve it for yourself. This effort of thinking gives you a feeling, a little joyous buzz as your synapses ping with connections. You feel the joy of understanding something neat, self-contained, and finite. The theories are also attractive to lecturers who hold idealised notions of 'the Law', or who feel the need to teach the cannon so that students can then understand the critique of it. This latter category is particularly familiar to me, as I have found myself (albeit with increasing agitation) within it for many years. The problem is that once hooked on the neat abstraction of law, it can be very difficult to let the world back in. In other words, the attraction turns to addiction. Students end up understanding the intricacies of the Hart/Fuller debate rather than being able to trace the dynamics of economic power, racial dominance, and patriarchy as they are threaded through their other legal subjects.

The theories will often say that 'What is Law?' is a first order question. This means that the task is simply to describe an aspect of reality. In this sense, isolating law from systemic injustice is simply a matter of describing one element of reality. Once the puzzle is solved, you are allowed back to look again at 'law in the wild'. But when you stop to think about it, it is actually quite strange to *have* to start with this sort of question. How often do you feel the need to ask yourself, 'What is a Society?' before you go out and meet your friends and acquaintances or, 'What is the Family?' before you relate to your parents and siblings? You are thrown into the world, and you find yourself always in the middle of things. The world already existed before you and you learn to exist within it. This is the same for law: you are thrown into law and you learn to exist within it and in relation to its institutions. This is to say, that you are likely to already have an inclination of your own position with relation to law. Perhaps your family is quite wealthy and you intuit that law will protect your property; maybe you know that if you were sexually assaulted there are unlikely to be prosecutions; maybe you have grown up in poverty and you have lived the power relations and precariousness of a zero-hours contract; maybe you understand that 'the Law' won't come down too heavily on you if you are caught with just a small amount of recreational drugs; maybe you know it will throw the book at you if you are carrying a knife when you are stopped and searched for the tenth time this month. Each of these are particular ways of being subjected by law. Each of your unique relations to it will contribute to your subjectivity. Because we are all always already thrown into 'the Law', each of us implicitly knows a lot about it. You have a relation to law, even if you have never specifically thought about it. On some level, you know this relation because law has given it to you. It is a gift, but not necessarily one that anyone might desire. Your relation may not be there in your conscious mind, but your body knows how to react in response to legal actors, your subconscious knows its relation to the norms and force of the state.

This is an affective and subconscious knowledge, which is to say that it is not really knowledge at all. You don't know it, but you feel it at particular moments. This feeling impacts your conscious thoughts and judgements. And if you had to think about it, you would probably be able to explain some of this attitude or inclination. This positional feeling towards the law is important to hold on to when you come to read the 'What is Law?' theories. They are very keen to exclude that sort of feeling. They seem to say, if you have to add all of these positional questions into the puzzle, it will never finally fit together. 'No,' they imply, 'it's best to just keep it simple: Let's not worry just yet about race or gender or sexuality or class, lets sort out what law really *is,* and then we can come back to those other questions.'

The critical response to this is expletive-ridden and, I'm told, unprintable.

On Attitude and Inclination

If 'What is Law?' is a first order question—a (not so simple) description of 'the Law' as it 'really' is—I want to propose a prior question. In a sense, it is really simple but it is not particularly easy to express. Maybe something like: 'What is your attitude to law?' or 'How do you feel about law?' But neither of these really get to the point. They seem to suggest that we are talking about some conscious rational thought about law, or some illegitimate emotional biases that would cloud your rational understanding of law. So by 'attitude' and 'inclination', I don't mean a conscious position or a bias that has to be overcome. I mean the relations to legality that you have found yourself enmeshed in. I mean the fact that you have already been thrown into law, and that law is always already shaping the world and our relations to it. There is no way to approach it without 'attitude' or 'inclination'.

This is important to remember, because almost universally the 'What Is Law?' theorists *like* 'the Law'—they are attracted or committed in some sense to it. They have an inclination which starts before their description of what 'the Law' is. Most 'What is Law?' theorists are broadly liberal in their politics, and a faith in law is a key tenet of liberalism. The conservatives amongst these theorists tend to also have a faith in law, although perhaps this might be a higher law or a love of authority, or indeed the type of control implied in the phrase 'law and order'. Either way, for vast swathes of people who write on the 'What is Law?' question, some sort of faith in law is essential. They are attracted to it, and keen to render it as an efficient or rational machine. This might seem like a slightly strange thing to say when people like H. L. A. Hart staked their careers on the argument that bad law (even Nazi law) was still law. But even if there was no inner morality to law, even if abhorrent law was still law, the inclination of these theorists was to identify the positive potential of law. Few have made this as explicit as Ronald Dworkin, who made an extraordinarily successful career by writing a detailed fantasy about an imaginary all-knowing judge who could always find the best possible light in which to see law, entirely collapsing law and justice together.

Few of the 'What is Law?' theorists will acknowledge their attraction to law. If they do, they tend to explain that it comes from their answer to that first order question. Something like, I love law because it is a fundamental good, it is above politics, it is neutral. They hint that the attraction stems from *what it is*. But I am suggesting that they can only come to this description of what it *is* (the first order question), based on their own prior attitude to 'the Law'. Let's face it, if someone is repeatedly stopped and publicly strip-searched because of their race, sexuality, or profession, they are unlikely to feel that the law these police deploy is entirely neutral. The idea of 'thrownness' (that we arrive always in the middle of things) insists that attitude and inclination *precedes* the description, because our attitude or inclination to law is a result of our lived experience. It is a singular expression of the social and political structures that we live through. And so, attitude and inclination are political.

What is more, the 'What is Law?' theorists do not have to acknowledge their attitude or inclination. The fairness, rationality, and legitimacy of 'the Law' are basic tenets of western liberal democratic societies. Law's goodness is 'hegemonic'. This means there is a sort of gut-feeling consensus in society about the basic value of law. It is a sort of 'obvious' position which does not need to be defended, just known. We see this when people try to protest peacefully and the police repress them with violence. Suddenly, great waves of armchair commentators will come forth to point to the danger of these few angry people in this small area of a large country. They call them 'rioters'; they discuss their 'animalistic' violence or their fundamental irrationality. And most of all they frame them as a threat to the very order of society. Irrespective of how terrible the cause that brought these people to the streets, the commentators will glorify 'the Law' (which shoots and gasses and beats these protestors). All the times these movements tried to use 'legitimate avenues' to effect change will become invisible, so too will the myriad of ways that the powerful blocked their very reasonable and piecemeal reforms. The commentators can decry the protest 'violence' (even if the police were the violent ones and the protestors were its victims) because law's goodness holds a hegemonic position in most Western societies. This makes a faith in the goodness of law very difficult to discern. It is just understood; people learn it without ever being told.

Generally speaking, critical legal theorists go against the grain of this hegemonic idea. They are suspicious of law. In the olden days (the 1980s), when critical legal studies began in the US, law schools were full of denouncements of nihilism and the bad faith of critical legal arguments. 'The Crits' (a cuss word, spat out by the academic establishment) had a 'bad attitude', apparently. It was somehow improper for lawyers not to believe in law. The Crits were happy to agree that they had an attitude, but only on condition that the mainstream should also see that their attraction was also an attitude: 'I'll show you mine, if you show me yours'.

Given that you have begun to study law, perhaps it is worth asking yourself about your gut feelings. Do you feel worry or anxiety when you see the police, or are you filled with a feeling of safety and calm? Do you look at judges and barristers and feel you don't belong, or recognise yourself in them? If your body is telling you that you don't trust them, then why would you trust the laws they make, interpret and enforce. If your body is telling you that you are going to be embraced by these arms of the state, you may want to ask whether it is just you that they look out for and whether your view would be the same if you were racially profiled, sexually assaulted, or extremely poor. Law school, as Duncan Kennedy once announced, is a 'training in hierarchy'.[1] While you learn the answers to the 'What is Law?' question (as well as many other details about law), Kennedy thought that that gut feeling about what was just or fair was gradually destroyed by the education process. In other words, in Law school you begin to lose your pre-university 'thrownness' as you are fashioned into another lawyer. Legal education is a training in legal hierarchy where you struggle to become a minor functionary of the state and/or of the structures of capital. He said that only as you truly let go of your own sense of justice would the legal profession begin to embrace you.

Suspicion

In any case, whether you trust 'the Law' or not, the critical legal attitude is to be suspicious. The first step is always to look behind the carefully crafted words and the imagined good intentions of law-makers and judges. It is important to see that the clean rational justifications that come with every judgment, have grubby, messy, and violent effects in the real world. It is important to understand that each law, each judgment, each minor administrative fiat, occurs in the context of structural injustice. Legal institutions have done immense social damage over time by amplifying and securing class, race, gender, sexuality, and ability-based discrimination, by developing rationalities that exclude the reality of those subject to oppression. And it has done this precisely as it claimed to embody the highest values of neutrality and fairness.

---

1. Duncan Kennedy, 'Law School as Training for Hierarchy' in David Kairy's *The Politics of Law* (Pantheon Books, New York, 1982), 54 (available at www.duncankennedy.net/)

James Baldwin put this particularly well, when in 1966 he said: 'I can't believe what you say... because I see what you do'.[2] His point was simply that fine words and individual good deeds should not distract from the structural violence of the racist social structure. His experience as a black man in the USA showed him the lie of white liberals' claims about racial justice. We might take this as a critical injunction: to look beyond the fine words of law; to try to see what is being hidden behind the abstract technicality of contract or criminal or public law. Baldwin's injunction is to pay attention to what is *done* by law, and not simply what it *says*. This means paying attention to the ways in which law's apparent abstract fairness disproportionately affects poor people, or people of colour, or women. For you as a law student, it means that it is *never* enough to read the case or the legislation. It is always necessary to explore the lived experience of law in whatever ways you can.

This sounds like an injunction to disregard the legal texts, but it's not. The way law frames problems is really important. The broad critical legal position is that 'law is politics, but by other means'. This means that legal texts are not just mystifications, they don't just hide what is really happening out there. They are also a different way of doing politics. For many people, politics is what happens in parliaments and capital cities around the world. It is done by politicians and lobbyists. But this critical position suggests that politics is much broader. If something is political, then it is contingent. This means that it is based on a series of positions which make it appear necessary. To say that law is political, simply means that the solid, unchanging foundation that it appears to build for itself through case law or legislation is not as solid as it seems. If something is contingent (rather than necessary), then it could be different.

To say law is political is to say that it can be remade. Domestic and international economic, political, and social systems *should* be torn down and rebuilt because they are structurally unjust—they cause untold damage to particular populations and to the planet. But of course, saying that something *could* or *should* be remade, tells us very little about the likelihood that it *will* be remade. It is necessary to see the play of power that effectively keeps unjust social structures in place. The self-protective powers of capitalism and the state are immense. Vast swathes of the world's populations are emotionally invested in social and economic systems that are destroying the earth and that render certain populations disposable. The task of the critical lawyer is to

---

2. James Baldwin 'A Report from Occupied Territory' *The Nation* (11/07/1965)

understand the role that law plays in all of this, and to try to change it. Getting stuck in the abstract and neutered 'What is Law?' question is likely to divert you from ever even seeing this task, never mind actually engaging in it now and throughout your life.

FURTHER READINGS

- Duncan Kennedy, 'Law School as Training for Hierarchy' in David Kairy's *The Politics of Law* (Pantheon Books, New York, 1982), 54 (available at www.duncankennedy.net/)
- Costas Douzinas & Adam Geary *Critical Jurisprudence* (Hart, 2005)
- Margaret Davies, *Asking the Law Question* (Thomson Reuters, 2017)

5

The Radical Lawyer

LEGAL PRACTICE, THE BAR, ACTIVISM

Zeenat Islam

I am a barrister operating within a system that I believe is fundamentally unjust not by accident but by design. I struggle with my complicity within the existing system and the enabling role I have, as a lawyer within it. Whilst I believe, there is a necessary role for lawyers to hold the state to account at every opportunity, I am less convinced about the idea of lawyers being able to make a *meaningful change* from within the current system. By 'meaningful change', I am not referring to the obvious 'wins' that we may have as lawyers and the difference we make to the lives of our clients. I am talking about the fact that in obtaining those small wins, we are navigating within and fighting against a system which does not want our client to win. Winning a case, in order to then fight again the next day, is not making meaningful change, because the arena in which we have to fight remains exactly as it was.

My journey to the Bar was motivated by an inherent sense of justice. I knew the world was unfair but in my early years I did not quite understand how the world related to me as a Brown, Muslim woman. One of my earliest recollections of experiencing racism is when I was walking home on 11th September 2001, and a boy from a local school spat the word 'Taliban' at me. This was the background that I and many others grew up in. In the shadow of 9-11 amidst the politicisation and demonisation of our faith and community. I believed being a barrister would be my way of defending my community, challenging injustice and making a difference in the world. In my youthful naivete, I did not understand then that the system I thought would ensure our fundamental rights and freedoms, was in fact, the very instrument that mandates our oppression. This is the problem with the conveyor belt approach to life we are blindly spoon-fed and conditioned to strive for. Where we have an uncritical view of the world and unconsciously accept and embody mainstream perspectives. One where the law is a force for good, courts guarantee justice and we all have an equal right to exist.

In this chapter, I share my experiences as a Muslim, British, Bangladeshi, woman barrister, advocate and activist. I share how I am continually finding my voice through navigating the Bar as an exclusionary space and witnessing how the law does not exist to serve us all the same, or at all. On this journey, I have had to unlearn much of what I believed to be true. Being a barrister and the law is not the vehicle of change I hoped it would be. I challenge the default idea that the law is a force for good using examples that resonate with me as a Muslim woman of colour in the UK today; the UK's counter-terrorism apparatus and the impact of emergency coronavirus legislation on communities of colour. In the second part, I offer some suggestions on how lawyers committed to meaningful social change, can use our platform and privilege to challenge the system from within and find ways of working, without legitimising it. Drawing on models of movement lawyering and cause lawyering, I argue that there is an imperative need for a new generation of courageous radical lawyers. Lawyers who are willing to boldly step outside of the traditional confines of what it means to be a lawyer. Lawyers with the courage to disrupt the status quo and defend what is just, rather than what is legal, despite the obvious conflict this creates. Lawyers that bravely reimagine our world, as an equitable and just place for all, and strive towards this goal each and every day, even though we may not see the fruits in our lifetime.

I hope that my reflections will be of benefit to others who may be on a similar journey and offer confidence for those looking to carve out a path on their own terms.

The Myth of Meritocracy

In accessing a career at the Bar, I was navigating a system which felt alien to me and represented nothing about who I am. The Zeenat on a CV part of me got me through the door, whilst the rest of me has very much remained on the periphery. Despite outward commitments to making the Bar accessible, and examples of those of us from 'non-traditional' backgrounds who make it into the profession, fundamental issues remain.

The Bar is not a meritocracy. Many believe that anyone can get to the Bar if you work hard—'if I did it, so can you.' This is simply not true.

You can have exactly the same qualifications with the same grades, but if you are White you are almost doubly more likely to get pupillage.[1] Yet there are many who will robustly defend the profession as not having a problem with race. There are systemic barriers in play which mean, it does not matter how good you are nor how hard you worked. The odds are simply worse for some, than others. The issue does not just stop at accessing the profession, it persists throughout. There are widespread issues in respect of retention and career progression for barristers from minority ethnic backgrounds[2] and particular faith groups[3] at QC level[4] and in the judiciary.[5] The use of the term 'BAME'[6] is problematic, not least because it is lazy homogenous labelling of huge swathes of people with very distinct life experiences, but it also masks the shocking lack of progress in improving representation and advancement for specific groups.[7] I have raised questions with organisations who claim their workforce is diverse at every level and publish statistics based on the

---

1. For example, of UK/EU domiciled BPTC graduates with an upper-second class degree and Very Competent overall BPTC grade, 45 percent of them from White backgrounds had commenced pupillage, compared to around 25 percent of the BAME cohort with the same degree class/BPTC grade. 'BPTC Key Statistics Report 2020,' accessed 12 April 2021, https://www.barstandardsboard.org.uk/uploads/assets/3f953812-cb0e-4139-b9dcc76f085de4e2/BPTC-Key-Statistics-Report-2020-All-parts.pdf

2. BSB Report on Diversity at the Bar 2020,' page 4, accessed 12 April 2021, https://www.barstandardsboard.org.uk/uploads/assets/88edd1b1-0edc-4635-9a3dc9497db06972/BSB-Report-on-Diversity-at-the-Bar-2020.pdf

3. For example although there are 338 Muslim barristers, there are only 11 QCs as compared to 129 Hindu barristers with 9 QCs, 93 Sikh barristers with 10 QCs and 250 Jewish QCs with 72 QCs. Table 8, page 22 'BSB Report on Diversity at the Bar 2020'. Please also note, whilst statistical data can be helpful in identifying patterns, it is important to remember the limitations including the limited monitoring questions, response rates and absence of sufficiently granular analysis for example on an intersectional basis.

4. The statistics reveal a particular disparity with the advancement of British Black African barristers to QC level. Page 4, 'BSB Report on Diversity at the Bar 2020.'

5. 'Diversity of the Judiciary: 2020 Statistics,' accessed 12 April 2021, Page 3 https://assets.publishing.service.gov.uk/government/uploads/system/uploads/attachment_data/file/918529/diversity-of-the-judiciary-2020-statistics-web.pdf

6. I have adopted the use of 'BAME' in this piece as this is the term used in the reports I have referred to which should not be taken as any agreement with or acceptance of this term.

7. For example 6.9% of barristers are from Asian British backgrounds compared to 3% from Black British backgrounds. Significant disparities exist within broader groups for instance when looking at barristers from South Asian backgrounds. There are 527 British Indian barristers, 322 British Pakistani barristers compared to 100 British Bangladeshi barristers—clearly progress is not equal across these groups. 'BSB Report on Diversity at the Bar 2020' 14.

entire organisation rather than disaggregating the information by levels of seniority and specific roles. In doing so, it would be clear that a high proportion of those from BAME backgrounds are most concentrated in the lowest levels of the organisational structure, begging the question of why are the people in the senior or more skilled positions White?

The importance of an intersectional analysis when considering these factors is laid bare in the 'Income at the Bar—by Gender and Ethnicity Report' 2020 which found that female BAME barristers are the lowest earning group and White male barristers are the highest earning group. Black African and Asian Bangladeshi barristers fare the worst and are particularly low earning groups.[8]

The issue is more than the statistics. The lived experience of people in the profession, speaks for itself. #Law_So_White is an online platform where people in the profession share anonymously their experiences of racism in the legal system.[9] From being mistaken for the defendant,[10] being told by Chambers that a candidate is more likely to be accepted 'the more you look like us'[11] and being told by a Crown Court judge that he does not believe in racially aggravated offences.[12] This is a minute snapshot of the daily realities of those from racialised backgrounds. I have suffered racism, sexism and Islamophobia. I have been gaslit when raising issues by colleagues and sometimes even friends who ask 'are you sure that's what they really meant?' I have been challenged for what I share on my public platforms, on one occasion being pulled up for a tweet about the Bar being racist, classist and sexist. Ironically, the challenge came from people working in equality and diversity. What has hurt most, is when those that I respect and consider friends have failed to have my back when something unacceptable has occurred. It is incredibly isolating. It has taken real strength and an acceptance

that the path of being unapologetic and uncompromising about the

---

8. 'Income at the Bar by Gender and Ethnicity,' accessed 12 April 2021, page 4 https://www.barstandardsboard.org.uk/uploads/assets/1ee64764-cd34-4817-80174ca6304f1ac0/Income-at-the-Bar-by-Gender-and-Ethnicity-Final.pdf
9. Twitter page, 'LawSoWhite,' accessed 12 April 2021, https://twitter.com/law_so_white?lang=en
10. 'Court Service Apologies After Black Barrister Assumed to be Defendant,' accessed 12 April 2021, https://www.theguardian.com/law/2020/dec/19/court-service-apologises-after-black-barrister-assumed-to-be-defendant
11. Twitter page, 'LawSoWhite,' accessed 12 April 2021,https://twitter.com/Law_So_White/status/1293089522373271552?s=20
12. Twitter page, 'LawSoWhite,' accessed 12 April 2021,https://twitter.com/Law_So_White/status/1278624454256537601?s=20

truth, is often a lonely one.

It was only in my later years in practice that I began to reflect on how truly conditioned we are to brush the constant microaggressions away and just carry on. It was not until I undertook anti-racism training, and considered more closely the idea of environmental microaggressions, that I realised how starkly the profession excludes so many of us in really obvious ways. Examples being the lack of representation in the judiciary, positions of leadership and so on, but also aspects such as the requirement to attend dining sessions at the Inns of Court, an intimidating prospect for many of us who will not have been sure what piece of cutlery to use for what, or what 'proper etiquette' is in these spaces. Not to mention the numerous portraits displayed in the Inns celebrating the 'greats' of the history of the Bar—do any of them look like us? Why is this significant? It tells us that a profession which prides itself on being a noble one, committed to achieving justice, is not immune from wider societal issues. The profession is a microcosm of society. Not only is it not immune, it is proactively exclusive and otherising.

'Diversity and Inclusion'—A Harmful Narrative

Many organisations are increasingly adopting trendy diversity and inclusion strategies. I believe that the diversity and inclusion narrative is more harmful than it is helpful. Even where there are efforts to address these issues, too often the burden falls on those from the particular excluded group. It is not uncommon for the person raising the issue to then morph into the 'diversity consultant' responsible for championing the change or educating others about the problems. Personally, I have withdrawn from events and awards that purport to celebrate and encourage 'diversity' when in reality they inherently contradict what they say they stand for, for example exorbitant ticket prices that most cannot afford. It is no surprise given what we have explored so far, that Black and Brown lawyers are often heavily represented in the diversity categories at Legal Awards, but less so in substantive categories. As Black and Brown lawyers, we have more to offer than expertise on experiences based on the colour of our skin.

The problem is more systemic than individual experience. Getting more diverse faces into the legal profession is not a solution as it does not address the root problem, why is there such a lack of diversity to begin with? In the same way, more representation in the profession will not change the lived experiences of many people who will continue to suffer racism and discrimination. Some suggest that 'representation in a system that is oppressive, may never be enough.'[13] In my view it is not. I do believe that it is important for the legal profession to be representative of the people that it serves. However, having more Black and Brown lawyers and judges will not make the justice system fairer. If the system itself is oppressive, it is that we must address rather than some of the components within the system.

Angela Davis describes this in the following way:

> I have a hard time accepting diversity as a synonym for justice. Diversity is a corporate strategy. It's a strategy designed to ensure that the institution functions in the same way that it functioned before, except now that you now have some black faces and brown faces. It's a difference that doesn't make a difference.[14]

We do not have to look too far for examples of those from minority backgrounds, who not only do not serve the interests of those from similar backgrounds to their own, but actively harm them. Priti Patel's policies and the recent Sewell Report claiming that there is no institutional racism in the UK, typify this point. Meaningful representation will not be achieved through the inclusion of those who are simply grateful for a seat at the table and who will do anything to get there. It will not be achieved through those who are unwilling to challenge the status quo but rather are happy for their presence to legitimise and reinforce it. We need more than the acceptance of the palatable voice of colour in the corridors of power and influence in our country. Through my experiences at the Bar, I have learned that I need to challenge my own consumption and acceptance of mainstream narratives.

The Need to Challenge Mainstream Narratives

The mainstream narrative is that law is good, police are our protectors, prison is for bad people and we all have the same rights. Where do these default positions in our understanding come from? I have referred to 'the system' but what exactly is it?

> The system is not just one 'thing,' it is an entire mode of knowledge production and narrative formation that works interdependently to
>
> reinforce the power of authority, over the bodies and minds of the

---

13. Asim Qureshi, *'Virtue of Disobedience'* (Byline Books 2018), 132
14. 'Civil Rights Leader Speaks at Bovard,' accessed 12 June 2020, https://dailytrojan.com/2015/02/23/civil-rights-leader-angela-davis-speaks-at-bovard/

disenfranchised.[15]

Our default positions come from the 'knowledge production and narrative formation' of the system. It is this which needs to be unpicked and unlearned. One example of a mainstream narrative is the idea that we are a democracy which promotes and protects human rights and equality for all. We have an internationally revered legal human rights framework that perpetuates this idea of us as a beacon of light. Our paternalistic superiority is such that we believe our way of doing things is the aspirational ideal.

As lawyers, one of our limitations is that we are only concerned with the black letter of the law, outside of the broader historical, social and political context. Most of have never inquired about or studied the roots of the laws with which we rely on in our legal work. Kehinde Andrews in his book 'The New Age of Empire: How Racism and Colonialism Still Rule the World' deals with the 'fatal weaknesses in the framework of human rights.'[16] He states that 'The West created a racial global order and then built a framework of rights that would maintain the status quo.'[17] In his view, 'to be a full human being is still defined in Whiteness' and 'all the founding texts upon which the human rights framework was built was designed as the rights of White men.'[18] A full analysis of this, is beyond the scope of this essay, but the point is, laws do not exist in a vacuum. They come with a history that remains relevant today.

If human rights really are universal, then why are so many living without their rights being fulfilled? There is an inherent contradiction between the emancipatory potential of the law and the lived reality of countless people and communities who are constantly discriminated against and vilified by the state, through the law. Consider for example, the gross overrepresentation of people from BAME backgrounds in the criminal justice system. The David Lammy Review in 2017 raised serious concerns about the proportion of young people from BAME backgrounds in custody which had risen from 25% to 41% between 2006-2016.[19] Despite the Review's recommendations for change, The Tackling Racial Disparity in the Criminal Justice System: 2020 Update reveals

---

15. Qureshi, *'Virtue of Disobedience'* 101
16. Kehinde Andrews, *'The New Age of Empire: How Racism and Colonialism Still Rule the World'* (Allen Lane 2021) 20
17. Andrews, *The New Age of Empire* 21
18. Andrews, *The New Age of Empire* 23
19. 'Lammy Publishes Historic Review,' accessed 19 June 2020, https://www.gov.uk/government/news/lammy-publishes-historic-review. Full report available here: https://www.gov.uk/government/publications/lammy-review-final-report

that this has continued to rise to 49% in 2018/19.[20] The latest Youth Justice Statistics for the year ending March 2020, report that now more than half of young people in custody are from BAME backgrounds, described by David Lammy as a 'national scandal.'[21] In particular, the proportion of children on remand who were Black has increased from 21% to 35% in the latest year.[22] This cannot be seen in isolation from institutional racism and the persistent criminalisation of communities of colour, in particular those from Black ethnic groups.

Similarly, the Lammy Review found that the number of Muslim prisoners had increased by nearly 50% in the last ten years, constituting 15% of the prison population but just 5% of the general population.[23] This shocking statistic must be contextualised against the background of the 'War on Terrorism' and consequent demonisation and profiling of the Muslim faith. The fact that particular communities are subjected by the system, is not an accident. It should call into question who the gatekeepers of the system are and who the system is designed to protect and serve. In this sense, the legal system has been described as being 'reflective of society's most destructive power imbalances and greatest injustices.'[24]

The Law as a Tool for Oppression

Laws are predicated on the power and politics of the day. The law is not a neutral arbiter, in a context which politicises and weaponises particular identities. Below I explore some examples that demonstrate that the operation of the law carries different ramifications dependent on who you are. We must consider intersections such as religion, race and gender in order to understand how the law is used as a tool for

---

20. 'Tackling Racial Disparity in the Criminal Justice System 2020 Update,' accessed 12 June 2020, https://assets.publishing.service.gov.uk/government/uploads/system/uploads/attachment_data/file/881317/tackling-racial-disparity-cjs-2020.pdf page 19, paragraph 68
21. 'National Scandal that more than half young people in custody are Black, Asian or minority ethnic,' accessed 21 April 2021, https://labour.org.uk/press/national-scandal-that-more-than-half-of-young-people-in-custody-are-black-asian-or-ethnic-minority/
22. 'Youth Justice Statistics 2019/2020,' accessed 12 April 2021, https://assets.publishing.service.gov.uk/government/uploads/system/uploads/attachment_data/file/956621/youth-justice-statistics-2019-2020.pdf, page 43
23. 'The Lammy Review,' accessed 12 April 2021, https://assets.publishing.service.gov.uk/government/uploads/system/uploads/attachment_data/file/643001/lammy-review-final-report.pdf, page12
24. Deborah Kenn, *Lawyering from the Heart* (Aspen Publishers 2009) 1

oppression. I have chosen examples that impact communities I belong to or am aligned with. First, I consider some aspects of the UK's counter-terrorism framework and its specific vilification of the Muslim community and secondly, I consider the disproportionate impact of the law on communities of colour as a result of the coronavirus pandemic.

The Counter-Terrorism Framework

The 'War on Terror' has seen the persistent expansion of exceptional legislation and policy becoming normalised and entrenched into our legal framework. The result has been the creation and reinforcement of the idea that Muslims are the 'suspect community.' One aspect of this framework is Schedule 7 of the Terrorism Act 2000.[25] Schedule 7 is a terrifyingly wide power which confers stop and detention powers at ports and airports, without the need for any reasonable suspicion. If stopped, an individual, although not under arrest, is legally required to answer questions and if asked, to provide biometric data such as fingerprints and DNA, give up electronic devices, be searched and potentially even strip searched. Non-compliance is a criminal offence.[26]

The case of Asiyah who was forced to take off her hijab, epitomes the truly dehumanising impact of Schedule 7 stops and in particular, how the law creates gendered and racial violence. The transcript of her conversation with officers records one saying:

> You might end up being arrested because you wouldn't let us take a photograph of your hair...I have no idea [of] the positioning of your ears on your face. Like, you might not even have any ears. We don't know what you look like.'[27] She describes being photographed without her hijab feeling like 'the police had taken a photo of me naked that was then being looked at by male officers....I felt my dignity had been taken

---

25. Terrorism Act 2000, Schedule 7 http://www.legislation.gov.uk/ukpga/2000/11/schedule/7
26. Despite concerns about the power being used arbitrarily and having insufficient safeguards in the European Court of Human Rights case *Beghal v UK* in 2019, Schedule 7 has been further expanded. Schedule 3 of the Counter-Terrorism and Border Security Act 2019 now confers the power to stop, question and detain to determine whether an individual has been engaged in 'hostile activity.'
27. 'Met police concedes forcing woman to remove hijab at airport was wrong,' *The Guardian*, accessed 12 June 2020, https://www.theguardian.com/law/2020/mar/14/metropolitan-police-concede-forcing-woman-to-remove-hijab-wrong

away and I had been stripped.[28]

The insidious growth of the counter-terrorism narrative, has pervaded all of the Muslim community. This is a global issue, with countless examples of state sanctioned frameworks that perpetuate Islamophobia from the hijab ban in France, to the genocide of the Uighur Muslims and the discriminatory citizenship laws in India.[29] In this way Kundani argues:

> Islamophobia is a form of structural racism directed at Muslims and the ways in which it is sustained through a symbiotic relationship with the official thinking and practices of the war on terror. Its significance does not lie primarily in the individual prejudices it generates but in its wider political consequences—its enabling of systemic violations of the rights of Muslims and its demonization of actions taken to remedy those violations. The war on terror—with its vast death tolls in Afghanistan, Iraq, Pakistan, Somalia, Yemen and elsewhere—could not be sustained without the racialized dehumanization of its Muslim victims.[30]

It is no longer just about the archetypal radicalised bearded man in an orange jumpsuit, but about the average Muslim woman too, from hijabs, to niqabs to burkinis, even our bodies are politicised. And our choices too as if we need liberating from the oppressive shackles of our faith. On this topic, Hoda Katebi writes 'The hijab, women's bodies, and fashion at large have long been battlegrounds for political power, colonisation, and state control.'[31] It doesn't stop with women, they want our children too.

The PREVENT duty codified in the Counter Terrorism and Security Act 2015, requires public bodies to have 'due regard to the need to prevent people from being drawn into terrorism.' This has meant 'that the counter-terrorism apparatus has spread from its traditional home in the police and intelligence services, to occupy almost every branch of the state, from schools and universities, to GP surgeries, social care,

---

28. 'Met police concedes forcing woman to remove hijab at airport was wrong,' *The Guardian*
29. 'Discrimination Against Muslimsunder India's New Citizenship Policy,; accessed 12 April 2021, https://www.hrw.org/report/2020/04/09/shoot-traitors/discrimination-against-muslims-under-indias-new-citizenship-policy
30. Arun Kundani, *The Muslims are Coming*, (Verso 2015) 11
31. 'Writer, Entrepreneur, and Activist Hoda Katebi on France's Proposed Hijab Ban,' accessed 20 April 2020, https://www.vogue.com/article/france-hijab-ban-hoda-katebi-personal-essay

opticians, libraries and even nurseries.'[32] Schools, supposed to be safe spaces for learning and intellectual inquiry have become surveillance operations. The Muslim Council of Britain reports a number of troubling cases e.g. a two year old with a learning disability sang an Islamic song containing 'Allahu Akbar'—a means of praising God, was referred to social services and in another case, a police officer accused a schoolboy for having 'terrorist like' views for having Free Palestine badges, which were deemed extremist.[33] More recently, in light of sanctions that students have faced in schools for expressing Palestinian solidarity, 'there has been a rapidly growing number of cases where children are being spoken to and surveilled through the lens of PREVENT.'[34]

Despite long awaited promises of conducting a review of the PREVENT strategy, the government has selected reviewers that actively support the government's agenda. The appointment of Lord Carlisle first and then William Shawcross has led rights groups to rightly boycott the review.[35] An example of how we can choose not to engage with a system that is not designed to be neutral. It is the law that has created, enabled and legitimised the discrimination and vilification of Muslims in the UK today. Massoumi, Mills and Miller state:

> We regard the state and more specifically the sprawling official 'counter terrorism' apparatus to be absolutely central to the production of contemporary Islamophobia—it is the backbone of anti-Muslim racism.[36]

Statistics confirm this. Hate crime has more than doubled since 2012/13 and analysis confirms that there have been spikes in hate crime following the EU Referendum and terrorist attacks in 2017.[37] As of 2019/20, 50% of religious hate crime offences were targeted against

---

32. Narzanin Masssoumi, Tom Mills and David Miller, 'Islamophobia, Social Movements and the State: For a Movement-centred Approach' in *What is Islamophobia? Racism, Social Movements and the State*, (pluto Press 2017) 12
33. 'Concerns on Prevent,' accessed 12 June 2020, https://www.mcb.org.uk/wp-content/uploads/2015/10/20150803-Case-studies-about-Prevent.pdf
34. 'Why pro-Palestine Activists are targeted in schools and society' https://www.middleeasteye.net/opinion/uk-pro-palestine-activists-targeted-in-schools (Accessed 15/06/2021)
35. 'Rights Groups Boycott Prevent Review,' accessed 12 April 2021, https://www.libertyhumanrights.org.uk/issue/rights-groups-boycott-prevent-review/
36. Masssoumi, Mills and Miller, 'Islamophobia, Social Movements and the State' 8
37. 'Hate Crime, England and Wales, 2018 to 2019,' accessed 19 June 2020, https://assets.publishing.service.gov.uk/government/uploads/system/uploads/attachment_data/file/839172/hate-crime-1819-hosb2419.pdf, 1

Muslims, continuing to rise from the previous year.[38] The numbers speak for themselves.

A Pandemic of Inequality

The coronavirus pandemic has exposed in ghastly terms what we already knew. How racial injustice really is a matter of life and death for some and the severity of the health inequalities in this country. Public Health England's 'Beyond the Data: Understanding the Impact of COVID-19 on BAME Communities' revealed that people from BAME backgrounds are up to twice as likely to die of coronavirus.[39] Analysis from the Office of National Statistics shows that people from a Black ethnic background are at a greater risk than all other ethnic groups, the risk for Black males being more than three times higher than White males.[40] The PHE report confirms that the pandemic has 'exposed and exacerbated long standing inequalities affecting BAME groups in the UK.' It states that 'change needs to be large scale and transformative. Action is needed to change the structural and societal environments such as the homes, neighbourhoods, workplaces...there is a legal duty and moral responsibility to reduce inequalities.'[41] However, rather than effective and prompt intervention to protect communities of colour and mitigate these disparities, the system has continued to criminalise them. The Coronavirus Act 2020 and Health Protection Regulations 2020 emergency legislation brought in a number of measures including sweeping police powers, with little scrutiny or accountability. Liberty describes the Act as a 'unprecedented assault on civil liberties' and in response has worked with human rights groups to campaign for the

---

38. 'Hate Crime, England and Wales, 2019 to 2020,' 10
39. This review found that the highest age standardised diagnosis rates of COVID-19 per 100,000 population were in people of Black ethnic groups. An analysis of survival among confirmed COVID-19 cases showed that, after accounting for the effect of sex, age, deprivation and region, people of Bangladeshi ethnicity had around twice the risk of death when compared to people of White British ethnicity. ('Beyond the data: Understanding the impact of COVID-19 on BAME groups,' https://assets.publishing.service.gov.uk/government/uploads/system/uploads/attachment_data/file/892376/COVID_stakeholder_engagement_synthesis_beyond_the_data.pdf, 4)
40. 'Coronavirus deaths by ethnic group,' accessed 19 April 2021, https://www.ons.gov.uk/peoplepopulationandcommunity/birthsdeathsandmarriages/deaths/articles/coronaviruscovid19relateddeathsbyethnicgroupenglandandwales/2march2020to15may2020
41. 'Beyond the data: Understanding the impact of COVID-19 on BAME groups,' 6

'Protect Everyone Bill.'[42] The Act enables and legitimises the further marginalisation of already marginalised groups as evidenced, in figures which revealed that people from BAME backgrounds have been disproportionately impacted.[43] In London, despite making up 12% of the population, 26% of black people received fines. Asian people who make up 18% of the population, received 23% of fines. White people were 23% less likely to be fined.[44] Further, there has been disproportionality in arrests where Black people have been overrepresented.[45] A review by the CPS revealed that all 44 cases that were brought under the Act were incorrectly charged.[46]

The pandemic has been used as a trojan horse for the continued infringement of civil liberties and human rights. Discriminatory and racist policing, mass surveillance, impinging on the right of protest and talks of tampering with the right to trial by jury are just a few examples, all of which disproportionately affect people of colour. One of the starkest recent examples of how the law is a tool of oppression is the Police, Crime, Sentencing and Courts Bill 2020. The Bill proposes a number of draconian measures including: serious restrictions on the fundamental right to protest, extending police powers even further to police and restrict protests, criminalisation of Gypsy, Roma and Traveller communities, sentences of up to ten years for defacing a statue and the introduction of an extraordinarily broad stop and search power without a reasonable suspicion requirement.[47] This stark disparity in power and who it rests with, is not by accident but by design. It reinforces and maintains the prevailing gatekeepers of the system, who are the subjectors and who are the subjected. Reminding us at every turn,

---

42. 'Liberty calls for new pandemic laws that protect everyone,' accessed 12 April 2021, https://www.libertyhumanrights.org.uk/issue/liberty-calls-for-new-pandemic-laws-that-protect-everyone/
43. 'Met police twice as likely to fine black people over lockdown breaches—research,' *The Guardian*, accessed 12 April 2021, https://www.theguardian.com/uk-news/2020/jun/03/met-police-twice-as-likely-to-fine-black-people-over-lockdown-breaches-research
44. Met police twice as likely to fine black people over lockdown breaches—research,' *The Guardian*
45. Met police twice as likely to fine black people over lockdown breaches—research,' *The Guardian*
46. 'CPS announces review findings for first 200 cases under Coronavirus Act,' accessed 12 June 2020, https://www.cps.gov.uk/cps/news/cps-announces-review-findings-first-200-cases-under-coronavirus-laws
47. For more see https://www.libertyhumanrights.org.uk/wp-content/uploads/2021/03/Libertys-Briefing-on-the-Police-Crime-Sentencing-and-Courts-Bill-HoC-2nd-reading-March-2021-1.pdf

of the relative little worth of the lives of people who are not White.

The examples I have explored demonstrate how law is used as a 'method of social control by the powers that be who are determined to perpetuate themselves by any means necessary.'[48] As Reni Eddo-Lodge states:

> We must see who benefits from their race, who is disproportionately impacted by negative stereotypes about their race, and to who power and privilege is bestowed upon—earned or not- because of their race, their class and their gender. Seeing race is essential to changing the system.[49]

The Limitations of Institutionalised Lawyers

We have explored some ways in which the law itself vilifies and discriminates but what has been the role of lawyers operating within the system? In my experience, one of the issues we have is that lawyers have become institutionalised. We defend people's rights but only insofar as the law permits. There is no real engagement with a wider conversation about the need for systemic change or the fact that the law itself is the problem. There is a reluctance to appear 'political'—which is ironic given inequality is exactly that, political. We reassure ourselves by the idea that we are pursuing justice. Some of us really believe that the British justice system is an institution to be revered and that working within it, is doing something noble. But an unjust justice system cannot dispense justice. So are we doing something good or are we actually complicit?

Many lawyers are also institutionalised within the profession. They uphold systems of power and privilege within chambers, firms, membership organisations and the Inns of Court. Despite an outward commitment to equality and fairness, there are questions to be asked about; how they support colleagues from diverse, ethnic and religious backgrounds, the work they are willing to put in to ensure fair recruitment and allocation of work, creating an inclusive environment, retention of diverse talent, processes to widen access to the profession and so on. In my view, how the legal profession operates and how the legal system operates are intrinsically linked. The issues in the profession mirror society more broadly, and the issues in society are

---

48. Michael Steven Smith, *Lawyers for the Left: In the Courts, In the Streets, and On the Air*, (OR Books 2019) 34
49. Reni Eddo-Lodge, *Why I am no Longer Talking to White People about Race* (Bloomsbury Publishing, 2018) 84

perpetuated by the system.

The Need for Critical Reflection

I am continuing on my path as a barrister, because the system will continue to marginalise and oppress. Whilst this remains the case, there must be a community of lawyers who are willing to critically examine the harsh realities of the status quo, challenge the system from within and hold it to account. As critical lawyers we must be prepared to unlearn and challenge our mainstream legal education and be willing to honestly examine and interrogate our norms. We need to be introspective about our platform and privilege as lawyers, and how we can utilise these to best serve others without paternalistic superiority. We need to understand that the world relates to us all in different ways, based on the privileges we hold. In doing this, whether it be colleagues or the clients and causes we represent, we must not take away from the lived experiences of others, when we simply cannot relate. Instead we must learn how to be allies, the non-performative kind. We cannot look at the law independently of the various aspects of our identity that make up who we are. An understanding of intersectionality is crucial.

We have to accept that the legal system is one of the components of the wider system and question the enabling role that we play within it. We need to be lawyers that have the courage not only to challenge how systems and spaces of power and influence have been set up, but also have a role in dismantling them and reimagining a different way. What does this look like in practice?

An Alternative Model of Lawyering

I learnt about 'movement lawyering' when undertaking a Legal Fellowship at the Centre for Constitutional Rights in New York City in 2016. This experience was transformative for me in helping me to reconcile my activism with my role as a lawyer. I worked with a community of exceptional lawyers who were driven by their values, politics and activism. A dynamic I have seen less of in legal practice in England. This model of lawyering has been referred to in a number of ways including cause lawyering, people lawyering, radical lawyering and rebellious lawyering. Essentially, the model is focused on changing the system, rather than just operating within it.

Michael Steven Smith describes these lawyers as 'lawyers for the left.' These lawyers '...challenge traditional notions of how one must practice law...their moral compasses gravitate to issues and people...rather than practice a form of conformist lawyering... they take their cues from communities in need...they ask themselves how law can be adapted to help to rectify injustice... They provide a critical check on society's dominant powers... something in their DNA animates them to challenge privileged viewpoints.'[50] Furthermore, 'what distinguishes cause lawyers from 'conventional lawyers' is that the former apply their professional skills in the service of a cause other than—or greater than—the interests of the client in order to transform some aspect of the status quo, whereas the latter tailor their practice to accommodate or benefit the client within the prevailing arrangements of power.'[51] Rather than dealing with just individuals, they deal with entire systems. In addition to challenging state power and institutions, movement lawyering goes beyond the traditional transactional lawyer client model. Lawyers work with social movements and communities, not just individuals.

Smith states that 'lawyers for the left take an activist and oppositional, albeit auxiliary role. We recognise that great movements of the people 'from below' are fundamental to social change...we use our legal training to carve out space for; defend the legitimacy of, and give legal expression to the fundamentally political movements for social transformation. On a more mundane level, we provide legal services and hence some possibility of justice to individuals who would otherwise have to suffer.'[52] In this way, it is people centred and people led, rather than driven forward by lawyers.

Lawyers alone cannot achieve social change. Nor can governments. Angela Davis states 'I don't think we can rely on governments, regardless of who is in power, to do the work that only mass movements can do...mass movements can indeed bring about systemic change.'[53] A recent example of this in the UK can be seen from the Black Lives Matter protests following the killing of George Floyd. The statue of slave trader Edward Colston was pulled down in Bristol by protestors. This subsequently led to authorities removing similar statues, renaming schools and university buildings and so on. These crucial changes were triggered by a movement.

---

50. Smith, *Lawyers for the Left* 1-2
51. Austin Sarat and Stuart Scheingold, *Cause Lawyering and the State in a Global Era*, (Oxford University Press, 2001) 68
52. Smith, *Lawyers for the Left*, 11
53. Angela Y. Davis, *'Freedom is a Constant Struggle: Ferguson, Palestine, and the Foundations of a Movement'* (Haymarket Books, 2016) 35, 37

Yet the response to the action was divided. People in government, in the legal profession and much of the public condemned the criminality of the action, whilst others praised what the movement has achieved in highlighting how deeply embedded the legacy of slavery remains in our society today and that it must not be celebrated. I am often deeply troubled by the misplaced emphasis many lawyers have in these conversations. Where the emphasis is on the toppling of a statue, rather than slavery. Where the emphasis is on looting rather than the killing of Black people in the street. This encapsulates the institutionalisation of lawyers I explored earlier and an unwillingness to step outside, the carefully crafted boundaries of what the law says is right, as opposed to what equity and justice demands.

This is why those of us who find ourselves in situations where we disagree with the black letter of the law must 'use the law in a radical way to empower people to help build movement, and to challenge in fundamental ways how state power is used.'[54] We must 'work in contradiction' and use our legal skills 'to serve the very populations that our law and justice systems are precisely designed against.'[55] In doing so, we may be 'uniquely placed not simply to serve justice and democracy but to reformulate and thus to destabilise them.'[56] This is precisely what is needed.

How do we 'Reformulate and Destabilise'?

Whilst we continue to have to work within the system, we must destabilise from within. Below I explore what some efforts to destabilise might look like. However, it must be understood that the work to destabilise alone is not enough. We cannot accept the system the way that it is, and whilst we work within it, we must be calling for and working towards wholesale systemic reformulation, not reform. We cannot expect the system to hold itself to account.

Starting with Ourselves

---

54. Smith, *Lawyers for the Left*, 15
55. 'Movement lawyering, what's that?' Accessed 12 June 2020, https://dukeengage.duke.edu/movement-lawyering-whats-that/
56. Stuart A Scheingold and Austin Sarat, *Something to Believe In, Politics, Professionalism and Cause Lawyering* (Stanford Law and Politics 2004) 125

Mariame Kaba, activist, organiser and author of 'We Do This 'Til We Free Us' says that if we want to transform society, we have to transform ourselves. She says 'our imagination of what a different world can be is limited. We are deeply entangled in the very systems that we are organising to change. White supremacy, misogyny, ableism, classism, homophobia and transphobia exist everywhere. We have all so thoroughly internalised these logics of oppression that if oppression were to end tomorrow, we would be likely to reproduce previous structures.'[57] She argues that we must imagine ourselves differently, be intentional in relation to each other, join collectives, organisations and faith groups that are committed to learning and unlearning.[58] As lawyers committed to social change, we have to willingly embrace the fact that we have much to learn and unlearn. We have to allow our deeply held perspectives, views and values to be challenged and learn to sit with the discomfort that this may bring. We must actively commit to working alongside, organising with and learning from others who are deeply invested in this work and find new ways of introducing these perspectives into our legal practice.

Critical Legal Education

We must study and learn critical perspectives of the law and the wider system. We need to accept that the system is not just broken, or flawed but that it is designed to perpetuate the oppression that it does. We must divest from the system despite working within it. We have to discard the lofty ideals that our justice system is one to be revered and that by being a lawyer within it we are a fundamental part of ensuring justice. Our legal work must be done based on this crucial understanding. We must have conversations about how mainstream legal education reproduces hierarchy. We need to push for critical legal education for aspiring lawyers much earlier on in their journeys, so these perspectives are brought into the profession from the earliest stage. In addition to our own critical education as lawyers, we need a transformative and nationwide public legal education programme that enables people to understand and enforce their rights, rather than a deliberate attempt

to keep people in a state of ignorance so they can never change their condition.

---

57. Mariame Kaba, 'We Do This 'Til We Free Us' (Haymarket Books, 2021) 4
58. Kaba, *We Do This 'Til We Free Us*, 4

Beyond the Courtroom

We must understand that our role transcends beyond cases and the courtroom, into the community and the wider world. In order to truly commit to working towards social change, we must accept that law alone will never be enough. We need to work closely with others that are working towards change in their respective spaces; educators, activists, advocates, grass root organisations and storytellers. We need to build coalitions for change. We need to be in these spaces in order to bridge the gap between people and the legal system which remains impenetrable leaving people unable to access any semblance of justice. We need to build trust with the people we say we serve. We must learn how to create and hold space for others and know when to step back.

We must be advocates for more than our clients. We have to be involved with wider conversations and calls for change, beyond our individual cases. What broader causes do our cases represent? What systemic injustices, do our cases point to? This approach would lead to more sustained engagement with and understanding of, for example, calls to decolonise the curriculum, to scrap PREVENT, abolish prisons and to defund the police—rather than dismissing these movements as wildly misguided.

A People Centred Approach

As lawyers for social change, we must decentre ourselves and centre the causes and the voices of those directly impacted. We need to demonstrate humanity in how we conduct our cases and interact with people and constantly humanise the person and/or cause we are representing. All too often as lawyers, we become case hardened and desensitised. Empathy and compassion from advocates is imperative as we are often our clients' only hope of being heard in a system which continually silences them.

Using our Platform and Privilege

With every platform our privilege as a lawyer gives to us, we must use it responsibly and honestly, explaining the realities of the injustice that the system perpetuates as opposed to promoting the idea of law as a saviour. We must use it to champion entry into the profession of people traditionally excluded, bringing with them their unique life experiences allowing us to better serve the people and causes we represent. As a profession, we must be less resistant to change and be willing to learn from others. In our own professional institutions we must demand change and challenge our peers and our superiors fearlessly. When we think about change, we should think about our various spheres of influence and also how change needs to occur on a personal, organisational, institutional and structural level.

Re-envisioning Our World

I choose to re-envision our world as one where we all exist in equal humanity. I have to, because it is this hope that keeps me going. A truly just world may not be possible in our lifetime but we must strive for more. Even in a world which does not value us all equally, we have a duty to act. We must choose not to watch in silence and complicity in the face of so many grave injustices. In the words of American, Palestinian activist, Linda Sarsour, we are not here to be bystanders.

When we discuss 'reformulate and destablise,' reformulation, is a system which gives us more. The guilty verdicts in the case of Derek Chauvin for George Floyd's murder, is not a vindication of the system. One correct conviction, does not make a justice system based on centuries of oppression, just. Nor will it change the lived reality that Black people face of being killed on the street for being Black. Mariame Kaba says that 'we need to use our radical imaginations to come up with new structures of accountability beyond the system we are working to dismantle.'[59] The question is not 'what do we have now, and how can we make it better? Instead, let's ask, 'what can we imagine for ourselves and the world? If we do that, then the boundless possibilities of a more just world await us.'[60]

My call to action for courageous radical, activist lawyers is to understand our role as being the thorn. To question. Challenge. Agitate. To disrupt from within. Where there is a tension between law and justice, we have a duty to defy what is unjust. In the words of Angela Davis, 'we have to act as if it is possible to radically transform the world and we have to do it all the time'. To some, 'activist' is a suspicious word with connotations of being a troublemaker or a nuisance. For me, it is foundational to my identity as a Muslim, Brown woman having to navigate the world we live in today. Being an activist for me, means

---

59. Kaba, 'We Do This 'Til We Free Us' 65
60. Kaba, 'We Do This 'Til We Free Us' 5

standing firm for justice, even if it be against myself [61] which is the biggest honour and privilege I could ever hope for.

Further Readings

- Kehinde Andrews, *The New Age of Empire: How Racism and Colonialism Still Rule the World* (Allen Lane 2021)
- Paulo Frierre, *The Pedagogy of the Oppressed* (Continuum, 2005)
- Mariame Kaba, *We Do This 'Til We Free Us* (Haymarket Books, 2021)
- Asim Qureshi, *A Virtue of Disobedience* (Byline Books 2018)
- Michael Steven Smith, *Lawyers for the Left: In the Courts, In the Streets, and On the Air,* (OR Books 2019)
- Ibram X. Kendi, *How to be an Rnti-Racist* (Random House, 2019)
- Linda Sarsour, *We are Not Here to be Bystanders* (37 Ink, 2020)
- Reni Eddo-Lodge, *Why I am no Longer Talking to White People about Race* (Bloomsbury Publishing, 2018)
- Angela Y. Davis, *Freedom is a Constant Struggle: Ferguson, Palestine, and the Foundations of a Movement* (Haymarket Books, 2016)

---

61. Quran, Chapter 4, Verse 135

6

Concept: A Deviant Student

Stephen Connelly

Ideology—comes from outside of the mainstream. In fact, conservative lawyers have long known what they were doing. Take Gottfried Wilhelm Leibniz, for example, who presented his *New Method for Teaching and Learning the Law* to the Archbishop of Mainz in 1667. Now, Leibniz understood that to really train lawyers it was not enough to instil rote learning. Impressing the rules into impressionable young minds, punishing them when they were wrong, rewarding them when they remembered the law—all this was training in the sense that one trained a dog. It kind of works, but Leibniz thought that to capture a mind you had to go deeper. Leibniz proposed a method of recognition: to present the law in such a way that it reflects something conceptual that subsists in the student. One such concept, Leibniz believed, was the rational activity which he regarded as common to all humans and their God. Of course, what Leibniz was actually doing was assuming a common or public reason and then instructing students that they should see they own thinking reflected in it.

This, as Giorgio Agamben tells us, is a classic manoeuvre of indoctrination: in order for contingent hierarchies to continue, they must present themselves as having always been the case. Indeed, in many philosophies (such as that of Leibniz) 'having always been the case' is transmuted into 'eternally necessary'. The net result for the student of law is that they are taught not just the law as content of thought, but are instructed how to reason about law as if that 'how to reason' were prior and immutable. The deviant, Canguilhem might say pathological, student is then just that one who questions the non-fit of their own way of thinking about the world with the pre-set 'common sense' to which all law students are expected to accede.

One of the archaeological tasks of critical legal theorists is not just to be attentive to the sedimentation of codes and other materials from which modern normative hierarchies are built, but also carefully to excavate these in search of the conceptual artefacts underpinning them all—concepts such as public reason, power, norm and authority—and to observe how these too have evolved over time to meet the needs of transient human masters.

Concept: Positivism

Ben Golder

Being a critical student means always asking questions of law. Sometimes the most important questions you can ask are about how things are presented to you. Are they presented as self-evident and simply common-sensical? And therefore not worth questioning? A critic is not necessarily someone who opposes something. Rather, a critic is someone who asks why a debate is constructed in the way it is, or why certain authors are chosen to represent a viewpoint, or why we are asking the same old questions time and again. The young Karl Marx, before he got bored with law and moved on to political economy, once wrote in a very important text that 'to formulate a question is to resolve it'.[1] That is to say, the ways in which we construct our inquiries are not only revealing but determinative. Asking the same old questions leads us to come up with very predictable answers.

University jurisprudence courses, especially in the United Kingdom, are a case in point. Legal positivists are frequently presented in the form of a debate that runs for most of the course with a different group of thinkers called natural lawyers. The legal positivists have names like Thomas Hobbes, John Austin, Jeremy Bentham, and Herbert (Lionel Adolphus) Hart. The natural lawyers have names like Thomas Aquinas or John Finnis. They argue passionately with each other. The

---

1. Karl Marx, '*On The Jewish Question*' [1844], at: https://www.marxists.org/archive/marx/works/1844/jewish-question/

positivists think that law is either the will of the sovereign or a set of rules, and style themselves as models of austere analytical clarity. They scrupulously separate law and morality, carefully extracting law as it really is from law as it might or ought to be—supposedly to set the world to rights. Against the moralistic natural lawyers, they are hard-headed chroniclers of law-in-the-real-world.

But it turns out that both sides of the debate are furiously answering the same (old) question: what is law? In this way jurisprudence is 'the theorized prejudice of lawyers,'[2] it is lawyers speaking to lawyers about the eminently important question of what law really is. But what if there were other questions worth asking? What if we wanted to ask questions about why certain groups always managed to evade the law, or to make it in their image? Or whether we really needed law at all? Whether we should tear it up (or down?) and start again? Then we would have to go beyond positivism's 'what is?' question. And maybe realise that asking the 'what is law?' question is a way not to ask the more pressing political questions.

You will find positivism in many of your substantive legal subjects, but it will rarely be identified even as the question. Positivism is the approach to law which imagines a self-contained legal science. From the background, it will whisper: You need only read cases and legislation, and that will give you all you need to know about law. But every time you come up against a module like this, you need to remember all that is being silenced. You need to remember whose voices made the law as it is, you need to remember the structural violence that law hides and the cruel and competitive subjectivities that it encourages.

---

2. Peter Fitzpatrick, 'The Abstracts and Brief Chronicles of the Time: Supplementing Jurisprudence,' in Peter Fitzpatrick (ed.), *Dangerous Supplements: Resistance and Renewal in Jurisprudence* (London: Pluto Press, 1991), p. 1.

8

How to Run an Empire (Lawfully)

PUBLIC INTERNATIONAL LAW, INTERNATIONAL ECONOMIC LAW

Ntina Tzouvala

The primary focus of contemporary legal education is domestic law. Think of your own curriculum: it certainly includes the national laws on contract, property and torts as well as the legal dimensions of the state's political architecture and of the relationship between individuals and governments. Indispensable as it may be, this state-focused idea about law and legality ignores the fact that in a globalized capitalist economy like ours, assets, goods and (some) people constantly cross borders, and so does law. Public international law attempts to regulate this conflictual reality: the world is connected through unequal economic relations, violence, human mobility, and ecological interdependence, but at the same time it is fragmented in almost two hundred national jurisdictions with their own laws and enforcement mechanisms.

Most international law textbooks share some basic ideas about the field. One of these ideas is that international law basically regulates (or at least it did traditionally) the relationships between sovereign states. Areas like the law of the sea or the protections afforded to diplomats and embassies abroad (immunities) are typical examples of these traditional areas regulated by international law. States are important in another way, since they are in the peculiar position of being both the recipients of the law, the legislators, and often the judges and the enforcers of the law. The basic presumption is that since all states are sovereign and equal they can only be bound by rules they have specifically consented to. This consent can take many different forms. The most common is the international treaty (also known as convention or covenant). Nowadays, treaties have proliferated to cover a wide range of matters that involve anything from international trade and investment to the preservation of biodiversity and the protection of human rights. Despite this prevalence of the treaty-form, other sources of international law retain their importance. Notably, states are also bound by international custom, the existence and content of which is much more elusive than that of treaties, since it is unwritten. Custom emerges when states act uniformly over a matter and they do so out of a sense of legal obligation, and not, for example, out of good will or habit. Finally, general principles of law adopted by (civilized) nations are also a source of international law. The idea here is that some core legal principles, such as the idea that agreements must be kept, are so common in domestic legal systems that they also become important for the international realm.

The above-summarized standard view has some serious blind spots, which enable us to approach international law critically. To begin with, the idea that only states can create international legal obligations is a common, yet not obvious one. Indeed, the modern nation-state is a fairly new form of organizing our common lives. It only first emerged three hundred years ago and became the dominant form of political community after decolonization in the 1960s and 1970s. This state-centrism of international law does not simply reflect this reality of the world. International law contributed to this proliferation of statehood by incentivizing peoples struggling against empires and colonialism to organize themselves in the form of states in order to enjoy the rights and privileges afforded to this form of political community by the law. In this process, other forms of human co-existence were marginalized. In the course of the 19th century Western states and lawyers argued that the systems of legality that had regulated for centuries the interactions between different communities, such as the Sino-centric view of order in East Asia or Indigenous laws in what became Australia, New Zealand or Canada, were not 'really' laws since they were purportedly barbaric or unsophisticated. Therefore, the (Western) state was elevated into the only conceivable source of international legality. What appears obvious and straightforward today was in fact the product of a long, arduous and often violent process.

Besides the fact that communities who are not states are excluded from the law-making processes of international law, the common idea about sovereign equality and legal obligation summarized above has other problems too. Even if we accept this state-centric view of legal sources, it is undeniably the case that not all states are equal when it comes to the creation of the law. This is clear in the case of international custom. For a state not to be bound by emerging custom, it needs to constantly register its objections to this rule, both verbally and in practice. This is possible (yet quite burdensome) for a handful of states that employ an army of lawyers. However, it is virtually impossible for developing states who struggle to keep up with the proliferation of international law with only a handful of lawyers in their employee. To make matters even worse, the majority of academic international lawyers and international courts pay disproportionate attention to the practice and legal opinions of the former group of states. A good example here is the law pertaining to the prohibition of the use of force in international relations. This rule has two significant exceptions: states are allowed to use force to defend themselves and also pursuant to being authorized to do so by the UN Security Council. A handful of states, including the USA, the UK and Israel, have put forward very broad interpretations of this right to self-defense, which essentially erode the default rule of the prohibition of force. These interpretations have become increasingly popular in the context of the 'war on terror' after 9/11, even though the number and geographic/cultural distribution of states that support them remain quite limited. It would be unimaginable that an interpretation supported, for example mainly by Myanmar, Lesotho and Argentina would ever gain the same traction. Therefore, even within a statist framework, some states are more equal than others in their capacity to influence the formation and interpretation of the law.

The persistence of both factual and legal inequalities is evident in the third source of international law mentioned above: the general principles of law recognized by civilized nations. Students are often instructed to read out the qualification 'civilized' as an anachronism that is irrelevant for modern international law. However, the persistence of this uncomfortable phrasing is a useful window to the imperial past of international law and, more importantly, to its ongoing legacies for the field. Despite the commonly-held belief that international law has historically regulated the relationships between sovereign states, in reality its fundamental doctrines were forged in the context of Western imperialism and as responses to radical changes, such as revolutions and wars of decolonization. This process involved not only states, but also companies, mercenaries, merchants and preachers. In the process, lawyers insisted that political communities formed a hierarchy: on the top one would find white-majority, Christian states with the laws and institutions necessary for sustaining a modern capitalist economy (private property, contract laws, protection of individual rights etc). In the middle of the pyramid (or 'semi-civilized') were polities like

Japan, China or the Ottoman Empire. They enjoyed some rights under international law, notably the right to conclude treaties with imperial powers that restricted their rights to impose import and export tariffs and posed limits to their jurisdictions over foreigners that resided in their territory. Finally, at the bottom of this juridical pyramid were the so-called 'savage' or 'uncivilized' states, which were only afforded the basic protections of humanitarianism, but did not enjoy legal status under international law.

This strict hierarchy between political communities is no longer explicitly part of the architecture of international law. This does not mean that the international legal order is as egalitarian as its proponents imagine it to be. The proliferation of national sovereignty during the de-colonization period was a historical victory of radical decolonization movements that challenged the old structures of international law and led to the establishment of new principles, including that of self-determination. However, as the historic alliance between decolonized states unraveled in the late 1970s, Third World sovereignty became a tool to bring about and justify domestic and international oppression and exploitation. The idea of the state as the primary subject of international law is indeed a powerful ideological tool. By assuming that a people are unitary and represented by the structures of the state in the international realm, international law invites those oppressed on grounds of class, gender, ethnicity etc. to identify with their oppressors within the legal personhood of the state. In this respect, domestic ruling classes have often embraced international law (for example, international trade or investment agreements). Despite the fact that the elites of weaker states might use international law to improve their relative position in the global economic structures, this does not automatically mean that these legal arrangements are beneficial for the most oppressed and marginalized within such states, let alone for non-human animals and the environment as a whole. Therefore, an analysis of international law that only focuses on the diplomatic, statist-level is a product of the ideology promoted by international law itself that transforms the will and interests of the state (or of its ruling classes) into the interests of the community as a whole.

Furthermore, this proliferation of state sovereignty coupled with material and political inequality is crucial for the functioning of modern imperialism. Indeed, imperialism does not usually simply involve brute coercion, but it deploys a combination of violent and non-violent techniques, with law being a very important amongst them. In the aftermath of the 1980s debt-crisis in Latin America and of the collapse of the Soviet Union, numerous post-socialist and decolonized states became dependent on the International Monetary Fund (IMF) and the World Bank for loans. These loans came with strings attached: the so-called 'conditionalities' made payments dependent of states reforming their economy along neoliberal lines. Privatizations, deregulation of the labour market, and trade and investment liberalization became necessary preconditions for the states to receive loans from the international financial institutions and to remain solvent. Since the 2008-2009 financial crisis, this linking between international finance and domestic reform has also become highly relevant for the states of the European periphery, such as Greece, Portugal or Ireland. These agreements were, of course, not imposed by force, but thanks to the sovereign consent of these states. Nowadays, it is precisely equal sovereignty that sustains a profoundly uneven global political economy that prioritizes the interests of private and public lenders over those of borrowers and promotes a very particular form of statehood that is subsumed to the necessities of market competition and capital accumulation.

The role of sovereignty as an enabler of empire extends beyond the realm of political economy too. Think, for example, of extra-territorial detention of refugees and migrants or the USA 'extraordinary rendition' program in the context of the 'war on terror'. In both cases, powerful states such as Australia, the EU member-states or the US, use strategically the sovereignty of other states to avoid legal responsibility for their policies. Through a series of bilateral agreements, Australia ensures that individuals who attempt to reach the country by boat are detained in Nauru or Papua New Guinea, often in desperate conditions that violate fundamental human rights rules. Therefore, even though Australia remains largely in control of the situation (and Australian corporations are heavily involved in the detention schemes, often returning a handsome profit), it can claim that, in fact, it is Nauru or Papua New Guinea that exercise jurisdiction over these individuals and are, therefore, responsible for their treatment.

This is, of course, not to say that international law has not changed since the 19th-century or that asymmetrical relations of wealth and power explain every aspect of it. In fact, international law is today a very diverse field that covers a wide range of matters. These different fields (international economic law, international human rights law, international environmental law etc) have developed with a degree of autonomy from each other and merit closer examination in their own right. That said, it is important to proceed with such detailed studies keeping in mind that international law carries certain biases that permeate its very core. This is perhaps the first step into reconfiguring the international legal order toward a more just and equitable direction that safeguards not only human flourishing, but also the future of the planet as a whole.

BIBLIOGRAPHY

- Antony Anghie, *Imperialism, Sovereignty and the Making of International Law* (Cambridge University Press, 2004).
- Bhupinder S. Chimni, 'Customary International Law: A Third World Perspective' *American Journal of International Law* 112(1) (2018), 1-46.
- Daria Davitti, Marlene Fries, 'Offshore Processing and Complicity in Current EU Migration Policies-Part 1' *EJIL:Talk!*, 10 October 2017, accessed 19 August 2020 https://www.ejiltalk.org/offshore-processing-and-complicity-in-current-eu-migration-policies-part-1/.
- Darryl Li, 'From Exception to Empire: Sovereignty, Carceral Circulation, and the "Global War on Terror"' in Carole McGranahan, John F. Collins (ads.), *Ethnographies of U.S. Empire* (Duke UP, 2018).
- Anne Orford and Jennifer Beard, 'Making the State Safe for the Market: The World Bank's Development Report 1997' *Melbourne University Law Review* 22 (1998), 195–216.
- Sundhya Pahuja, *Decolonising International Law: Development, Economic Growth and the Politics of Universality* (Cambridge University Press, 2011).
- Rose Parfitt, 'The Spectre of Sources' *European Journal of International Law* 25 (1) (2014), 297-306.
- Ntina Tzouvala 'Civilisation' in Jean D'Aspremont and Sahib Singh (eds) *Concepts for International Law: Contributions to Disciplinary Thought* (Edward Elgar, 2018), 83-104.
- Illan rua Wall, 'The Irish Crisis: Europe Colonises Itself' Critical Legal Thinking, 7 December 2011, accessed 19 August 2020 http://criticallegalthinking.com/2011/12/07/europe-colonises-itself/

FURTHER READINGS

- Tendayi E. Achiume, 'Migration as Decolonization' (2019) 71(6) *Stanford Law Review* 1509.
- Hilary Charlesworth, 'International Law: A Discipline of Crisis' (2002) 65(3) *Modern Law Review* 377.
- Michael Fakhri, 'Third World Sovereignty, Indigenous Sovereignty, and Food Sovereignty: Living with Sovereignty despite the Map' (2018) 9(3-4) *Transnational Legal Theory* 218.
- David W. Kennedy, *Of Law and War* (Princeton UP, 2006).
- Martti Koskenniemi, *From Apology to Utopia: The Structure of International Legal Argument* (2nd edn, Cambridge UP, 2005).
- Robert Knox, 'Valuing Race? Stretched Marxism and the Logic of Imperialism' (2016) 4(1) *London Review of International Law* 81.
- Karin Michelson, 'Rhetoric and Rage: Third World Voices in International Legal Discourse' (2002) 16(2) *Wisconsin International Law Journal* 353.
- Makau Mutua, 'Savages, Victims and Saviours: The Metaphor of Human Rights' (2001) 42 *Harvard International Law Journal* 201.
- Usha Natarajan, 'A Third World Approach to Debating the Legality of the Iraq War' (2007) 9(4) *International Community Law Review* 405.
- Anne Orford, 'Feminism, Imperialism and the Mission of International Law 71(2) (2002) *Nordic Journal of International Law* 275.
- Sundhya Pahuja, 'Conserving the World's Resources?' In James Crawford, Martti Koskenniemi (eds.), *The Cambridge Companion to International Law* (Cambridge UP, 2015).
- Teemu Ruskola, 'Raping Like a State' (2010) 57 *UCLA Law Review* 1477.
- Guy Fiti Sinclair, 'State Formation, Liberal Reform and the Growth of International Organizations' (2015) 26(2) *European Journal of International Law* 445.
- Ntina Tzouvala, *Capitalism as Civilisation: A History of International Law* (Cambridge UP, 2020).
- Irene Watson, *Aboriginal Peoples, Colonialism and International Law : Raw Law* (Routledge, 2016).

9

Law In The Anthropocene

CLIMATE CHANGE, ENVIRONMENTAL ACTIVISM & LAW

Daniel Matthews

We are currently living through a period of profound transformation within the Earth's climatic system. Human activity, primarily by burning fossil fuels, is altering the chemical composition of the atmosphere and oceans in a way unprecedented for millions of years. CO_2 concentration has passed the 400 parts per million mark that many climatologists take to be a signal of irreversible change beyond the nominally 'safe limit' of a 2°C increase above pre-industrial averages. The last time atmospheric CO_2 was at this level was during the Pliocene epoch, 4 million years ago, when humans didn't exist and sea levels were 25 meters higher than today. Leading climate scientists paint a bleak picture of our current and expected climatic conditions. We are already seeing widespread extinctions with some claiming that we have begun the sixth 'mass extinction event' in planetary history, comparable with the period of change that killed off the dinosaurs. Along with biodiversity loss, there are unprecedented pressures on freshwater systems; the phosphorous and nitrogen cycles, essential for the production of fertilisers; and the range of habitability for basic food stuffs like wheat and rice. These changes within the Earth's climatic system will dramatically impact human societies and prompt a fundamental reassessment of extant modes of production, consumption and habitation in so-called 'developed' economies.

Changes within our climatic system are so significant that many scientists working in the fields of geology and earth systems science have suggested that the Earth has entered a new geological epoch, brought on by human action, called the Anthropocene. Geologists, who are interested in the 'deep history' of the planet, divide planetary history into various segments—eons, eras, periods, epochs and ages—that denote periods of relative stability within the earth's climate. This chronology, stretching over many millions of years, is called the Geologic Time Scale. The movement from one climatic condition (and age or epoch) to another is usually marked by some fundamental shift within the Earth system, like a change in the chemical composition of the atmosphere and oceans, the end or onset of an ice age, massive volcanic activity or the widespread extinction of species. Until recently, most geologists agreed that we were living in the Holocene epoch, a period of some 11,700 years, marked by the end of the last ice age. The Holocene has provided the largely benign climatic conditions that allowed for the growth of agriculture and the flourishing of human civilisation. The Anthropocene thesis contends that this period of stability has ended. There is much debate about exactly how to define this new epoch—particularly on the question of its date of origin, with anything from the early 17th century to the middle of the 20th century being suggested as possibilities. As yet the Anthropocene does not form part of the official Geologic Time Scale as the details of this designation continue to be debated. Nonetheless, the Anthropocene offers a useful shorthand for the radicality of the current disruptions taking place within the planet. The Anthropocene indicates that the actions of 'modern man'—arguably over the course of the last two hundred years and attributable to a fraction of the global population—have diverted the course of planetary history. The social relations that define the contemporary world economy have acquired so much power that the climatic conditions of the last twelve millennia have been displaced and we have entered the decidedly uncertain conditions of a new climatic regime.

Beyond the specialist domains of geology and earth system science, the Anthropocene concept has been discussed by a number of writers within the humanities and social sciences. This is partly because the concept disrupts commonplace assumptions about the distinction between the 'social' and 'natural' domains, a presupposition that structures so much of the writing in Western philosophy and social theory. Nature is often thought to be somewhere 'out there', obeying certain 'natural laws' (the laws of physics and evolution for instance) that are largely (or entirely) indifferent to human intervention. In this sense, the natural world is often taken to provide the 'backdrop' or 'staging' for human social life. The social sciences and humanities are exclusively concerned with the human dramas that take place, set against this 'natural' scenography. These latter disciplines are interested in human-made phenomena and human-to-human networks that are subject to more or less conscious decisions that are detached from the 'natural world'. The Anthropocene appears to disrupt this bifurcation by showing that the organisation of society—in the form of production, consumption and habitation practices, amongst other things—has a profound impact on nature's deep structures. The 'natural backdrop' to our human dramas has suddenly become highly mobile and reactive, not nearly as stable or as indifferent to our actions as we once thought. Indeed, our very sense of the 'social domain' is disrupted by the Anthropocene thesis, suggesting the need to account for networks and entanglements between the human and a range of non-human forces, constituting 'geo-social' or 'socio-ecological' formations.

In legal scholarship and practice, questions pertaining to the environment are often thought to be the preserve of the specialist field of environmental law. But the issues thrown up by the Anthropocene transcend any one legal field and encourage us instead to reflect more deeply on the relationship between legal concepts, traditions, institutions and practices and those ecological and geological forces that are increasingly shaping social life. The challenge is to understand how legal practices, theories and concepts are woven into the planetary web of life. Legal scholarship is only beginning to turn its attention to this challenge and there is much work to be done in this area. However, we can point to two routes into these issues; the first is *historical* and the second *theoretical*.

Re-Reading the History of Modern Law

Regardless of the official date given for the onset of the Anthropocene, it is clear that profound climatic change is attributable (to a very large degree at least) to the massive increase in fossil fuel consumption beginning in the late 18th century and accelerating dramatically from the mid 20th century. In this sense, the Anthropocene is rooted in the history of capitalist social relations. Indeed, many commentators argue that the Anthropocene should be renamed the 'Capitalocene' for this very reason. How, then, is law implicated in the processes of production, extraction and pollution that has tipped us into the current dangerous situation? How have extant approaches to property law, the law of corporations, legal personality, and tortious liability helped to *facilitate*, *obscure* or *resist* those processes that have so destabilized the climate? In thinking about these questions, two themes stand out.

The first is how the distribution of responsibilities that the law achieves embeds a form of *anthropocentricism* within social life. The much vaunted (and critiqued) 'age of rights' has been central to this process. Individual human rights, for instance, promote a view of the human that is disarticulated from the ecological relations on which all of us ultimately depend. The protection of basic human freedoms—the freedom of assembly, free speech, conscience and so on—is precious and should, of course, be defended. But a focus on such rights and freedoms perhaps too readily ignores the obligations and debts that all of us owe to the Earth's environmental and climatic conditions. In this sense, the historical trajectory of rights beginning in the late 18th century and fundamentally re-articulated after 1945 (dates, it should be noticed, that precisely coincide with dramatic increases in global fossil fuel consumption) perhaps helps us understand how an anthropocentric world view has become normalized within Western law and culture where the vulnerabilities of the environment, ecosystems and non-human forms of life are routinely ignored.

A second theme concerns the way in which legal concepts and practices help to entrench the *nature/culture* distinction in a way that posits the natural environment as something to be exploited and controlled, rather than cared for and respected. In this context, property law looms large. It is, after all, modern property regimes that guarantee the rights to clear land, extract minerals and fossil fuels, and restrict common use and accesses. The historical imposition of Western property regimes on indigenous land and communities in the context of colonialism is particularly significant in this context. The legal orders that justified the displacement of indigenous peoples from their land—often under the guise that indigenous people were merely part of 'nature' and therefore could be readily disposed of—have facilitated high pollution extractive industries within colonial and post-colonial states. Indeed, indigenous land rights, which offer some resistance against the imposition of settler property law, is at the forefront of many campaigns aimed at resisting mining and fracking practices in the USA, Canada and Australia, where the enduring questions of colonial injustice are particularly raw.

These brief examples illustrate the way in which the history of some of our most basic legal concepts and principles is implicated—sometimes in unintended or unexpected ways—in the social and economic processes that have shifted the earth's climate beyond the conditions associated with the Holocene. Many issues deserve further thought and attention. How have the rights and duties elaborated within corporations law, property law, contracts and torts (the fields of law crucial to sustaining capitalistic societies) been implicated in either inuring us from a proper sensitivity to ecological relations, or actively legitimating the exploitation of the environment in the name of 'business efficacy', 'economic growth' or a bourgeois conception of 'freedom'? And how has the evolution of public law principles like territorial jurisdiction, popular sovereignty and the right to non-intervention shaped a perception of political life in which environmental harms are obscured or devalued? One of the provocations of the Anthropocene is that it encourages us to re-read the history of modernity less as a history of 'progress' but as a history of ever accelerating environmental destruction that has taken on geological and planetary proportions. The history of modern law, in this sense, becomes one way of understanding the history of our new entry into the Anthropocene. As we face a highly uncertain future, understanding the role that law has played in producing the current crisis is going to be essential if we are to avoid repeating the mistakes of the past.

Theoretical Innovations

An alternative route into these issues is *theoretical* rather than *historical*. If the modern 'age of rights' either ignores or sidelines environmental concerns, one area of theoretical innovation lies in broadening our conception of fundamental rights to apply to aspects of the 'natural world'. This approach has been taken up within the Earth Jurisprudence movement, which aims to articulate the basic 'rights of nature' where ecosystems and non-human animals are all considered to have rights that could—ideally—be enforced by the courts in an effort to sustain ecological integrity. Enlarging the scope of rights in this way helps to challenge the anthropocentricism of modern 'rights talk' and forces us to consider the inherent dignity and worth of aspects of the natural world. But a number of difficulties remain. How do we balance the rights of non-human animals or ecosystems with human rights? And in making this calculus is it likely—or even desirable – that we stop privileging the rights of humans? Does it make sense to impose the Western notion of individualized and justiciable 'rights' onto non-human animals and ecosystems that are subject to patterns of behaviour that are largely alien to human cognition? And in the context of a highly complex and dynamic earth system where species, ecosystems, climatological and geological forces all interact in ways that the best contemporary science struggles to understand, is the goal of 'ecological integrity' even meaningful, let alone amenable to legal reasoning?

Notwithstanding these difficulties, the 'rights of nature' have been given some judicial and legislative approval; most prominently in New Zealand where the legal personality of Te Awa Tupua (Whanganui River) has recently been recognized and a statutory framework established by which the rights of the river can be represented and defended. Here, courts will be able to adjudicate over the competing rights claims by the river, on the one hand, and those human actors that engage with it on the other. Whilst this move might open the door to further innovations in this direction, more work is needed in order to understand the theoretical basis for these emergent 'rights of nature' and how they intersect with existing forms of legal reasoning.

Beyond extending rights to non-human actors, a more general theoretical concern lies in re-thinking the context in which law is situated. It is now commonplace to think of law less as a hermetically sealed bubble of 'black letter' rules and regulations, but as something that is embedded in social, cultural, political and economic contexts. In this sense, a 'law and society' or 'law in context' approach to legal scholarship has become *de rigueur*. But as we indicated above, the new climatic regime challenges us to re-think the very nature of 'society' itself, suggesting that social life is not neatly separated from 'nature' but is embedded in reactive and dynamic relations with ecological and geological forces.

One key insight that has emerged from 'law and society' approaches has been the notion that legal power is embedded in the social milieu, traceable within cultural and artistic practices, as well as the patterns and perceptions of everyday life. Equally, changing social practices and values have been shown to play an important role in shaping legal development. If we embrace a view that 'society' is a matter of 'geo-social' or 'socio-ecological' relations, then we must

understand how law emerges out of and is disseminated within the more-than-human networks that constitute these forms. This might involve an inquiry into the norms, customs or other forms of ordering that are inherent within our contemporary geo-social formations, or within the planetary climate system itself. This perspective might reveal new obligations that human societies owe or new goals towards which they ought to be directing their energies. In exploring these themes, insights from indigenous legal knowledges, which tend to be far more sensitive to the entanglements between human and non-human relations, and the normativity that such imbrications infer, are particularly apposite. In this sense, contemporary Western legal theory has much to learn from these traditions.

The key theoretical challenge in this context is to think of law as being deeply entwined, not just with 'social life', but with ecological and geological forces too. How we bring these non-human forces into the scope of our legal theorising remains a challenge that is only beginning to be addressed. But with the onset of a new climatic regime, where questions of the environment, ecology and climate change are increasingly dominating our everyday experiences and are at the forefront of contemporary political campaigns, such innovations are urgently needed.

FURTHER READINGS

- Kathleen Birrell and Daniel Matthews (eds) 'Laws for the Anthropocene: Orientations, Encounters, Imaginaries' *Law & Critique* (2020) 31(3).
- Margaret Davies, *Law Unlimited: Materialism, Pluralism and Legal Theory* (Routledge, 2018)
- Jason W. Moore, *Capitalism in the Web of Life: Ecology and the Accumulation of Capital* (Verso, 2015).
- Nicole Rogers and Michelle Maloney (eds), *Law as if Earth Really Mattered: The Wild Law Judgment Project* (Routledge, 2018).
- Will Steffen et al, 'The Anthropocene: Conceptual and Historical Perspectives' *Philosophical Transactions of the Royal Society* (2011) 369.
- Jorge E. Viñuales, 'Law and the Anthropocene' *C-EENRG Working Paper* (2016).

10

Concept: Neoliberalism

Jessica Whyte

In the past decade, scholars have argued about how best to characterise neoliberalism. Is it an economic reductionism that transforms all values into cash value? A flimsy ideology grasped by a capitalist class to wage war against organised labour? A political rationality? A way of governing? A zombie, that staggers on long after it should have been put to rest by financial crises? Or perhaps a figment of the imagination of scholars who use the term as a swear-word for anything they dislike?

In cutting through this tangle of definitions, we could do worse than consult a short text written by a paradigmatic neoliberal: the Chicago School economist Milton Friedman. Back in 1951, a young Friedman provided one of the clearest descriptions of this new liberalism. The 'basic error' of nineteenth-century liberalism, he wrote in 'Neo-Liberalism and its Prospects', was to confine the role of the state to the maintenance of order and enforcement of contracts. This was the *laissez-faire* principle. Friedman framed neoliberalism as a reaction to this basic error: 'Neoliberalism would accept the nineteenth-century liberal emphasis on the fundamental importance of the individual', he wrote, 'but it would substitute for the nineteenth-century goal of *laissez-faire* as a means to this end, the goal of the competitive order'. This entailed much more scope for state intervention to create the conditions for competition than nineteenth-century *laissez-faire* had countenanced.

Despite excellent recent studies, a common view still treats neoliberalism as simply a doctrine of free markets, an economic fundamentalism, or a rigid commitment to *laissez-faire*. Such a view has profoundly distorted our understanding of neoliberalism. For all their undoubted diversity, those liberals who gathered in 1947 to found the Mont Pèlerin Society (what Philip Mirowski and Dieter Plehwe have called the 'neoliberal thought collective') were largely united by the programme outlined in Friedman's short text. Their central concern was the active production of the conditions of market competition. Early neoliberals were convinced that markets were not natural; rather, they required adequate legal, political, and moral conditions.

Early neoliberalism was upheld by true believers who felt besieged by what Michel Foucault dubbed 'an anti-liberal invariant'—this encompassed not only National Socialism and Soviet Communism, but also the US New Deal and the British welfare state. In the wake of the Great Depression, faith in liberalism had dissipated, and the neoliberals saw the need for concerted political transformation to bring about the conditions in which markets could thrive again. It would be several decades before the intellectual project they initiated would gain political traction. Although there is no one-to-one correspondence between the political project of early neoliberalism and neoliberal policies of austerity, privatization, and deregulation, the former deeply influenced regimes as different as Augusto Pinochet's Chilean dictatorship and Tony Blair's British 'New Labour'.

11

Concept: Hegemony

Henrique Carvalho

What does it mean to say that the law is hegemonic? To say that is to suggest that the law enjoys a certain status in our social lives, in which it appears as something not only naturalised, as part of the way things are, but also something with which we feel we need or might desire to identify, as part of who we are or long to be. This status gives law power. At its core, the idea of hegemony highlights that political power is ultimately not about force; rather, it is primarily about values, beliefs and affects. This is very clear with regards to the law: even though the legal system is replete with sanctions that are applied in case of violation or disobedience (most notoriously and violently embodied in the apparatus of punishment), which are backed up by significant force, this only covers a very small fraction of the scope in which the law operates in society. And even punishment would be impossible to enforce if most people were not ready to accept it as necessary, normal and unavoidable. Therefore, law derives most of its power from its hegemonic status.

But to say that the law is hegemonic is also simultaneously to open this status to question. It is to acknowledge that the authority of the law is the consequence of a series of processes which culturally and socially enable an atmosphere of acceptance and compliance for those in positions of dominance to operate the way they do—what Antonio Gramsci called the 'manufacture of consent'.[1] Hegemony heavily relies on processes of socialisation and institutionalisation, through which ideas and the values associated with them acquire an aspect of 'givenness' as they appear as intrinsic aspects of social life, and are symbolically given legitimacy and importance. This is true for most conventions in society, from the 'right' or 'proper' way to eat, to when we should laugh or cry, to where and when we should cross the road. However, 'hegemony' associates specific ideas and practices directly with issues of ideology, as it understands them to be linked to dominant interests and structures of oppression. To say that the law is hegemonic is therefore to suggest that there is something deeply problematic about its authority, in that it constrains other possibilities and entraps people's consciousness in a worldview that is reductive and exclusionary, and thus inherently violent.

To say that the law is hegemonic is to say that its authority must be challenged, scrutinised, deconstructed and contextualised. It is to invite us to uncover its biases, its complicity with other hegemonic ideas—such as masculinity and whiteness. Ultimately, to say that the law is hegemonic is to push for the possibility of people's social experiences to be disentangled from its affective hold, and to be given different voices---which, perhaps with enough effort, can become counter-hegemonic.

---

1. Antonio Gramsci, *Selections from the Prison Notebooks of Antonio Gramsci*, (International Publishers, 1971)

12

Controlling Refugees

REFUGEE LAW, MIGRATION, INTERNAL DISPLACEMENT

Simon Behrman

What is the purpose of Refugee and Asylum Law? The straightforward answer, which is to be found in most standard approaches to the topic, is that it exists to extend protection to people escaping from persecution. Certainly, there is evidence to support this proposition. All states that are party to the main international refugee law treaties are bound to consider claims for asylum, and if those claiming it can prove to the authorities that they indeed are refugees, then they have a right to stay. Refugee and Asylum Law modules will always lay out the various criteria that need to be met to gain refugee status. This will usually centre around the definition of a refugee contained in Article 1A of the 1951 Refugee Convention.[1] In addition, they should also illustrate how both the refugee law treaties, and a whole battery of related human rights law that interact with them, guarantee a set of substantive rights in the country of asylum.

And yet, there is a curious anomaly. On a regular basis, the top hosting countries for refugees are states which either are not part of the international refugee law regime such as Pakistan and Jordan, or, like Turkey, only formally recognize a very limited scope for refugee law. Other states that currently host some of the largest numbers of refugees include Sudan, Uganda and Kenya, who have adopted a much wider refugee definition that is contained in Article 1(2) of the Organization of African Unity (OAU) Refugee Convention. Alternatively, Germany has effectively suspended the normal operation of refugee law to allow

---

1. UN General Assembly, *Convention Relating to the Status of Refugees*, 28 July 1951, United Nations, Treaty Series, vol. 189, 137.

Syrian refugees to enter in 2015. On the other hand, the states that are founding signatories to the 1951 Refugee Convention and are central to the international refugee law system, particularly those in Europe and North America, are often the most parsimonious when it comes to hosting refugees. Globally, only around a third of forced migrants each year are included within the category of refugee, according to statistics compiled by the UN High Commissioner for Refugees (UNHCR).[2] The rest are excluded usually because they lack some requirement contained in the 1951 Refugee Convention definition: they have not left the country of their nationality—hence, they are 'internally displaced persons' (IDPs)—or they are fleeing the generalized effects of war rather than any persecution directed specifically at them. It is estimated that by the middle of this century, one of the largest groups of forced migrants will be people fleeing the effects of climate change, and yet it is commonly accepted that they will not fall within the remit of refugee law.

At first blush, the obvious point is that those excluded are not refugees because they do not fit the relevant legal definition. But when such a high proportion of people fleeing danger of one sort or another are excluded from this definition, and when states who use this definition as a gateway to asylum end up accepting so few as compared to those without any operating legal framework to distinguish refugees from other migrants, we need to challenge the circular logic that says someone qualifies for refugee status because refugee law says they are indeed a refugee.

There are two main responses from scholars to this problem. First, it is argued that refugee law has a very specific remedial purpose, which is to protect those most at risk e.g. people fleeing persecution by their governments or those from whom their governments cannot or will not provide protection.[3] This argument embodies a classic idea of the relationship between the state and the individual, which says that our rights to a life free from violence are guaranteed by our state of nationality. It is only when that relationship breaks down—when the state turns on its own citizens causing them to flee their country of nationality and seek protection elsewhere—that international refugee law steps in to fill the gap in protection. From this perspective, the exclusion of IDPs

---

2. UNHCR maintains a very useful database of current and historical statistics on forced migration https://www.unhcr.org/uk/data.html Accessed 29 April 2020.
3. E.g. Matthew E. Price, *Rethinking Asylum: History, Purpose, and Limits* (Cambridge: CUP, 2009).

is justified on the basis that so long as forced migrants remain within their own state, this relationship has not been definitively broken. It also explains why people fleeing natural disasters, such as earthquakes or volcanic eruptions, do not come within the purview of refugee law. As traumatic and disrupting as those events are, they do not necessarily involve the breakdown of the state/citizen relationship. Less clear is why victims of generalized violence such as armed conflict should also be excluded. After all, in many cases civil war effectively diminishes or destroys the state's capacity to protect its citizens.

The second response is to argue that protections for forced migrants extend well beyond the main refugee law conventions. This idea has become known as 'complementary protection'.[4] It is argued that the huge expansion of human rights law in recent decades has effectively created a body of law independent of the 1951 Refugee Convention that is also far more expansive in its coverage.[5] Here the principle of *non-refoulement* has been of the greatest importance. The origins of *non-refoulement* can be found in the abortive 1933 Refugee Convention, but was also included in Article 33 of the 1951 Refugee Convention. The substance of this principle is that states are prohibited from sending people back to a place where there would be a threat of serious harm. While the 1951 Convention only refers to the threat of persecution, the wider meaning has been developed to interpret the duties of states in regards to more general human rights norms. For example, in two landmark cases the European Court of Human Rights held that states would be in violation of the right to freedom from torture by sending people back to conditions which would amount to cruel and inhuman conditions.[6] Much more recently, the Human Rights Committee of the UN has ruled that sending people back to conditions in which climate change has degraded the environment to such an extent as to pose a threat of serious harm, would also be in violation of the principle of *non-refoulement*.[7]

In my view, both these arguments present a skewed approach to ideas

---

4. Jane McAdam, *Complementary Protection in International Refugee Law* (Oxford: OUP, 2007).
5. Vincent Chetail, 'Are Refugee Rights Human Rights? An Unorthodox Questioning of the Relations between Refugee Law and Human Rights Law,' in *Human Rights and Immigration*, ed. Ruth Rubio-Marin (Oxford: OUP, 2014).
6. *Soering v UK* [1989] ECtHR 14038/88; *Chahal v UK* [1996] ECtHR 70/1995/576/662.
7. *Ioane Teitiota v. New Zealand*, CCPR/C/127/D/2728/2016, UN Human Rights Committee, 7 January 2020.

of violence and protection. In the first case, an artificial delineation is made between violence suffered as a result of direct persecution that leads to displacement across borders, and that of people suffering less direct structural forms of violence. We are used to the discourse in which 'refugees' are to be given preferential treatment as distinct from 'economic migrants'; the implication being that the latter group are made up of people who have left their countries of origin merely for personal convenience. But this ignores things such as poverty as forms of structural violence. Not only can poverty itself reduce life expectancy and lead to substantial physical and psychological harm, but things such as race and gender will often intersect to exacerbate the effects of poverty on certain groups of people. Yet, none of this is captured in the prevailing idea that refugee protection must be predicated on 'persecution', which insists on direct violence only.

The human rights argument does carry some weight, and it is certainly true that the principle of *non-refoulement* has served to effectively prevent states deporting people back to face serious harm. In particular, it has often provided an effective shield even in the post-9/11 period when states have claimed that individuals must be sent back on grounds of national security. But it is also important to recognize that *non-refoulement* only provides a break on deportations, but does not guarantee anything beyond that. It is for this reason that many terrorist suspects, for example, while not being deported back to their countries of origin are kept in detention for extended periods or are otherwise subjected to stringent restrictions on their rights of movement, access to work or state support. Protection, if it is to have any substantive meaning, is not merely about preventing serious harm, but also about providing the conditions in which people can live as normal and fulfilling a life as possible.

So, if protection is not the guiding principle of international refugee law, then what is? In my view, it is primarily about control of access to asylum.[8] Once we start to look at refugee law in this way, many of the contradictions I highlighted earlier resolve themselves. This argument can be advanced in the first instance by simply correcting a widespread misnomer which refers to a 'right of asylum'. In fact, there is no right of asylum in international law. The closest we come is Article 14 of the Universal Declaration on Human Rights (UDHR), which refers to the right to 'seek and enjoy in other countries asylum from persecution'.

---

8. My argument is fully fleshed out in *Law and Asylum: Space, Subject, Resistance* (Routledge, 2018).

Notwithstanding the fact that the UDHR is not binding on states, this formulation is fundamentally different from the original draft, which promised a right 'to seek and *be granted*' asylum. The rather more nebulous 'enjoy' obscures the key need of the refugee who presents themselves at the border: the right of entry. Later binding human rights instruments such as the European Convention on Human Rights or the International Covenant on Civil and Political Rights completely omit any mention of asylum. Even the 1951 Refugee Convention contains no legal right to asylum, nor even any standard practices or monitoring of the process for applying for asylum. State parties to the Convention are only bound to grant asylum to those whom their own procedures determine fits the definition in Article 1A. The link between all these gaps and failures to guarantee asylum is one of the central pillars of sovereign right in international law: the right of each state to control entry into its territory. Indeed, you will find this right repeatedly referred to by judges in asylum cases. Thus, the claims of people seeking asylum must always be secondary to this right of states, and it therefore follows that international law, which after all is created by states themselves, reinforces that hierarchy of rights.

Clues as to the real priorities of international refugee law are dotted throughout its history: the collapse of the two precursors to the UNHCR, the United Nations Relief and Rehabilitation Administration, and the International Refugee Organization owed much to the emerging Cold War rivalry between the USA and the USSR; the view of one observer to the negotiations over the 1951 Convention that they 'had at times given the impression that it was a conference for the protection of helpless sovereign states against the wicked refugee'[9]; the paragraph of the Preamble to the 1951 Convention that asserts 'that the grant of asylum may place unduly heavy burdens on certain countries'; the placing of asylum policy in the European Union's 'third pillar' comprising issues of crime and security. All of these examples—and there are many more—point towards refugee law as primarily a means of control rather than of protection. In this sense, refugee law has been remarkably successful. The narrowness of the legal definition of the refugee coupled with the definition's hegemonic power provide an effective filtering mechanism for states to exclude most forced migrants from gaining asylum. This is one reason why those states that are not part of this international legal system—mainly in the Middle East

---

9. Quoted in James C. Hathaway, 'A Reconsideration of the Underlying Premise of Refugee Law,' *Harvard International Law Journal* 31 (1990), 145.

and South Asia—are much more generous in terms of the numbers of refugees that they admit. Indeed, perhaps one reason these states have rejected international refugee law is to preserve much stronger and more generous non-legal traditions of asylum.[10]

So, to return to the question I began with, the *primary* purpose of refugee and asylum law is not protection, but control. This does not mean that protection plays no part in how it operates—there are many subsidiary benefits, some of which I have mentioned—but it does force us to question whether we should defer to refugee law's, and by implication the state's, hegemonic claim to determining who qualifies or not for asylum. Of course, without refugee law, states still retain discretion to decide who gets asylum or not. This leaves us with some further questions that I think are worth considering when studying Refugee and Asylum Law: to what extent does it mitigate the capriciousness of states or mask the political prejudices of states? Should political, ethical or other approaches take precedence over legal ones when framing the concept of asylum? What does refugee reception look like in states without refugee law, and what are the relative benefits and drawbacks of their treatment of refugees?

Further Readings

- B.S. Chimni, 'The Birth of a 'Discipline': From refugee to forced migration studies', *Journal of Refugee studies* 22 (2009), 11.
- Liisa H. Malkki, 'Refugees and Exile: From "refugee studies" to the national order of things', *Annual Review of Anthropology* 24 (1995), 495.
- Andrew E. Shacknove, 'Who is a Refugee?' *Ethics* 95 (1985), 274.
- Patricia Tuitt, *False Images: Law's Construction of the Refugee* (Pluto 1996).

---

10. See, for example, Dallal Stevens, 'Shifting conceptions of refugee identity and protection: European and Middle Eastern approaches,' in *Refugee Protection and the Role of Law: Conflicting Identities*, eds. Susan Kneebone, Dallal Stevens and Loretta Baldassar (London and New York: Routledge 2014); Simon Behrman, 'Laws of Asylum and Protection: The Indian Experience in a South Asian Context', *Refugee Watch* 53 (2020), 15.

13

Law in the Climate Crisis

INTERNATIONAL ENVIRONMENTAL LAW

Sam Adelman

After banks and hedge funds exploded the global economy in 2008, paving the way for Brexit and authoritarian populists such as Trump, economics students in many universities asked why so much of their curriculum was dangerous, irrelevant or both, and challenged their universities to change. It is a challenge that too many law schools have evaded.

In Greek, *krísis* is a decisive turning point that requires a choice. Global heating is an existential crisis inextricably linked to biodiversity loss in the Sixth Mass Extinction, zoonotic transmission of viruses in pandemics, and injustices such as impoverishment and racial, gender and socio-economic inequality. Human hyper-agency and telluric power has altered the Earth's climate and geology and taken us into the Anthropocene, in which human and geological history are inseparable.[1] The Anthropocene destabilises existing ontologies and epistemologies as well as our understandings of history. It highlights the failings of Eurocentric rationality and western models of law and development,

---

1. The Anthropocene is the idea that we are in a new geological epoch in which human activity is the dominant influence on climate and the environment (Simon Lewis and Mark Maslin, *Human Planet: How We Created the Anthropocene*. Yale University Press, 2018.). The Great Acceleration, which began in the second half of the twentieth century, has led to the most profound transformation of the human relationship with the natural world in the history of humankind (Will Steffen et al., 'The trajectory of the Anthropocene: the great acceleration', 2015 *The Anthropocene Review* 2(1), 81-98. See Elizabeth Kolbert, *The Sixth Extinction: An Unnatural History*. A&C Black, 2014.)

and invites us to be open to the knowledge and wisdom of indigenous peoples who have lived in harmony with nature for millennia.

Critical environmental law (both domestic and international) examines the role that law plays in climate and ecological breakdown, and how law can be used in pursuit of climate justice. This applies to every module in all degrees because global heating impinges upon the entire curriculum.[2] Since climate breakdown affects everybody (albeit in very different ways), critical environmental law necessarily engages with an array of disciplines ranging across economics, moral philosophy, history, sociology and politics amongst others.

Business as usual is destroying the planet, regularly facilitated by law. A critical approach seeks to explain environmental law's lack of normative ambition, and why it is replete with unenforceable principles (such as the polluter pays and precautionary principles) that are hortatory and voluntary rather than binding and enforceable. The only enforcement mechanism in the Paris Agreement is naming and shaming. We live in a time of weak answers to hard questions, the foremost of which is whether a habitable planet is possible under capitalism?

How do we explain the mismatch between Earth System science and environmental law? Or the abyss between the core concept of sustainable development and ecological sustainability? Since the Industrial Revolution, the pursuit of endless fossil-fuelled growth on a finite planet has led to the breaching of four of nine planetary boundaries: biosphere integrity, climate change, biogeochemical flows, and land-system change.[3] To paraphrase von Clausewitz, law is the continuation of business by other means.

Legal education should enable students to develop their abilities to comprehend and critically analyse the causes of the climate crisis, its connections to other injustices, and how it shapes our collective future. For centuries, law schools have normalised and legitimised environmental destruction and the breaching of planetary boundaries, prioritising the teaching of ways evading responsibility for ecological degradation. Critical environmental law seeks to bring about a legal paradigm shift to prevent this crisis from becoming a catastrophe. Critical environmental law engages with mainstream legal theory,

---

2. Universities should be required to undertake annual sustainability audits of every module in every department.
3. Will Steffen et al., 'Planetary boundaries: guiding human development on a changing planet' (2015) 347(6223) *Science* 736; Johan Rockström et al., 'A safe operating space for humanity' (2009) 461 *Nature* 472.

examining the ways in which legal formalists and positivists have promoted the myth that law is neutral, objective and impartial rather than a set of human choices. Like critical legal theory, it identifies the contradictory nature of legal doctrine and rules, the ontological and epistemological assumptions upon which liberal law is constructed, and legal discourses that facilitate ecological destruction. If, in Einstein's words, 'No problem can be solved at the same level of consciousness that created it,' we need to change law's 'consciousness', its underlying assumptions and the way it is taught to reflect the scale and urgency of climate breakdown and the nature of the transformation required to bequeath a habitable planet to future generations.

Changing law's content—its rules and regulations—occurs through critique, dissent, resistance and struggle. Changing law's form is more difficult. Law schools perpetuate conceptions of law as neutral, impartial, and objective, and the obvious way of regulating human activities despite abundant evidence that it is regularly partisan, often subjective and consistently hierarchical. Scratching law's surface reveals the prevalence of instrumentalist and mechanistic reasoning, and the tendency to equate price and value. Modern western law promotes binary Cartesian thinking that pits humans, cultures and society against nature, and anthropocentrism against ecocentrism. Critical environmental law seeks ways of overcoming these problems without simply inverting them—the choice between anthropocentrism and eco- and biocentrism is false because human wellbeing is contingent upon the health of the planet and other species. Critical environmental law addresses the limitations of the law in relation to complex issues of governance for which law provides partial solutions. These include proposals to geoengineer the planet's climate using technologies that carry substantial risks. Who, if anyone, should have their finger on the global thermostat?

Law treats credit, debt, interest and rent as natural, inevitable and unavoidable, generally ignoring the fact that they require endless compound economic growth on a finite planet. Law prioritises the needs and interests of the owners private property. Company law thus privileges shareholders over other stakeholders including the public and the planet, tax law is more concerned with avoidance and evasion than carbon taxes, trust law promotes investments by pension funds in fossil fuels, and international economic law subordinates everything to trade and unsustainable investment. Despite its limitations, law plays an important role in dealing with climate breakdown through human rights law to protect people displaced by climate change, in legislation needed for a just transition to a post-carbon economy through a Green

New Deal, in punishing tax evaders and polluters, and attempts to constrain growth fetishism in pursuit of ecological sustainability.

Global heating is fundamentally a political problem in which law plays a central role. Law has played an important role in rights struggles, in overturning bad law and authoritarian legal systems. Human rights underpin struggles across the world from Black Lives Matter to gender and sexual equality. The focus of the work of the current and former UN special rapporteurs on human rights is the adoption and enforcement of the right to a clean, safe, and healthy environment. There is a growing movement to give rights to nature in Latin America, New Zealand and elsewhere. Law can make banks, private equity and hedge funds accountable; it can be used to clamp down on tax avoidance and evasion; and it can facilitate a global Green New Deal and environmentally friendly alternatives such as doughnut economics.[4]

Law is often reactionary, but it can be used tactically and strategically in pursuit of progressive ends: to alleviate suffering caused by climatic harms, to promote climate justice, and to bequeath a habitable planet to future generations. It can be used reactively to protect animals, humans and ecosystems and proactively to with the aim of preventing future harms. Law must be deployed in the 'fierce urgency of now', as Martin Luther King's words, in the little time remaining to avert cataclysm.

Critical environmental law examines multilateral environmental agreements, the growing amount of climate change legislation and climate litigation, the potential they provide for environmental and climate justice, and the urgent need to overcome the limitations of the law to prevent the catastrophic consequences of failing to keep global temperature from increasing by more than 1.5 degrees Celsius above preindustrial levels by the end of this decade.[5] The growing wave of climate litigation demonstrates the contradictory nature of law. It demonstrates that international environmental law can be effective despite the numerous legal obstacles in the way of successful climate litigation including standing, jurisdiction, and causation. Successful litigation relies upon effective legislation and enforcement. It is expensive and lengthy but landmark cases such as *Urgenda* in the Netherlands and *Ashgar Leghari* in Pakistan demonstrate the potential for success

---

4. Kate Raworth, *Doughnut Economics: Seven Ways to Think Like a 21st-Century Economist* (Chelsea Green Publishing, 2017).
5. The Grantham Research Institute on Climate Change and the Environment provides a database of legislation and litigation, http://www.lse.ac.uk/granthaminstitute/

using different sources of law such as tort, human rights and the Paris Agreement.[6] With notable exceptions such as the US, courts in many jurisdictions appear willing to respond positively to well-crafted arguments that reflect growing public alarm manifested in the school climate strikes and the civil disobedience campaign of Extinction Rebellion. There is growing evidence of the value of North-South and South-South collaboration and cross pollination on litigation strategies, often driven by civil society organisations and environmental lawyers. The history of the UN Framework Convention on Climate Change (UNFCCC) since 1992 suggests that bottom up activism is the only way of remedying the failure of states to negotiate an effective agreement.

Multilateral environmental agreements (MEAs) contain core principles such as sustainable development and common but differentiated responsibilities and respective capabilities (CBDR-RC) that have been honoured more in the breach than the observance. The CBDR-RC principle, which is at the core of climate justice, has been the most contentious aspect of the UNFCCC because it relates to all strands of justice: distributive, gender, global, reparative, etc. For better or worse, the UNFCCC and the Paris Agreement comprise the international legal framework within which our future will be decided in a flawed regime that nevertheless makes it possible to ascribe obligations according to a state's historical responsibility for greenhouse gas emissions, the benefits accrued from carbon-based industrialisation, and its ability of wealthy states to provide resources for a just transition to a greener world. It is the framework within which climate justice is pursued for the poor and vulnerable, especially in the global South, who are least responsible for the climate emergency but most vulnerable to the harms it causes.

Climate breakdown is driven by a broken system whose flaws are exposed by the pandemic and the need for fundamental transformation. Existential transboundary threats that intensify impoverishment and inequality within and between countries require global solutions. In early 2020, the seemingly impossible became possible within a few

---

6. *Ashgar Leghari v Federation of Pakistan* [2015] W.P. No. 25501/201, Lahore High Court, 4 April 2015; *The State of the Netherlands (Ministry of Economic Affairs and Climate Policy) v Stichting Urgenda* (case number 19/00135, 20 December 2019), Netherlands Supreme Court. The successful blocking of a third runway at Heathrow also demonstrates how the Paris Agreement may be used: *R (On The Application Of Plan B Earth) (Claimant) v Secretary Of State For Transport (Defendant) & (1) Heathrow Airport Ltd (2) Arora Holdings Ltd (Interested Parties) & WWF-UK (Intervener)*, Case Nos: C1/2019/1053, C1/2019/1056 and C1/2019/1145. The judgment is being appealed.

weeks as the Covid-19 pandemic spread, but responses to the pandemic also demonstrate how difficult transformation is in the face of calls for a return to the deeply dysfunctional 'normality' of the status quo ante. Critical environmental law seeks to provide students with a transdisciplinary framework for understanding how we arrived at the edge of the precipice and the contradictory role law can play in enabling us to step back. Climate breakdown is fundamentally a failure of political will because we have long understood its causes, what we need to do, and how to do it with existing technologies. Like many universities, Warwick has declared a climate emergency. That is the easy bit. Using law to hold governments accountable and destroy fossil fuel companies—the Holy Grail of climate litigation—is more difficult, which is why students should demand that law schools heed Che Guevara's injunction to 'Be realistic. Demand the impossible.'

Concept: Colonialism & Imperialism

Christine Schwöbel-Patel

To learn about imperialism is to learn about foreign domination. Perhaps you had an early sense of imperialism, prompted through growing up in a former European imperialist state—the UK, France, Germany, the Netherlands, or Spain. These states are, unsurprisingly, invested in placing imperialism in the *past*. The apologists for these states emphasise that formerly colonised states are now independent. But you might have asked yourself, why it is that people continue to be racialised in these countries? Or perhaps, an idea of foreign domination was formed through experience of a settler colony like Australia, the USA, or Canada. Here, domination of indigenous peoples is more difficult to place in the past, although the dominant story is often that the *violent* part of domination is in the past. You might have asked yourself how land could have been taken from the indigenous population, how settlers got away with killing and plunder, and why indigenous peoples continue to be oppressed? Finally, an idea of imperialism may be borne out of coming from a formerly colonised country. Here, it is likely more palpable that imperialism is by no means in the past—say, through the noticeable absence of looted riches or artefacts (now in European palaces or museums), or through the puzzle that many people are working for Western corporations, but that profits flow mostly to former imperial powers.

To encounter imperialism as a law student encompasses an understanding that foreign domination is both a historical account as well as a diagnosis of contemporary conditions of inequality in which law plays a central role. Law legitimises imperialism; but it can also be used to resist imperialism. Early theorists of imperialism, like Rosa Luxemburg, highlighted how imperialism was a condition of capitalism. Capital sought new opportunities for accumulation outside of the imperialist metropole, and it has done so consistently in a violent manner. International laws that fortified domination were generally those between imperial nations seeking a balance of power within Europe and designating the Global South for exploitation. Once former imperial states were forced to recognise independence, in the 1950s and 1960s, the Global South was deemed as de-colonised. However, a powerful and important movement of Third World resistance insisted that independence had given way to neo-colonialism. Radical thinkers of that time, like Kwame Nkrumah and Franz Fanon, have been key for understanding the continued imperial structures that persist until the present day.

15

Concept: Third World Approaches to International Law

Rohini Sen

Third World approaches to international law (TWAIL) is a theoretical, methodological and political process. Each of these terms are significant to understand the nature of TWAIL which envisions itself as dynamic, diverse and in dialogue with multiple forms of critique and conversations that interrogate international law's status quo. At its core, TWAIL stands for three fundamental things:

1. To identify and investigate how international law continues to disadvantage the Global South[1]
2. To question and challenge such structures and processes of oppression.
3. To offer reformative and inclusive possibilities both within and beyond international law.

Within this TWAILian approach, there are divergent views on the reformative potentials of international law[2]. There are those who believe it can be reformed and adapted to universal standards of practice. Then,

---

1. TWAIL uses Global South in recognition of all its complexity and the fact that it is not geographically rigid.
2. Mutua, Makau, What is Twail? (2000). American Society of International Law, Proceedings of the 94th Annual Meeting, pp. 31-39, 2000.

there are those who insist that it is structurally designed to oppress and benefit certain categories and, can only be dismantled and replaced. This spectrum of views simultaneously uses and disavows international law tactically to attain a range of outcomes in support of Third World[3] peoples and States, recognising conflict and dissonance as an integral part of this (any) movement.

Some of the core concepts of international law that are challenged by TWAIL include statehood, sources and doctrines of international law, territorial boundaries, international organisations and sovereign equality. Historically locating it in colonialism, TWAIL asserts that international law is eurocentric positivism that structurally and institutionally erases every other history and experience while universalising itself. 'Universal' international law is rooted in a politics of difference and continuous violence. And this form of violence is insidious, changing shape and form through the international legal system; masking the imperial, colonial, capitalist and patriarchal processes that sustain these differences.

In calling itself an approach, it allows for a range of modes through which to attain its core goals. Some are located in theoretical and methodological academic discourses while others in political and social movements. Since they are directed at hegemonic structures, these modes are equally mindful of not reproducing them within their own geopolitical spaces. To do this, TWAIL is constantly in conversation with queer and feminist approaches, Marxist approaches, Critical Race theory and other structural critical interventions that share similar aims. At its core, TWAIL is predicated on these relationships and processes of relationship making that challenge mainstream international law's purported objectivity and neutrality, no matter who inherit them and where they take place, including within TWAIL.

---

3. Third World is no longer understood to bear the same meanings as it did during the Cold war, or its subsequent evolution predicated on the developmental stereotypes. There is no agreed upon meaning and, the term is as contingent as Global South within TWAIL discourses. For the purposes of TWAIL, Third World is a space that generates/informs approaches in opposition to continued hegemony in international law.

16

Contract Law and Empire

CONTRACT LAW, LEGAL HISTORY

Máiréad Enright

Contract law imagines us as free, rational, and choosing beings. The ideal subject of contract law is both able to pursue contracts for himself and bound to perform them. He is free because he enjoys 'freedom of contract';[1] freedom from judicial or legislative interference with his commercial interests.[2] Contract law, on this account, is a body of essentially neutral background rules; the bare minimum regulatory framework necessary to enable us to engage in profitable economic exchange. In this short piece, I want to disrupt that story by discussing some other types of people who have a place in the history of contract law, and of contractual freedom.

Here, I want to focus on contract and Empire; a theme rarely encountered on standard courses in contract law.[3] There is not space

---

1. To read more about feminist critiques of freedom of contract, see Máiréad Enright, 'Contract Law,' in *Great Debates in Gender and Law*, ed. Rosemary Auchmuty (London: Palgrave, 2018), 1.
2. On the origins of this approach in law see Paul Johnson, *Making the Market: Victorian Origins of Corporate Capitalism* (Cambridge: Cambridge University Press, 2010).
3. There are very occasional indirect references to Empire in the standard curriculum, if you know how to identify them. One is *Tito v Wadell (No. 2)* [1977] 3 All ER 129 Ch 106. On one level this is a case about the measure of damages. On another, it is about the destruction of Banaba through guano mining, when what is now the Republic of Kiribati was under British rule. The mining produced rich phosphate fertilizer which was used to facilitate mass agriculture in New Zealand, and the Banabans were displaced to other lands. See further Dania Thomas, 'Contract, Context and Contest: Revisiting Tito v. Waddell,' *N. Ir. Legal Q.* 58 (2007), 406.

here to give a complete history of imperial capitalist contract law. In the footnotes, I have scattered a range of stories, but in the main text I want to use scholarship in legal history to retell two. The first is about enslaved people in eighteenth century Jamaica; people who by definition did not have any contractual freedom, but whose trafficking, purchase, and suffering was enabled by it. The second is about tenant subsistence farmers in rural Ireland in the decades after the Great Famine,[4] and how their agitation for secure rights to land interacted with a state commitment to contractual ideology. I want to show that the history of contract law has not been a simple journey from oppressive 'status' to unalloyed 'freedom'. Rather, 'freedom of contract' is of violent origin. It depends on inequality: freedom for some, at the miserable expense of others.

Dehumanizing Contracts: Enslavement and Marine Insurance

Contract was at the heart of the trans-Atlantic trade in enslaved people.[5] However, contract's reach is wider than the direct traffic in

---

Another is *Balfour v Balfour* [1919] 2 KB 571, a case about marriage and intention to create legal relations. Most case summaries explain that the husband was based in 'Ceylon', and leave the question of Empire aside. However, this case is inescapably about family and Empire. John Aylmer Balfour was Director of Irrigation for the Government of Ceylon (now Sri Lanka) from 1913-1918, and made a career in civil engineering in countries including South Africa and Mozambique. Irrigation was central to the colonial enterprise in Sri Lanka because it facilitated large scale cultivation of coffee, tea and rubber; work which was done by bonded migrant labourers who had little control over their working lives. John's wife, Clara Balfour, alone by the sea in Sussex, was not unusual in finding herself deserted when she could no longer perform her role in the domestic life of a colonial official; Marjorie Levine-Clark, 'From "Relief" to "Justice and Protection": The Maintenance of Deserted Wives, British Masculinity and Imperial Citizenship, 1870–1920,' *Gender & History* 22/2 (2010), 302–321.

4. This was a period of mass starvation in Ireland from 1845-1849. The potato crop failed repeatedly, and the consequences of crop failure were exacerbated by a government policy of *laissez-faire* capitalism. Less extensive, but similar famines took place in Scotland from 1846. See further John Crowley, William J. Smyth, Michael Murphy, and Tomás Kelly, *Atlas of the Great Irish Famine, 1845-52* (Cork: Cork University Press, 2012).

5. Enslavement here is distinguished from indenture. Colonial indentures were time-limited contracts. They were supposedly freely entered into. By entering into an indenture, the servant lost their right to dispose of their own services to another employer, or often even to marry without the employer's permission. The difference between indenture and slavery was that slavery was not voluntarily entered into and could not be ended without the master's consent. For a readable account of indenture in Papua New Guinea in the late 1970s, see Peter Fitzpatrick, 'Really Rather like Slavery:

human beings.[6] Standard form[7] marine insurance contracts[8] were developed and refined in the context of this trade.[9] Those who had purchased enslaved people could contract for insurance against the risk of their death on the Middle Passage. These insurance contracts were enforced even in periods when it was generally not permitted to take out insurance contracts on human lives.[10] This was because the law constructed the subject of the insurance contract in terms of 'chattels' rather than life. From the slave-traders' perspective, insurance was a means to mitigate the risks associated with the hazardous trans-Atlantic journey.[11] For underwriters, it was an especially lucrative industry; the

---

Law and Labor in the Colonial Economy in Papua New Guinea,' *Contemporary Crises* 4/1 (1980), 77–95.

6. A case with a complex connection to enslavement is *Harvey v. Facey* [1893] AC 552, which you may encounter in studying the law of offer and acceptance. Those familiar with Kingston Jamaica may know that, some decades before the case was decided, Bumper Hall Pen was a plantation where up to 30 enslaved people lived. "Pen" is a word for plantation. Raffael Nunes, a stockbroker then living in London, was compensated when they were 'emancipated', and became 'apprentices'; 'Details of Estate | Legacies of British Slave-Ownership,' accessed 17 August 2020, https://www.ucl.ac.uk/lbs/estate/view/20163. The plaintiffs were Larchin Mandeville Facey and his wife Adelaide Dacosta. Larchin's grandmother Elizabeth was manumitted in 1817. Some of her descendants became influential businessmen in Jamaica.

7. For a detailed discussion of these contracts and the surrounding insurance law see James Oldham, 'Insurance Litigation Involving the Zong and Other British Slave Ships, 1780–1807,' *The Journal of Legal History* 28/3 (2007), 299–318.

8. Some banks were also involved in mortgaging plantations where enslaved people were held. Enslaved people acted as collateral for the mortgage loans. When plantation owners defaulted on their debts, enslaved people were re-sold at the instance of the bank. John J Clegg, 'Credit Market Discipline and Capitalist Slavery in Antebellum South Carolina,' *Social Science History* 42/2 (2018), 343–376.
Naidu describes enslaved people in this position as 'collateralized human bodies'; Suresh Naidu, 'American Slavery and Labour Market Power,' *Economic History of Developing Regions* 35/1 (2020), 3–22.

9. For a detailed discussion see Robin Pearson and David Richardson, 'Insuring the Transatlantic Slave Trade,' *The Journal of Economic History* 79/2 (2019), 417–446. See also Tim Armstrong, Slavery, Insurance, and Sacrifice in the Black Atlantic, in *Sea Changes: Historicizing the Ocean*, ed. Bernhard Klein and Gesa Mackenthun (New York: Routledge, 2004), 167–85; Trevor Burnard, *Jamaica in the Age of Revolution* (Philadelphia: University of Pennsylvania Press, 2020), 174-194.

10. Geoffrey Wilson Clark, *Betting on Lives: The Culture of Life Insurance in England, 1695-1775* (Manchester: Manchester University Press, 1999), 17.

11. These risks are reflected elsewhere in the standard contract law curriculum; see e.g. *Cutter v. Powell* [1795] 101 ER 573 in which a ship's second mate, sailing from Kingston was not to be paid until he arrived at the port of Liverpool. Martin Dockray, 'Cutter v Powell: A Trip Outside the Text,' *The Law Quarterly Review* 117 (2001), 664–82. He points out that Cutter would have been especially important to his employer because

risks involved allowed them to charge high premiums. However, the common law insisted that traders could only claim on their insurance if the enslaved peoples' death was caused not by starvation or physical or mental illness,[12] but by some exceptional event; a 'peril of the sea', such as shipwreck or piracy.[13] In this way, the law set a basic limit to the exercise of contractual freedom.[14] At the same time, the law reflected the clear understanding that this trade was a brutal one; certain kinds of death were unexceptional, ordinary and tolerable. The notorious case of *Gregson v. Gilbert*,[15] concerning the slave-ship, the Zong, demonstrates how the contractual distinction between insurable and uninsurable events reinforced the status of enslaved people as commercial goods and non-persons.[16] Thomas Gilbert was a Liverpool merchant whose consortium insured slave ships. The Gregsons were leading Liverpool slave traders.[17] They and others had invested in enslaved people, who were first taken from Cape Coast Castle to Accra[18] and then to Jamaica, where the survivors were to be sold at a profit. Captain Luke

---

he was also a shipwright: he had a crucial function in maintaining the quarters where enslaved people were confined, and erecting the barricades which prevented insurrection. Sometimes a ship's master would promise sailors 'the price of one negro slave' as a bonus; *White v. Wilson* [1800] 126 ER 1188

12. *Tatham v. Hodgson* [1796] 101 ER 756; This is the distinction between 'inherent vices' and 'external accidents'; Tim Armstrong, 'Slavery, Insurance, and Sacrifice in the Black Atlantic,' in *Sea Changes: Historicizing the Ocean*, ed. Bernhard Klein and Gesa Mackenthun (New York, London: Routledge, 2004), 167–85, 172; Rupprecht, 'Excessive Memories: Slavery, Insurance and Resistance', 6–28.

13. See e.g. *Jones v. Schmoll* [1785] 1 Term Rep 130n., also decided by Lord Mansfield, in which an insurance policy was held to cover those who were lost by wounding during an insurrection, but not those who 'swallowed salt water, and died in consequence thereof, or who leaped into the sea and hung upon the sides of the ship...' Tim Armstrong,. 'Slavery, Insurance, and Sacrifice in the Black Atlantic,' in Klein and Mackenthum, *Sea Changes: Historicizing the Ocean*, 171.

14. Marouf Hasian Jr,, 'Domesticated Abolitionism, the "Human Cargo" of the Zong, and the British Legal Usage of Dehumanizing Rhetoric, 1783–1807,' *Western Journal of Communication* 76/5 (2012), 503–519.

15. *Gregson v Gilbert* [1783] 3 Doug 232 (KB)

16. For further context see Anita Rupprecht, '"A Very Uncommon Case": Representations of the Zong and the British Campaign to Abolish the Slave Trade,' *The Journal of Legal History* 28/3 (2007), 329–346.

17. See Ian Baucom, *Specters of the Atlantic: Finance Capital, Slavery, and the Philosophy of History* (Durham: Duke University Press, 2005), 47-49.

18. The *Zong* was a Dutch ship which had been captured with over 200 enslaved people already on board. They had been transported from Middelburg in the Netherlands. Additional people were purchased from the London Company of Merchants Trading to Africa, who held enslaved people at a range of forts including Fort William in Ghana; Baucom, *Specters of the Atlantic*, 10.

Collingwood had ordered 132 enslaved people thrown overboard, over several days in November 1781. Their names are not recorded, but we know that the first to die were women and children. Those enslaved on the ship had been valued at £30 a head.

The ship had missed Jamaica, perhaps through the captain's negligence. Water supplies on board were low. The owners argued that it had been essential to jettison some of the ship's human cargo to save the ship. The question was whether the owners of those drowned could claim on the insurance contract, and thereby recover their loss. To do this, they needed to persuade the court that people had been thrown overboard in circumstances of 'immediate peril', and not merely discarded because they were ill and were therefore likely to be more difficult to sell in Jamaica; worth less as damaged goods than as insured property.[19] The owners lost the case for two reasons. First, the emergency was not immediate—water was available within sailing distance, and killings continued even though supplies of water onboard were improved by heavy rain. Second, the captain had specifically and deliberately selected for death those enslaved people who were in the weakest condition; suggesting that he had not made the decision to sacrifice them under pressure. Nevertheless, the court found a breach of insurance contract and not a crime. Although abolitionists such as Granville Sharp emphasized that the case was ultimately about unjustifiable loss of human life, it was not treated as a murder case.[20] The logic of the court's analysis was inherently commercial. Thus, the Chief Justice, Lord Mansfield noted, that though the story of the *Zong* 'shocks one very much', the murder of those 132 people was no different, as a matter of contract law, than if horses had been thrown overboard.[21]

In this case, we can see how contract law removed enslaved people from the realm of ordinary human concern. As Baucom observes, the insurance transaction was entirely at 'arm's length'. The plaintiff and defendant in Liverpool had never seen the Zong. Captain Collingwood purchased enslaved people on behalf of the Gregson consortium. They were insured, not as individuals, but as commodities; as abstract

---

19. Tim Armstrong, 'Slavery, Insurance, and Sacrifice in the Black Atlantic,' in Klein and Mackenthun *Sea Changes*, 167–85, 173-174.
20. Marouf Hasian Jr. 'Domesticated Abolitionism, the "Human Cargo" of the Zong, and the British Legal Usage of Dehumanizing Rhetoric," 503–519.
21. James Walvin, *The Zong: A Massacre, the Law and the End of Slavery*, (New Haven: Yale University Press, 2011), 103; James Oldham, 'New Light on Mansfield and Slavery', *Journal of British Studies* 27/1 (1988), 45–68.

value.²² Lord Mansfield's judgment did nothing to improve matters; indeed, it enabled this dangerous trade to continue. The historian Saidiya Hartman argues that his decision confirmed that the deaths of people brought against their will across the Atlantic could be mere 'collateral damage', and made it possible for that killing to continue,²³ provided that slave-traders and their agents stayed within the lines drawn by law. The judgment protected, not the freedom of enslaved people, but the freedom of insurers and other 'businessmen'. In recent years, activists demanding reparations for enslavement have asked insurance companies including Lloyds of London and Royal Sun Alliance to divest themselves of some of the wealth obtained by enabling slavery and death.²⁴

Contract Law and Colonization: Irish Implied Terms

Contract law made tradeable 'things' of some colonized peoples. Others, by contrast, were given the role of subordinate contractors within the Empire. Under this, generally racialized logic, some peoples were denied contractual capacity, because they were considered unfit for it.²⁵ Others, by contrast, were placed under contract law's tutelage as it was exported across the Empire.²⁶ They were presented as imperfect, requiring training as rational capitalists and consumers.²⁷

---

22. Ian Baucom, *Specters of the Atlantic* (Duke University Press, 2005) 15; Robbie Shilliam, 'Forget English Freedom, Remember Atlantic Slavery: Common Law, Commercial Law and the Significance of Slavery for Classical Political Economy,' *New Political Economy* 17/ 5 (2012), 591–609.
23. Saidiya Hartman, *Lose Your Mother: A Journey Along the Atlantic Slave Route* (New York: Farrar, Straus and Giroux, 2008).
24. On reparations claims against insurance companies as claims of unjust enrichment see Paige A. Fogarty, 'Speculating a Strategy: Suing Insurance Companies to Obtain Legislative Reparations for Slavery,' *Connecticut Insurance L.J.* 211/9 (2002); Anita Rupprecht, 'Excessive Memories: Slavery, Insurance and Resistance,' *History Workshop Journal* 64 (2007), 6–28.
25. See e.g. the Kenyan Credit Trade with Natives Ordinances, which restricted 'natives' contractual activity and denied them effective access to credit, ostensibly to 'protect' them from unscrupulous money-lending.
26. Ritu Birla. 'Law as Economy: Convention, Corporation, Currency,' *UC Irvine Law Review* 1 (2011), 1015–1038; See Cecilia Morgan, *Building Better Britains?: Settler Societies in the British World, 1783-1920*, Vol. 4. (Toronto: University of Toronto Press, 2017).
27. Christopher Alan Bayly, *Imperial Meridian: The British Empire and the World 1780-1830*, (London: Routledge, 2016), 218; See also Peter Fitzpatrick,. *Modernism and the Grounds of Law* (Cambridge: Cambridge University Press, 2001), 206.

Their 'freedom of contract' was often used to justify the continued appropriation of their land.[28] This often entailed the abandonment and suppression of indigenous customs. British conceptions of freedom of contract stood in for modernity. Maine wrote that 'the society of our own day is mainly distinguished from that of preceding generations by the largeness of the sphere which is occupied in it by Contract.' He concluded that '[t]he movement of progressive societies has hitherto been a movement from Status to Contract'[29]; from obligations imposed by custom, tradition, kinship, or religion to those imposed by individual agreement.[30]

In pursuit of this vision of progress, colonized peoples were required to undergo processes already near completion in mainland Britain. British working people had gradually lost their rights under communal values systems; these were replaced by a centralized common law which cherished individualism.[31] In this way, contract law ensured that goods, property, and manpower[32] were unmoored from traditional communitarian notions of fairness and obligation, and, in this way, made easier to buy and sell.[33]

---

28. See e.g.Stuart Banner. 'Conquest by Contract: Wealth Transfer and Land Market Structure in Colonial New Zealand,' *Law & Soc'y Rev.* 34 (2000), 47., explaining how large tracts of land were exchanged for goods of limited value. See also Seuffert, Nan. 'Contract, Consent and Imperialism in New Zealand's Founding Narrative' *Law&history* 2 (2015), 1, 31.
29. Henry Sumner Maine, *Ancient Law, Its Connection to the Early History of Society, and Its Relation to Modern Ideas* (London: J. M. Dent and Sons, 1917), 101.This was originally a comment about the development of Roman law and, by analogy the development of European legal systems.
30. Karuna Mantena, *Alibis of Empire: Henry Maine and the Ends of Liberal Imperialism* (Princeton, Oxford: Princeton University Press, 2010), 110; Maine subsequently became a colonial administrator, and attempted to embed an ideology of 'freedom of contract' there. See Sandra Den Otter, 'Rewriting the Utilitarian Market: Colonial Law and Custom in Mid-Nineteenth-Century British India,' *The European Legacy* 6/2 (2001), 177–188.
31. This included ideas like 'moral economy', 'just price' and the 'prohibition against usury'. See generally E.P. Thompson, *Customs in Common: Studies in Traditional Popular Culture*, (New York: New Press/ORIM, 2015).
32. However, as Simon Deakin notes, workers were never as free as those who bought their labour; the rise in freedom of contract went hand-in-hand with new laws designed to punish non-participation in capitalist labour markets; Simon Deakin, 'Legal Origin, Juridical Form and Industrialization in Historical Perspective: The Case of the Employment Contract and the Joint-Stock Company,' *Socio-Economic Review* 71 (2009), 35–65, 53.
33. Patrick Selim Atiyah, *The Rise and Fall of Freedom of Contract*, Vol. 1. (New York: Oxford University Press, 1979), 167; For a more complex account see Warren Swain,

These tensions are visible in the debates over the Land Law (Ireland) Act 1881.[34] In the 1840s, and again in 1860, Britain had passed legislation which aimed to embed 'laissez-faire' capitalism in Irish land law. In particular, Deasy's Act[35] and Cardwell's Act[36] attempted to transform the relationship between landlord and tenant into a contractual one.[37] This was an attempt to impose British conceptions of property rights on a populace, many of whom believed that the right to use land for subsistence farming was not dependent on ownership.[38] British reforms strengthened landlordism; the exploitation of Irish farmers by absentee landlords. They also undermined communal forms of ownership, enabling easier eviction of small farmers and repurposing of the land to grow profitable crops such as flax and corn, or to facilitate large-scale

---

'Power History and the Law of Contract in Eighteenth Century England,' in *Private Law and Power*, ed. Kit Barker, Simon Degeling, Karen Fairweather and Ross B. Grantham, (Oxford: Hart, 2017), 31-51.

34. Land Law (Ireland) Act 1881

35. Landlord and Tenant's Act (Ireland) 1860. This Act established that the only tenant's rights recognized in law must be based in a contract with the landlord.

36. Tenure and Improvement of Land (Ireland) Act 1860. This Act provided for limited compensation for improvements carried out by the tenant.

37. See generally Rachael Walsh and Lorna Fox O'Mahony, 'Land Law, Property Ideologies and the British-Irish Relationship,' *Common Law World Review* 47/1 (2018), 7–34.

38. This was not, of course, the first attempt to achieve this; Gaelic land law had been unenforceable in the King's Courts since 1605. See generally Laird, Heather. *Subversive Law in Ireland, 1879-1920: From 'unwritten Law' to the Dáil Courts*. Four Courts Press, 2005. Especially before the Famine, older Gaelic models of land occupation survived in parts of the country such as Galway and Kerry. These resisted enclosure and division by retaining a rundale system of distributing land held in common to the community –often a community with close family ties– for co-operative farming. Often large groups would pool their labour, and farm together as joint leaseholders, and no individual could point to a plot of land which was exclusively his. An individual farmer might be responsible for several plots of land of varying quality distributed across a shared area, rather than a single plot. This allowed all members equal access to the different types of land available to the group. There was also an expectation that all of the sons of a deceased father would share his lands equally by subdivision, instead of passing his lands as a whole, by primogeniture to the eldest son. Of course, this system was not universally retained, and was often heavily contested, even if it was idealized and simplified in nationalist rhetoric. Nevertheless, many landlords discouraged these practices as inefficient, and in the 1890s, the Congested Districts Board deliberately encouraged systems of enclosure, allocating distinct plots to individual households. See further Eoin O'Flaherty, 'Geographies of Communality, Colonialism, and Capitalism: Ecology and the World-System,' *Historical Geography* 41 (2013), 59–79; O' Flaherty, Eoin O'Flaherty, 'Rundale and 19th Century Irish Settlement: System, Space, and Genealogy,' *Irish Geography* 48/2 (2016), 3–38.

grazing. Moderating legislation passed in 1870 had not adequately addressed these abuses.[39] The law was inherently coercive: the inequalities between landlord and tenant were so great that the tenant's only choices were to accept the rent his landlord proposed or face either eviction, destitution or emigration.[40] By the 1880s, the movement for land reform had gathered strength. The Land League pursued a 'Land War', using tactics such as boycotts, rent strikes, and setting up non-state arbitration courts to undermine reliance on official law. Much of the British Press presented this movement in terms of terrorism, associating it with the Fenian Rising of 1867.[41] One *Punch* cartoon showed Liberal Prime Minister Gladstone as a noble hero, competing with a simian Irish terrorist for the love of Hibernia.[42] In response to the demands of the Irish Land League, the Gladstone proposed a Land Bill which would have altered the terms of leases in Ireland, including by adding three statutory implied terms. These were known as the or '3 Fs'; fair rents which could be set by land courts, fixity of tenure provided the rent was paid, and free sale. The Liberal Party's argument was not that freedom of contract should be rejected, but that it should be modified where it was impossible to maintain in its purest form. In Ireland, Gladstone believed, 'the old Irish notion that some interest in the soil adheres to the tenant, even though his contract has expired, is everywhere rooted in the popular mind.'[43] This reform did not go as

---

39. Landlord and Tenant (Ireland) Act 1870; the 1870 Act included recognition of the 'Ulster custom', in areas where it could be proven that it applied. This referred both to fixity of tenure and to the tenant's right of free sale, which allowed him to exact significant compensation from any tenant replacing him on his land. Tenant right is complex because it is associated with the rights of less wealthy landowners of Ulster-Scots origin, who came to live in Northern Ireland from Scotland as part of early waves of plantation and colonization.
40. An 1882 cartoon from the nationalist *Weekly Freeman* shows a tenant farmer reluctantly signing a lease, while he is threatened with eviction notices, rent increases, and the possibility of the workhouse Irish Comics Wiki. 'Weekly Freeman/Cartoons 1882,' accessed 17 August 2020, https://irishcomics.fandom.com/wiki/Weekly_Freeman/Cartoons_1882. See further discussion of Ireland in Karl Marx, *Capital: Volume I* (Modern Barbarian Press:Champaign, 2018) 482-489.
41. At this time, only around 50% of Irish men were entitled to vote, as voting rights were dependent on wealth.
42. See 'The Rivals', *Punch* 13 August 1881 https://www.gettyimages.co.uk/detail/news-photo/the-rivals-1881-the-liberal-prime-minister-gladstone-news-photo/463930395
43. Cited in Heather Laid, 'Time and the Irish: An Analysis of the Temporal Frameworks Employed by Sir Henry Maine, Eóin MacNeill, and James Connolly in Their Writings on Early Modern Ireland,' *Proceedings of the Harvard Celtic Colloquium* 28 (2008), 128–41.

far as the Land League wanted: it did not promise to improve farmers' conditions so that large numbers could be genuinely free to purchase their land and secure a permanent connection to it. It did not make provision for farmers who could not pay their rents because of bad harvests. It merely improved the basis on which leases could begin and end; maintaining the regime of freedom of contract by making it marginally more accessible.[44]

Parliamentary debates around the Act show how contract was ideologically associated with civilization and freedom, while the demand for intervention was made to seem weak and pitiable. Conservatives opposed the idea that fair rents should be determined by a court-imposed external standard rather than bargained for by the landlord and the tenant, within the context of the wider market. They argued not only that land reform in Ireland would undermine freedom of contract, but that it was paternalistic.[45] Lord Carnarvon argued that 'if it be true that you think freedom of contract is impossible in Ireland, then you mean that the Irish people are not fit for free institutions, and are not a free people.'[46] However, there was also concern that reforms in Ireland would feed demand for similar reform at home. Tellingly, Lord Salisbury warned that change in Ireland would encourage English radicals: 'the earthquake wave which has been fatal to his Irish brother... is travelling slowly towards [the English landowner].'[47] The *Economist*, by contrast, reassured its readers that 'the farmers of Great Britain are quite able to make their own bargains with landlords, and stand in no need of a legal tribunal to tell them what rents they ought or ought not to pay'.[48] In these statements, we can see how a thin notion of 'freedom of contract' was used to diminish working class political movements and justify colonial exploitation. 'Freedom of contract' was conflated with peaceable acceptance of economic exploitation.[49] It served to

---

44. It was passed in parallel to the Coercion Act, 1881 which allowed those active in the Land War to be interned without trial. CS Parnell was arrested and jailed under the Act when his newspaper criticized the Land Act 1881.
45. Andrew Phemister, '"The Grandest Battle Ever Fought for the Rights of Human Beings": Radical Republicanism and the Universalization of the Land War,' *Éire-Ireland* 51/1 (2016), 192–217.
46. Hansard Column 1183, Volume 264, 8 August 1881.
47. Cited in Ewen Green, *The Crisis of Conservatism: The Politics, Economics and Ideology of the Conservative Party, 1880-1914*, (London: Routledge, 2005), 72.
48. Cited in Helen Merrell Lynd, *England in the Eighteen Eighties*. (London: Routledge, 2019) 138.
49. Robert Nichols, *Theft Is Property!: Dispossession and Critical Theory* (Durham, London: Duke University Press, 2020), 141-143.

naturalize inequality;[50] farmers under Empire had 'freedom' to contract into continued poverty and hierarchy.[51]

Conclusion

In her work on the Zong case, the poet M. NourbeSe Philip writes that the language of the contract law judgment 'promulgates the non-being of African peoples, and I distrust its order, which hides disorder.'[52] Studying the history of contract law should encourage us both to distrust its promises and to consider the disorder it may hide. Today, contract law continues to impose and enforce racial hierarchy. Consider, for example, the habitual 'contracting out' of services for asylum seekers in Britain to private companies; the lives of a new generation of racialized subjects are minutely governed by contracts which they cannot negotiate or enforce.[53] Contractual rhetoric is also used to justify maltreatment and exclusion of poor people—for example those who are unemployed, or those engaged in 'anti-social' behaviour—as 'contracts' and 'agreements' are used to codify new obligations to the neoliberal state.[54] For law students, a sense of how contract has been used in the past can sharpen awareness of how it may conceal injustice in the present—clothing inequality, poverty, and powerlessness in the language of freedom.

---

50. Tal Kastner, 'Deviance in Nineteenth-Century American Law and Culture,' in *The Routledge Research Companion to Law and Humanities in Nineteenth-Century America*, ed. Nan Goodman and Simon Stern, (Routledge, 2017), 56-72.
51. Similar legislation, the Crofter's Holdings (Scotland) Act 1886, was passed in Scotland at the end of the Highland Clearances, and in Bengal (Bengal Tenancy Act 1885) following working class uprising.
52. M. NourbeSe Philip and Setaey Adamu Boateng, *Zong!* (Middletown: Wesleyan University Press, 2008), 197.
53. Jonathan Darling, 'Privatising Asylum: Neoliberalisation, Depoliticisation and the Governance of Forced Migration,' *Transactions of the Institute of British Geographers* 41/3 (2016), accessed 17 September 2020, https://doi.org/10.1111/tran.12118, 230–43.
54. See e.g. Tom Boland and Ray Griffin, 'Making Sacrifices: How Ungenerous Gifts Constitute Jobseekers as Scapegoats,' *Distinktion: Journal of Social Theory* 17/2 (2016), accessed 17 September 2020, https://doi.org/10.1080/1600910X.2016.1198920, 174–91.

FURTHER READINGS

- M. NourbeSe Philip and Setaey Adamu Boateng, *Zong!* (Wesleyan University Press, 2008)
- Ritu Birla, *Stages of Capital* (Duke University Press, 2009)
- Robbie Shilliam, 'Forget English Freedom, Remember Atlantic Slavery: Common Law, Commercial Law and the Significance of Slavery for Classical Political Economy,' *New Political Economy* 17/ 5 (2012), 591–609.

17

Unreasonable Expectations

CONTRACT LAW

Sahar Shah

Where do we begin?

I mean this as both a musing (where should *I* begin) and a challenge: where does any contract law textbook begin? What does it take for granted; what does it presume goes without saying?

I want to begin exactly where Contract Law textbooks never begin: by breaking the fourth wall of the core law modules[1] and providing some account of who I, the writer, am. This will, I think, explain a lot of what is to follow in this chapter. I am a young(ish) woman of colour, a former Contract Law student, and a current Contract Law seminar tutor. I have no shocking anecdotes of overt, 'inelegant'[2] racism from my time as a law student to impart. But what I can recall from my time as a Contract Law student is a persistent and nebulous sense of *unfitness*. My law school years were riddled with moments of feeling slightly misaligned, intellectually awkward and *not quite right*. This stemmed not necessarily from 'impostor syndrome', a term used commonly today, but the simple fact of *actually being an impostor*: it was not that I *felt* I was impersonating a law student; it was that I *was* impersonating a law student. The law student's clothes were ill-fitting, itchy, and uncomfortable on me because they were not made for me. I felt this keenly in the smallest of moments—when I would see nonwhite-sounding

---

1. On a standard UK undergraduate qualifying law degree (LLB). Core modules generally include Contract Law, Tort Law, Criminal Law, Trusts Law.
2. Ta-Nehisi Coates, 'This Town Needs a Better Class of Racist', *The Atlantic*, 1 May 2014, accessed 1 July 2021, https://www.theatlantic.com/politics/archive/2014/05/This-Town-Needs-A-Better-Class-Of-Racist/361443/.

names in Contract Law case names and brace myself slightly, waiting to see if this party to the case would be deemed 'the wrong one' in the judgment (and for some reason expecting this). When I would read classical Western jurisprudential theory and not fully be able to digest it because the thinking seemed abstruse[3] and unsatisfying, stemming exclusively from an archetype of man that I had only ever seen from afar. These theories (for instance, notions of society as comprised of individual, autonomous men, with inherent rights to appropriate 'the earth, and all inferior creatures [that] be common to all men'[4]) also seemed unable to account for, and crucially, *unconcerned with accounting for* historical or social facts as they pertained to subaltern and marginalised peoples—nevertheless, they formed the foundation of modules like Contract Law. (I would later learn that these theories were not necessarily unconcerned with subaltern peoples; many were, in fact, obsessively applied to projects to subordinate subaltern peoples, or alternatively to remake them in the image of the white man.)[5]

The iconic feminist and critical race theorist Patricia Williams describes her own jarring experience of encountering the intellectual leaps of doctrinal law for the first time:

> I learned about images of power in the strong, sure-footed arms' length transactor. I learned about unique power-enhancing lands called Whiteacre and Blackacre, and the mystical fairy rings which encircled them, called restrictive covenants. I learned that excessive power overlaps generously with what is seen as successful, good, efficient and desirable in our society.[6]

The study of doctrinal law in most modern law schools is not necessarily an exercise in character development; law schools are not finishing schools. However, law schools are concerned with character production in that they (like law itself!) tell the same types of stories

---

3. My sincerest apologies for using this word—an ironically obscure one, considering its meaning is 'difficult to understand; obscure'.
4. John Locke, *Second Treatise of Government* (Hackett Publishing Company, 1980), Project Gutenberg E-Book #7370, accessed 1 April 2021, https://www.gutenberg.org/files/7370/7370-h/7370-h.htm, sect. 27.
5. See Mills (Charles W. Mills, *The Racial Contract* (Cornell University Press, 1997)) for a brilliant, scathing critique of Western philosophy, riddled with sarcasm and moments of levity. The reading experience of *The Racial Contract* is an eye-opening and rewarding one. I draw on Mills at various points throughout this chapter.
6. Patricia J. Williams, 'Alchemical Notes: Reconstructing Ideals from Deconstructed Rights', *Harvard Civil Rights-Civil Liberties Law Review* 22 (1987), 401.

repeatedly, populated by the same kinds of characters. Some law students are able to identify themselves in these characters and embark upon trajectories of intellectual character development that match the narratives in law schools. Others cannot (or will not) do this. What kinds of characters do the stories of modules like Contract Law narrate and reproduce—and how?

To consider this, I want to take a look at some of the materials that have shaped my experience of Contract Law (textbooks and influential essays) and place these in conversation with the fascinating work of critical and decolonial theorists.

Beginnings

The majority of Contract Law textbooks introduce themselves by noting the ubiquity of contracting in everyday life, opening with some variation of the sentence: 'Contracts are made and performed every moment of every day and affect every aspect of life, whether you are purchasing food in a supermarket, taking a bus or train journey, booking tickets for the theatre on the internet, or leasing a flat.'[7] The contractual form constitutes an essential logical (and ideological) building block of much of English commercial law and thus, given our[8] deep embeddedness in commercial structures, has an immense impact upon our lived experience of the world. However, despite (or perhaps because of) this ubiquity, there is significant doubt (raised even in most standard Contract Law textbooks) that there *is* a coherent body of law, singularly extricable from the overlapping bundles of rules that constitute English law more broadly, that can be productively categorised as 'contract law'.[9] One of the first orders of business for textbooks, then, is to summon some justification as to why contract might be treated as a distinct area of study, i.e. why these books should exist at all.

Contract law is said to emerge from the 14th century law of *assumpsit*, meaning 'he undertook'– under this form of law, actions could be brought against those that failed to make good on their promises or assurances.[10] This sheds some light onto the nature of not only

---

7. Janet O'Sullivan, *O'Sullivan & Hilliard's The Law of Contract*, 9th ed. (Oxford University Press, 2020), 1.
8. The 'us'/'our' here is fraught, of course. Who do I mean by 'us'? Why do textbooks unthinkingly invoke 'us' in these contexts without any qualifiers or contingencies?
9. Mindy Chen-Wishart, *Contract Law*, 6th ed. (Oxford University Press, 2018).
10. Paul S. Davies, *JC Smith's The Law of Contract*, 2nd ed. (Oxford University Press, 2018), 2.

contract law, but also *Contract Law*, the core legal module. It is the role of consent (he *undertook* suggests that 'he' did so of his own volition), born from a notion of individual autonomy, that supposedly marks contract law out as distinct from all other forms of law (including those grouped within the general 'laws of obligations')[11]—'[w]hereas contractual duties are voluntarily undertaken, many duties are imposed upon us by the law whether we like it or not'.[12] Thus, the idea of individual freedom brings contract law into existence in the law school and in the pages of legal textbooks.

'Free market' ideology and an emphasis upon contract-making emerged alongside the empire-building activities of countries like the United Kingdom.[13] A textbook image from this period is perhaps one of a ship journeying to distant shores to bring the notion of free contracting to the 'natives' of faraway lands. Mutually beneficial trade relationships thus ensue; the world is made smaller and more peaceful—thanks, in part, to the logic of free contracting.[14]

Charles Mills conceptualises this period somewhat differently, explaining that:

> the golden age of contract theory (1650 - 1800) overlapped with the growth of a European capitalism...the evolution of the modern version of the contract, characterized by an antipatriarchalist Enlightenment liberalism, with its proclamations of the equal rights, autonomy, and freedom of all men, thus took place simultaneously with the massacre, expropriation, and subjection to hereditary slavery of men.[15]

This points to a clear hypocrisy (and a glaring logical inconsistency) at the philosophical heart of 'freedom' of contract. The co-emergence and imbrication of ideas of freedom of contract with the forcible appropriation of human lives, labour, land, and nature might justifiably rob 'freedom of contract' of its explanatory power. However, it has not, for most standard Contract Law curricula and textbooks, which neglect to mention this historical context.

The fact that textbooks can continue to recount the origins of freedom of contract without noting the coercion and violence that

---

11. Davies, *The Law of Contract*, 2.
12. Davies, *The Law of Contract*, 2.
13. Mills, *The Racial Contract*.
14. See Jessica Whyte, *The Morals of the Market: Human Rights and the Rise of Neoliberalism* (Verso, 2019).
15. Mills, *The Racial Contract*, 18.

fuelled it, and the coercion and violence that gave the idea global prominence, can perhaps be explained in part by Quijano's understanding of coloniality. Quijano explains that the subject/object divisions that characterised (and characterise) colonial knowledge generated 'a new radical dualism: divine reason and nature'. In this dualism, '[t]he 'subject' is bearer of 'reason', while the 'object', is not only external to it, but [of a] different nature. In fact, it is 'nature".[16] In a cyclical way, the non-subject status of subaltern peoples was historically linked with the very absence of binary subject/object dichotomies and rationalities in pre-colonial societies.[17] To the colonial mind, if subaltern groups did not constitute themselves in opposition to land and nature (objects) - if in fact, their onto-epistemologies are constituted in terms of *relationality* and *reciprocity* with land and nature - then Indigenous people must also be objects (a point made in different ways by Harris[18] and Mills).[19] The lives, lands, and labour of subaltern peoples could thus be coercively and/or violently appropriated without ever contravening the principles of free contracting.[20]

This is a well-established idea in coloniality and critical race theories. The experiential and conceptual validity of the notion of 'freedom of contract' has also been brilliantly critiqued by a range of theorists[21],

---

16. Aníbal Quijano, 'Coloniality and Modernity/Rationality,' *Cultural Studies*, 21 (2007), 173.
17. A number of Indigenous epistemologies are instead premised upon relationality, adopting a more complex view of relationships than the transactional, bilateral formulations that characterise English contract law. The objectives of relationships (within these epistemologies) include ideas such as preservation, protection, sustainability, the well-being of all living and non-living things, and balance—a distinct difference from the contractual, free-market understanding of relationships predicated upon individual self-interest. For instance, within the Indigenous conception of *buen vivir*, the individual is inextricable from their social context (Eduardo Gudynas, 'Buen Vivir: Today's Tomorrow', *Development* 54 (2011), 441-447). The Bantu conception of *ubuntu* ('I am because you are') is premised upon the existential *oneness* of humanity (Nonceba Nolundi Mabovula, 'The erosion of African communal values: a reappraisal of the African Ubuntu philosophy', *Journal of Humanities and Social Sciences* 3 (2011), 38-47). English contract law's vision of society as composed of autonomous, arms-length transactors acting in their own self-interests might appear ridiculous and short-sighted through the lenses of these epistemologies.
18. Cheryl Harris, 'Whiteness as Property,' *Harvard Law Review* 106 (1993), 1707-1791.
19. Mills, *The Racial Contract*.
20. Mills, *The Racial Contract*, 60.
21. E.g. Robert L. Hale, 'Bargaining, Duress, and Economic Liberty,' *Columbia Law Review* 43 (1943), 603—628; Máiréad Enright, 'Contract Law,' in *Great Debates in Gender and Law*, ed. Rosemary Auchmuty (Palgrave Macmillan, 2018), 1; Patricia

and the hypocrisy of the notion in light of its intertwinement with empire has been brilliantly considered by Enright in this very book.[22] I focus instead in this chapter on the ways in which the colonial and capitalist configurations of contract law are reproduced *in Contract Law modules*. I want to take the origin of modern contract law—*assumpsit*—and instead follow a different path from the etymological route of this word (*assumere*). Stemming from *assumere*, 'to assume' can mean to undertake voluntarily, the meaning ascribed to it in Contract Law. However, it can also mean 'to take as given, without proof'. What is *taken as given* and what is obscured from view in Contract Law modules? And, importantly, *how is this done* in the face of the increasing gap between lived reality and the presumptions underpinning Contract Law?

This is crucial because, it is important to remember, 'contract law' exists as a distinct, cordoned-off body of law *only in Contract Law modules*.[23] What is done within a Contract Law module, then—the stories told, the narratives privileged, the presumptions calcified—has ideological significance for each generation of law students. While Contract Law pedagogically asserts itself as purely pragmatic[24], with the implication that it is merely equipping students to navigate the legal landscape in the 'real world', it contradictorily acknowledges (as noted above) that contract law as 'contract law' does not necessarily exist in the world beyond the law school. Its existence in the law school, then—and in particular, its position as a *core module*—is thus an ideological statement with pedagogical consequences.

Reasonable Expectations and Objectivity

The ideal (or perhaps the only truly aligned and legitimate) subject of contract law (the white man) is reproduced in Contract Law modules as the ideal subject from which reasonableness, rationality, and knowledge more broadly stem. This 'subject' is embodied primarily in the theorists and judges to whom contract law modules and textbooks invoke almost exclusively. For instance, a highly influential theory in Contract Law is one set out by Johan Steyn, a former UK House of Lords judge, in his

---

J. Williams, 'Alchemical Notes: Reconstructing Ideals From Deconstructed Rights,' *Harvard Civil Rights-Civil Liberties Law Review* 22 (1987), 401.
22. Chapter **X**
23. E.g. Enright, 'Contract Law', 1.
24. E.g. TT Arvind, *Contract Law*, 2nd ed. (Oxford University Press, 2019), 1–17.

famous essay, *Fulfilling the reasonable expectations of honest men*. The idea of 'reasonable expectations' is considered helpful within doctrinal accounts of contract law, as the idea combines elements of both the former 'classical' theory of contract and subsequent reliance-based theories.[25] These theories both, as contract law textbooks formulaically illustrate, have their explanatory pitfalls. The idea of reasonable/legitimate expectations is of central contemporary importance in the doctrinal study of contract law[26] as it is perceived to transcend some of these explanatory pitfalls - it is thus useful for our purposes because its purported explanatory power provides us with an expedient route to an epistemological critique of contract law.

In his essay on the idea, Steyn aims to set forth a unifying explanation of contract law (through his famous thesis statement that '[a] thread runs through our contract law that effect must be given to the reasonable expectations of honest men').[27] He opens with:

> It is a defensible position for a legal system to give predominance to the subjective intentions of the parties. Such a policy can claim to be committed to the ideal of perfect individualised justice. But that is not the English way. Our law is generally based on an objective theory of contract. This involves adopting an external standard given life by using the concept of the reasonable man.[28]

Steyn thus begins by ascribing a sense of exceptionalism to English law—whilst appearing to concede that other approaches to law might be 'defensible', the implication is clearly that 'perfect individualized justice' is a lofty and naiive goal. This quickly sets the stage for Steyn to position *the English way* as one based on *objectivity* and thus superior. Steyn uses the word *external* to show that while this is 'the English way', the knowledge produced is nevertheless separate from English *people and culture*. Steyn proceeds to introduce us to the Reasonable

---

25. Séverine Saintier and Robert Merkin, Poole's *Textbook on Contract Law*, 14th ed. (Oxford University Press, 2019), 9-10.
26. Catherine Mitchell, 'Leading a Life of Its Own? The Roles of Reasonable Expectation in Contract Law', *Oxford Journal of Legal Studies* 23 (2003), 639—655, 640. Mitchell is critical of the role of 'reasonable expectation' in contract law, arguing that its usefulness as a unifying concept is undermined by the fat that 'the differently grounded expectations of the contracting parties are usually the precise site of conflict between them'.
27. Johan Steyn, 'Contract law: fulfilling the reasonable expectations of honest men', *Law Quarterly Review* 113 (1997), 433—442, 433.
28. Steyn, 'Fulfilling the reasonable expectations of honest men', 433.

Man, telling us that 'the hypothetical reasonable man pursues his own commercial self-interest' but 'he is by definition not dishonest'.[29] What, necessarily, links the pursual of commercial self-interest with honesty? Steyn does not explain, though we are left with the sense that Steyn is describing his ideal friend/business partner.

For instance, Steyn disagrees with the resistance to a broad doctrine of 'good faith' in English contract law. Steyn considers it 'surprising that the House of Lords in *Walford v Miles* held that an express agreement that parties must negotiate in good faith is unenforceable' and that 'Lord Ackner observed that the concept of a duty to carry on negotiations in good faith is inherently repugnant to the adversarial position of the parties when involved in negotiations'.[30] However, Ackner's observation of good faith in relation to commercial bargains seems to make sense: parties *are* positioned as adversarial in contractual dealings[31] and are attempting to act in their own commercial self-interest—*why* then must they necessarily be honest, aside from that Steyn would like it to be that way? This points to a tautology at the heart of Steyn's understanding of 'objectivity'. Objectivity for Steyn again comes back to *his* idea of a reasonable person. This tautology, and Steyn's seeming unwillingness to identify it, forces Steyn to take us in circles throughout this essay (e.g. 'The law does not protect unreasonable expectations. It protects only expectations which satisfy an objective criterion of reasonableness').[32] After nine pages, we are left with no substantive clue as to what reasonableness *is*. We get only this: 'Reasonableness is a familiar concept and no definition is necessary... It is concerned with contemporary standards not of moral philosophers but of ordinary right thinking people'.[33] This one gesture towards elucidation begs more questions than it resolves: who are right-thinking people? What is 'right thought'?

It becomes apparent that by 'reason', Steyn simply means *his own* emotion/intuition. 'One of the first lessons you learn' in Contract Law, Enright explains, 'is that subjective intentions do not matter to contract doctrine: only the outward 'objective' appearance of agreement

---

29. Steyn, 'Fulfilling the reasonable expectations of honest men', 434.
30. Steyn, 'Fulfilling the reasonable expectations of honest men', 438.
31. English contract law facilitates this dynamic by, for instance, not placing a broad/active duty upon parties to disclose material facts in contractual dealings (e.g., *Smith v Hughes*), and by generally refraining from enquiring into the nature of the bargain struck between contracting parties (e.g., *Chappell v Nestle Co*).
32. Steyn, 'Fulfilling the reasonable expectations of honest men', 434.
33. Steyn, 'Fulfilling the reasonable expectations of honest men', 434.

counts'.[34] This 'performs a political function' in that 'it allows courts to bypass detailed engagement with the conditions in which contractual intention is formed, producing rules that are 'singular, daunting, rigid and cocksure"'.[35] Through this process, 'the preferred practices of some are made the universal rule in order to discipline others'.[36]

MacKinnon explains that so-called '[o]bjectivity is liberal legalism's conception of itself. It legitimates itself by reflecting its views of society, a society it helps make by so seeing it, and calling that view, and that relation, rationality.'[37] However:

> Like the science it emulates, this epistemological stance cannot see the social specificity of reflexion as method or its choice to embrace that which it reflects. Such law not only reflects a society in which men rule women; it rules in a male way insofar as 'the phallus means everything that sets itself up as a mirror'.[38]

Despite their inherent *subjectivity*, notions of 'reasonableness', 'rationality', and 'objectivity' generate predictability in the law rather than randomness because '[i]n this hall of mirrors, only in extremis shall any man alter what any other man has wrought'.[39] (What MacKinnon says about *law itself* can also be said about *legal textbooks*. Consider the textbooks I have cited in this chapter—all published in Oxford, by Oxford University Press, most written by men. Textbooks are iterative and reproductive, just like legal precedent. The tone found within textbooks is deeply reverent - intellectual forefathers are idolised; their words and ideas lovingly recalled, respected, defended. Subsequent generations of textbooks might bear the names of these forefathers, despite being written by new authors).[40] The reasonable man is not 'external', as Steyn claimed—it is in fact Steyn, and men just like him—Steyn's friends, Steyn's colleagues, Steyn's progeny. It is the men of Steyn's ilk that find their expectations *legitimised* by contract law. It is their

---

34. Enright, 'Contract Law', 2.
35. Enright, 'Contract Law', 3. (Citing Mary Joe Frug, 'Rescuing impossibility doctrine: A postmodern feminist analysis of contract law' (1992) 140 University of Pennsylvania Law Review 1029, 1035.)
36. Enright, 'Contract Law', 3.
37. Catharine A. MacKinnon, *Toward a Feminist Theory of the State* (Harvard University Press, 1989), 162.
38. MacKinnon, *Toward a Feminist Theory of the State*, 163.
39. MacKinnon, *Toward a Feminist Theory of the State*, 164.
40. See, e.g. Davies, *JC Smith's The Law of Contract* or Saintier and Merkin, *Poole's Textbook on Contract Law*.

subject status *prior to contract law* that imbues their 'expectations' with legitimacy and reasonableness.[41]

Women do not have the same subject status as men prior to the law.[42] Within colonial formulations of race, it is only white people that are imbued with subjectivity - 'others' thus constitute objects that might, like land and nature, be appropriated by white subjects to varying degrees.[43]

The de-subjectification of women and subaltern peoples is reproduced when contract law modules obscure certain facts from view. The colonial context of the emergence of contract law warrants no mention in any textbook. Numerous landmark cases are set against a backdrop of colonial exploitation[44], and this exploitation is rarely noted, let alone unpacked, in conventional textbooks. The image created by *Bell v Lever Brothers* is particularly stark: the case centers on a 'golden parachute agreement' made between two Englishmen at the Savoy Grill in London.[45] Behind the scenes of this case: Lever Brothers (now Unilever) was (when the Court of Appeal decision was delivered in 1931) building significant wealth through the use of forced labour by its subsidiary Huileries du Congo Belge in the Congo from 1911—1945.[46] By what trick of the mind is the historical and social context of *Bell v Lever Brothers* rendered invisible in Contract Law textbooks and modules?

Patricia Williams considers the word I (*toi*) in Vietnamese, which translates to 'your servant'—'[s]uch a self-concept', Williams says, 'is a way of experiencing the other, of ritualistically sharing the other's essence and cherishing it'.[47] By contrast, in the English language (and

---

41. 'Ideal contractual subjects are strong, independent, self-possessed and productive. They are autonomous beings who possess and trade in concrete legal rights.' Enright, 'Contract Law', 3.
42. MacKinnon, *Toward a Feminist Theory of the State*, 163.
43. E.g. Quijano, 'Coloniality and Modernity/Rationality'.
44. E.g. *Bell v Lever Brothers* [1931] 1 KB 557, CA; [1932] AC 161, HL, *McRae v Commonwealth Disposals Commission* [1957] HCA 79 (an Australian case that forms a key part of the doctrine of common mistake in English contract law), and *Raffles v Wichelhaus ('The Peerless')* (1864) 2 H & C 906s.
45. [1931] 1 KB 557, CA; [1932] AC 161, HL
46. RIAO-RDC & GRAIN, 'Agro-colonialism in the Congo: European and US development finance bankrolls a new round of agro-colonialism in the DRC', 2 June 2015, accessed 21 September 2020, https://www.grain.org/en/article/5220-agro-colonialism-in-the-congo-european-and-us-development-finance-bankrolls-a-new-round-of-agro-colonialism-in-the-drc.
47. Williams, *The Alchemy of Race and Rights*, 62.

perhaps Western culture and rationality more broadly), there is little that 'encourages looking at others as parts of ourselves'.[48] We can see this operating even in ways that are not overtly racialised or gendered in Contract Law—for instance, one influential Contract Law textbook poses the following question in its discussion of events that might 'frustrate' a contract (i.e. render contractual performance impossible):

> If the contract is to be performed by a person known to be a sole trader, and that person is unable to complete the contract because they suffer a major heart attack and have to give up work, is that sole trader in repudiatory breach of contract, or could they succeed in a claim that the contract was frustrated?[49]

Coming across this statement in the ordinary course of reading is jarring. There appears to be a gaping chasm between the premise (the end of a human life) and the subsequent question (regarding the particulars of how a contract might come to an end). It is a painstakingly built ideological and spiritual apparatus that links these clauses. This apparatus enables the question-asker to position themselves at a cool distance from human life, a mere conduit of a specific, teleological market-based rationality. (By the time a Contract Law student arrives at page 487 of their textbook, does this statement appear intuitive and natural to them, too?)

When it comes to those that are *racialised*, the consequences of the Western (in this case, English) separation of the *I* from the *whole* of life are drastic, because:

> some I's are defined as 'your servant', some as 'your master'... some serve without ever being served; some master with no sense of what it is to be mastered; and almost everyone hides from the fact of this vernacular domination by clinging to the legally official definition of an I meaning 'your equal'.[50]

About some lives, jarring questions are asked. About Other lives, no questions are asked at all. The rhetoric of formal, liberal equality in which Contract Law textbooks are sheathed enables these books to reproduce colonial capitalist relations of power in the minds of students without ever making explicit statements to this effect. By excluding historical and sociological context from their remit, textbooks reinforce

---

48. Williams, *The Alchemy of Race and Rights*, 62.
49. Saintier and Merkin, *Contract Law*, 487.
50. Williams, *The Alchemy of Race and Rights*, 63.

the notion that some lives are *irrelevant to the terms of the discussion of* Contract Law. Coercion perpetrated by Lever Brothers in the Congo may amount to coercion, or it may not: to Contract textbooks and Contract classrooms, this is simply irrelevant. What *matters*, students are told, is the agreement made between the two men party to the discussion. The people of colour on whom these men might have stepped to arrive at a place of agreement is not only peripheral: it is invisible, or more accurately, *invisibilised*. This is not an exercise in pure, passive disregard—when Others are excluded from the terms of discussion in this way (present in the periphery, the subconscious, but not as subjects), an active statement is made, however quietly: that some *can* inherently contract, and others cannot. And by virtue of this 'inability', those that 'cannot' are (as was proclaimed loudly and emphatically through the civilising mission of European colonialism) objects.

In a fantastic pedagogical resource on decolonising core UK law modules, Jivraj considers the 'key' case *Harvey v Facey*,[51] cited generally to distinguish clear contractual 'offers' from other forms of communication. A fact not mentioned or elaborated upon in most textbooks is that the case involves the sale of the former slave plantation 'Bumper Hall Pen' in Jamaica.[52] Again, the Contract textbook tells us, what is relevant in this context is the nature of the agreement between two white men. What else *might* be visible here if, for a moment, we were to discard the parameters of the discussion set by 'Contract Law', and instead (briefly) adopt a contextual view of human relationships as embedded in society and history? The case is dated 30 years after the Slave Compensation Act 1867 paid compensation (upon the abolition of the trans-Atlantic slave trade) to the owners of enslaved people (both those living in the Caribbean and the many 'absentee owners' living in the UK). The UCL Centre for the Study of the Legacies of British Slavery shows compensation for the loss of enslaved persons in Jamaica awarded to at least 5 people with the surname 'Facey'.[53] Whether or not any of these people were related to the Facey of *Harvey v Facey* fame, the wealth from the appropriated and bloodstained land that formed the 'object' of *Harvey v Facey* and the compensation meted out to the Faceys 30 years earlier for the loss of 'their property' (for

---

51. [1893] UKPC 1 (29 July 1893)
52. Suhraiya Jivraj, *Towards Anti-Racist Legal Pedagogy: A Resource* (2020), https://kar.kent.ac.uk/id/eprint/82763, accessed 1 July 2021, 39.
53. Centre for the Study of the Legacies of British Slavery, accessed 1 July 2021, https://www.ucl.ac.uk/lbs/search/.

which they will have 'freely' contracted), has no doubt 'trickled down' to diffuse descendants in the UK today, enhancing the subjectivity of these descendants and fortifying their ability to contract 'freely'.

The tidy and effortless means by which the contexts or key Contract cases are obscured from view—the terms of the discussion structured in such a way as to render certain lives, certain histories, certain subjectivities *immaterial*—reproduces the colonial sense that some people are *objects*, rather than subjects. I say 'sense' here because invisibilisation of this kind, so deeply and habitually deliberate that it is casual, can have affective significance in a classroom. And it is this affect—the atmospheres produced when Contract Law 'knowledge', and the genetic material this 'knowledge' carries, percolate in the classroom and in the collective and individual student body/mind—that can perhaps explain in part why Contract Law, despite its clear logical and philosophical inconsistencies, has been so successfully able to reproduce itself through generations.

Distortion, Disorientation, and Unreasonable Expectations

Like MacKinnon, Frantz Fanon uses the metaphor of 'mirrors' to discuss how people interact with their social context. MacKinnon uses the metaphor of the mirror to illustrate the ways in which a distinctly male epistemology is reproduced through jurisprudence as 'objective' and neutral (insofar as it reflects existing social conditions without disrupting/altering them). Fanon uses Jacques Lacan's notion of a 'psychological mirror stage' to argue that the ego-formation of Black children is interrupted by the strength of the white gaze. In their formative 'mirror stage' just after infancy, during which time all humans first develop a unified sense of ego/self, Black children are prevented, by societal structures of white supremacy, from fully and accurately *seeing* themselves.[54] White gaze continues to reflect distorted images of Black people back to themselves, as they are 'dissected under white eyes, the only real eyes'.[55]

It is possible to apply Fanon's thinking to the operation of the intellectual white gaze in law schools. When subaltern students (or perhaps female students, or students that for any reason do not fit into the container of the ideal contracting subject/producer of contractual

---

54. Frantz Fanon, *Black Skin, White Masks*, trans. Charles Lam Markmann (Grove, 1967), 161.
55. Fanon, *Black Skin, White Masks*, 116.

knowledge) are presented with ideas of 'free contracting' and 'reasonableness' devoid of empirical evidence, context, contingency and history—ideas that might fly in the face of their own lived experience and reality—it is likely to produce distortions in these students' understanding of *themselves* as subjects and 'knowers'. If what they *know* to be true (intuitively, viscerally, experientially, factually) does not match what Johan Steyn and his ilk 'know' to be true intuitively and viscerally, then their knowledge is reflected back to them as *unreasonable* (or at the very least, *not quite reasonable*), tangential—'reduced to the 'intuitive' rather than the 'real".[56] Williams recounts the jarring sensation she felt when her sister visited the US National Archives and 'found something which may have been the contract of my [enslaved] great-great grandmother Sophie's sale (whether hers or not, it was someone's)'.[57] What might somebody like Williams be expected to feel when they are asked to critique notions of 'freedom of contract' against only non-contextual, ahistorical benchmarks (perhaps, in the same exam, being prompted to cite *Harvey v Facey*)? Fanon describes the feeling that might arise within us when we are faced with distorting, fracturing experiences such as these: 'I am made of the irrational; I wade in the irrational. Up to the neck in the irrational'.[58]

At the university stage, it is possible that the prescribed processes of knowledge conveyance and reception in core modules like Contract Law produce a sense of alienation in certain students, interrupting their capacity to identify themselves as knowers or knowledge-producers. Jivraj and Memon, in an account of their work on Decolonising the University, speak movingly of the 'sense of dysphoria rather than belonging' encountered in UK universities by law students.[59]

Drawing on Fanon's work, Ahmed considers the ways in which:

> bodies are shaped by histories of colonialism, which makes the world "white" as a world that is inherited or already given. This is the familiar world, the world of whiteness, as a world we know implicitly. Colonialism makes the world "white," which is of course a world "ready" for certain kinds of bodies, as a world that puts certain objects within

---

56. Williams, *Alchemy of Race and Rights*, 63.
57. Williams, 'Alchemical Notes', 420.
58. Fanon, *Black Skin, White Masks*, 123.
59. Ahmed R. Memon and Suhraiya Jivraj, 'Trust, courage and silence: carving out decolonial spaces in higher education through student-staff partnerships', *The Law Teacher* 54 (2020), 476.

their reach. Bodies remember such histories, even when we forget them.[60]

This manifests in the university, in which "whiteness' is both ever present—looming, visible and subsuming the everyday life of students—yet it will not and cannot name itself for what it is and what it perpetrates—institutional racism'.[61]

Ahmed examines the ways in which some bodies might not 'fit' into or align with their environments, whilst others do by virtue of the ways in which they embody their environments due to social, environmental, and historical factors - the "upright' body is involved in the world and acts on the world, or even 'can act' insofar as it is already involved'. Bodies that do not 'fit' cannot be 'involved' in their surroundings in the same way - this 'causes the body to collapse, and to become an object alongside other objects. In simple terms, disorientation involves becoming an object'.[62]

It is perhaps this *disorientation* and consequent *objectification* of certain students that enables Contract Law to continue reproducing a subjective rationality as objective, universal, and transcendent.

There is also a material element to this. The very power relations woven into the ideological substance of Contract Law are materially replicated in the classroom because of the environment in which the Contract Law classroom is in turn embedded - the neoliberal university, and more broadly, the neoliberal and tyrannical job market, the neoliberal world. And who, more than anyone else, is shackled to the whims and ways of the neoliberal job market (one that demands, for a commercial training contract, a strong performance in Contract Law)? The most marginalised students, of course. For these students, the possibilities to *challenge* are limited—their intellectual and spiritual energies *must* remain focused on participating in the mirroring exercises required to perform well in standard Contract Law modules. The keys that modules like Contract Law provide to the exclusive kingdom of the British legal profession also has seductive appeal, bolstered by the sublime aesthetics of law schools, law libraries, and legal professional institutions (combining elements of awe, fear, and beauty). As Quijano says: at first, European culture was placed out of reach for subaltern peoples—'[t]hen European culture was made seductive: it gave access to power. After all, beyond repression, the main instrument of all power

---

60. Sara Ahmed, *Queer Phenomenology: Orientations, Objects, Others* (Duke University Press, 2006), 111.
61. Memon and Jivraj, 'Trust, courage and silence', 480.
62. Ahmed, *Queer Phenomenology*, 159.

is its seduction'.⁶³

The 'neoliberal university model where the hierarchy of student–staff is dictated by the specific purpose of 'assessing' the value of students—or 'clients'—in order to give them a return for their 'investment" further reinforces the logic of contracting in the classroom. It not only enfolds students, but also *teachers* into a narrow educational transaction.⁶⁴ Like law itself, *teachers of core modules* generally posture as neutral. Feminist and critical race scholarship, for instance, brings the researcher into the picture. But this presence of the knower as a person with context is not present in the way that core modules are taught. Why do we allow certain schools of thought to occupy the center ground in or classrooms (often through teachers as conduits) without demanding that the true thinkers of these thoughts name themselves and explain themselves? This is, of course, the ultimate genius of the colonial claim to 'objectivity': when the thinkers are not identified, contextualized, provincialized, the 'thought' can lay claim to a universality—in the course of a legal education, we might even be tricked into believing these thoughts have come from our own minds. The classroom is thus one site at which colonial modernity continues to 'conscript the very subjects called to resist and overthrow it.'⁶⁵

I have largely been addressing students throughout this chapter, but in closing I turn to other teachers: what if we, as those that do not comfortably and naturally 'fit' the contours of contractual rationality, were to respect ourselves as knowers, as Fanon called on subaltern and colonized peoples to do? What would happen to the elements of the Contract Law curriculum that did not hold up against our expectations? Would anything of the module survive? We are generally encouraged not to ponder such remote possibilities because they are naiive and outlandish. But, for now, simply as a thought experiment: what would the world (or, dreaming smaller, the Contract Law classroom) look like if we asked it to give effect to our unreasonable expectations?

---

63. Quijano, 'Coloniality and Modernity/Rationality,' 169.
64. Memon and Jivraj, 'Trust, courage and silence', 478.
65. Foluke Adebisi, 'Decolonising the law school: presences, absences silences… and hope', *The Law Teacher* 54 (2020), 472. Excerpt from keynote address, titled 'Cacophony, Autocritique and Abolition: Impression Points on Decolonisation and the Law School', delivered by Joel Modiri, a senior lecturer in the Department of Jurisprudence, University of Pretoria, South Africa.

18

Decentering Property Norms

Property Law, Land Law

Smith Ouma

The dominant textbooks in property or land law that are used in British universities understand the enactment of property rights in land through a limited and individual-centric perspective. The approaches taken in these texts have been informed by the restricted definitions to land that are contained in the current legal and economic systems. Under these systems, the individual property owner, with a singular title, is favored and idealized. Individual ownership has been ascribed with moral superiority and proffered as the natural order. In short, these textbooks and the legal system they describe, are infused with a limiting worldview as certain knowledge sources have been disqualified as inadequate. Implicit within property law as it is taught in the UK, there is a hierarchy on *knowing*. It endorses particular knowledge registers, and insists that any theory of property must emerge from this tradition. The tradition itself has deep Judeo-Christian theological origins. Theorists like John Locke bear an enduring influence on how property is understood and taught. Contemporary property law then tends to be constructed through the architecture of 17th and 18th century liberal ideology. But an outcome of embracing the limiting Lockean traditions on property rights has been the ruthless dislocation of forms of *knowing* and *being* that could potentially provide a greater diversity to our understanding of property. The ensuing ideological enactments of property are then structured around a monolithic approach or what Carol Rose calls 'the standard story about property.'[1]

---

1. Rose, C. 'Property as Storytelling: Perspectives from the Game Theory, Narrative Theory, Feminist Theory', (1990) 2(37) *Yale Journal of Law and the Humanities*, 51.

Possessive Individualism in Property Theory

Locke's works laid the foundations to the current hegemonic conceptions of property (or land to be more specific). In his *Second Treatise of Government*, he advanced what would become the classical property view where he foregrounded labour as the foundation to property and proclaimed appropriation of property as a necessity, or even more a moral duty, to tame and 'make use of the waste'.[2] He considered land which was unowned in the western sense as lying waste and in need of appropriation. Locke developed his theory at a time when European colonial settlement was advancing in the North American mainland and there was need for an ideological justification for the colonial ventures and acquisition of land. The colonial doctrine of *terra nullius* (land belonging to no one) was advanced to provide the moral and legal justifications for dispossessing indigenous peoples and extinguishing native title. Extending such doctrine to spaces with subsisting indigenous peoples' rights was oriented at providing legalistic rationale for colonial expropriation and the erasure of natives from their lands.[3] Erasure has been the hallmark of settler colonialism. It has been facilitated by tools like registration and issuance of paper deeds. Issuance of deeds over colonized lands signaled colonial understanding of colonized land as 'new and without history'.[4]

Law became a tool and a medium for unilaterally producing 'empty spaces' or 'waste', imposing new meanings and sovereignty over these spaces, and ultimately converting the colonized spaces into a form that valorized commercial exchange, and hence an object of English attention.[5] According to Tomlins, 'English notions of legal sovereignty, of rightful occupation, and of exclusive possession were central to the discourse of American colonizing.'[6] Locke embraced these notions and in his view, possession defined property and anything that was not

---

2. Locke, J. *Two Treatises of Government*, Peter Laslett, ed. (Oxford University Press, 1988) II, para. 184.
3. Corcoran, P. 'John Locke on the Possession of Land: Native Title vs. 'Principle' of Vacuum Domicilium', available at https://digital.library.adelaide.edu.au/dspace/bitstream/2440/44958/1/hdl_44958.pdf accessed May 4, 2021, 2.
4. Keenan, S. 'From Historical Chains to Derivative Futures: Title Registries as Time Machines', (2019) 20(3) *Social and Cultural Geography*, 283.
5. Tomlins, C. 'In a Wilderness of Tigers: Violence, the Discourse of English Colonizing, and the Refusals of American History', (2003) 4(451) *Theoretical Inquiries in Law*, 474.
6. Tomlins. 'In a Wilderness of Tigers', 454.

individually possessed was 'lying waste in common'.[7] Appropriation then takes an elevated place in Lockean accounts of property. He argued that appropriation is limited to the extent that one has mixed their labour with land.[8] In Locke's estimation, an individual will be able to make use of property once '...it becomes part of him, that another can no longer have any rights to it, before it can do him any good for the support of his life.'[9]

Within market societies, Locke's philosophy may find some normative legitimacy. For these societies, Lockean views provide the ideological scaffolding from which property arrangements are constructed. Hence property will, in western societies, often be constructed through its metonymic association with possessive individualism. Under common law, possession is credited as the origin of property and as the basis for a claim to title.[10] Enforceable property rights emerge from possession once an individual has met the formality requirements that are prescribed by law. Ultimately, the registration of an individual as a proprietor under the established registration systems acts to extinguish any other claims that may be advanced by others towards the land. But still, any paper deed issued to a proprietor will in most cases carry more value when it is backed by physical possession.[11] It explains the relevance of adverse possession in land law teaching and why a considerable amount of time is often spent to explain and justify the concept.

Locke's views were instrumental in shaping the approaches adopted by William Blackstone, an English jurist whose *Commentaries on the Laws of England* best describe the doctrines of English law, including English property law. For Blackstone the right to property represents 'that sole and despotic dominion which one man claims and exercises over the external things of the world, in total exclusion of the right of any other individual in the universe.'[12] We can then trace the logics of possessive individualism in the ideological language that Blackstone

---

7. Locke, J. *Two Treatises of Government*, para. 37.
8. Macpherson, C.B. *The Political theory of Possessive Individualism: Hobbes to Locke* (Clarendon Press, 1962) 214.
9. Locke, J. *Two Treatises of Government*, sect. 26.
10. Blackstone, W. *Commentaries on the Laws of England in Four Books* (JB Lippincott Company, 1893) para. 8.
11. Keenan, S. 'From Historical Chains to Derivative Futures: Title Registries as Time Machines', 284.
12. Blackstone, W. *Commentaries on the Laws of England in Four Books, Vol. 1*, para. 2.

adopts here and particularly from his use of terms like *sole and despotic dominion, one man, total exclusion*, etc. Indeed, Blackstone's Commentaries is in many institutions treated as a mandatory statute book which students taking land law must purchase and constantly make reference to.

Are There 'Other' Ways of Seeing/Knowing Property?

Lockean views may fail to find resonance in non-market societies. This is particularly the case in contexts where the commons are the defining proprietary system. There commons act as 'the creative force in social production and reproduction.'[13] By locating possessive individualism high up on the hierarchy that he devises, Locke presupposes its moral superiority over ownership types such as communal tenure. Indeed, Locke already assigned common property a subordinate place to private property when he argued that the commons represent that which is residual to what has already been appropriated by an individual.[14] Locke's writings must then be understood in the context of the European settler-colonialism ongoing at the time on the American continent as it provided justification for the expropriation of land that native communities held in common.

Rose has examined how early modern theorists like Locke framed their discussions in a narrative mode that was infused with theoretical self-interest. She argues that during this time, the dominant group of storytellers like Locke made their position on possessive individualism seem to be the natural one.[15] According to Crabtree, such discursive representations like the ones depicted by Locke 'creates a heady mix in which the colonial appropriation, enclosure, and modification of commons or Indigenous lands is undertaken, promoted, and justified...'[16] Locke then set the basis for an economic defence of colonialism as 'the colonizers merely fulfill their obligation under natural law to prevent land from lying in waste.'[17]

---

13. See Okoth-Ogendo, H.W.O. 'The Tragic African Commons: A Century of Expropriation, Suppression and Subversion', (2003) 1 *University of Nairobi Law Journal*, 107.
14. Locke, J. *Two Treatises of Government*, ch. 5 sec. 27.
15. Rose, C. 'Property as Storytelling', 54.
16. Crabtree, L. 'Decolonising Property: Exploring Ethics, Land, and Time, Through Housing Interventions in Contemporary Australia', (2013) 31 *Environment and Planning*, 101.
17. See Winter, Y. 'Conquest', available at http://www.politicalconcepts.org/issue1/

In the context of such colonially delineated knowledge paradigms, the colonized have no history and cannot speak.[18] The teaching of property has not adequately acknowledged this epistemic violence. Instead, it participates in the reinscription of the Anglo-American way of seeing the institution of property without critically assessing the implications of this single-lens approach and adopting Western views on property as the normative yardstick. Our current property law curriculum is laden with the discursive debris of classical property theorists whose views are treated as unimpeachable and the filter for the values that we must adopt. We can see this in the key texts that we use in property law. Any critical engagement with these texts would reveal that they are cast in colonial and neo-colonial traditions. Such examination would enable one to see how the literature on land law remain beholden to the narrow hegemonic conceptions in which individualism is maintained as the metaphor for property.

This has an alienating outcome for students from backgrounds where the institution of property is experienced differently. It also fails to acknowledge the variety of ways in which property can exist, even within Western societies. Additionally, we can no longer consider it innocuous that the leading texts on property that are used in our law schools fail to acknowledge the dispossessory logics that lurk behind Lockean traditions. These kinds of failures of imagination have led Suhraiya Jivraj to conclude that, 'there is significant scope for teaching property law through a historical lens and socio-economic context that places all aspects of property law in its global and colonial context.'[19] Similarly, for Ncube and Mbembe, we must adopt 'decolonizing methodologies' which deconstructs 'a canon that attributes truth only to the Western way of knowledge production' and which treats 'other' knowledge systems as mere appendages to the Euro-American world.[20]

---

conquest/ See also Arneil, B. 'The Wild Indian's Venison: Locke's Theory of Property and English Colonialism in America', (1996) XVLIV *Political Studies*, 70.
18. Spivak, G.C. 'Can the Subaltern Speak', available at http://abahlali.org/files/Can_the_subaltern_speak.pdf 82.
19. Jivraj, S. 'Towards Anti-Racist Legal Pedagogy: A Resource', available at https://research.kent.ac.uk/decolonising-law-schools/wp-content/uploads/sites/866/2020/09/Towards-Anti-racist-Legal-Pedagogy-A-Resource.pdf 42.
20. Ncube, C. 'Decolonising Intellectual Property Law in Pursuit of Africa's Development', (2016) 8(1) *The WIPO Journal*, 36. Mbembe, A. 'Decolonising Knowledge and the Question of the Archive', available at https://wiser.wits.ac.za/system/files/Achille%20Mbembe%20-%20Decolonizing%20Knowledge%20and%20the%20Question%20of%20the%20Archive.pdf accessed May 10, 2021.

Conclusion

Acknowledging the diversity in forms of knowing and broadening our analysis of property rights may enable us to reorient our focus to the original sin of dispossession and acknowledge its ongoing manifestations. By unmuting 'other' knowledge archives, we could perhaps take cognizance of and grapple with the multiple implications of adopting insular property norms. We may then be able to open our outlooks to the world to cross-fertilization by views that have historically been othered. We may then start viewing property as a transgenerational asset, which would impose obligations on present generations to conserve it for the yet-to-be born. By eschewing the view of property as a sole and despotic dominion, we can foreground use rights by radically restructuring the power relations that define production of space and maintaining focus on the utility value of space. My invitation here is for us to be conscious of the ruse of single-lens epistemologies. It is an appeal to unshackle ourselves from narrow conceptions on property which fail to acknowledge its colonizing attributes or which treats them as peripheral or aberrational. Ultimately, we should be unremitting in our pursuit of liberatory epistemologies which properly equips us to recognize, name and critique exclusions.

Further Readings

- Musila, G.A. 'Navigating Epistemic Disarticulations', (2017) 116 (465) *African Affairs*.
- Modiri, J.M. 'Conquest and Constitutionalism: First Thoughts on an Alternative Jurisprudence', (2018) 34 *South African Journal on Human Rights*.
- Wa Thiongo, N. *Decolonising the Mind: The Politics of Language in African Literature* (Heinemann, 1986).
- Bujo, B. *The Ethical Dimension of Community: The African Model and the Dialogue Between North and South* (Paulines Publications Africa, 1998).
- Nyamu-Musembi, C. 'Breathing Life into Dead Theories about Property Rights: De Soto and Land Relations in Rural Africa', (2006) *Institute of Development Studies Working Paper*.
- Kariuki, F. et. al. *Property Law* (Strathmore Press, 2016).

- Bhandar, B. *Colonial Lives of Property: Law, Land, and Racial Regimes of Ownership* (Duke University Press, 2018).
- Lefebvre, H, *Writings on Cities* (Blackwell Publishers, 1996).

19

The Radical Fringes of Tort Law

TORT LAW, LITIGATION

Colin Murray

Tort is not radical; for many it wears its conservatism on its sleeve. As a branch of law left in large part to judicial development it makes a virtue of incrementalist fine tuning of causes of action and glories in the maintenance of floodgates even on the most inherently constrained channels for challenging harms.[1] Many proposals to radically reform tort law are in reality proposals to abolish tort law and replace it with something else.[2] But even within the bounded reality of tort this jurisprudential space is both less radical, and sometimes more radical, than one might presuppose.[3] Here, I want to explore tort law as a means of addressing wrongs perpetrated by, or in some way involving, state actors, focusing on how tort operates in the jurisdictions of England and Wales.[4] I also reflect on efforts to use tort to open up avenues for

---

1. See Carl Stychin, 'The vulnerable subject of negligence law' (2012) 8 *International Journal of Law in Context* 337-353, 338 and L. Dolding and Richard Mullender, 'Tort Law, Incrementalism, and the House of Lords' (1996) 47 NILQ 12. For a counter argument, which treats these developments as 'a rearguard battle against an ever-expanding tort law', see Dan Priel, 'A Public Role for the Intentional Torts' (2011) 22 King's Law Journal 183, 185.
2. See, for example, Stephen Sugarman, 'Doing away with tort law' (1985) 73 California Law Review 555 and Peter Cane, 'Reforming Tort Law in Australia: A Personal Perspective' (2003) 27 Melbourne University Law Review 649.
3. See also Denis Brion, 'The chaotic indeterminacy of tort law: between formalism and nihilism' in David Caudill and Stephen Gold (eds.), *Radical Philosophy of Law: Contemporary Challenges to Mainstream Legal Theory and Practice* (Humanities Press, 1995) pp. 179-199.
4. For an early alternate account of tort's public function, see A. Linden, 'Tort Law as Ombudsman' (1973) 51 Canadian Bar Review 155. The influence of this account

challenging wrongs that are ineffectively dealt with by other branches of law (and thereby addressing omissions or shortcomings by public bodies). In other words, this account explores the factors which have left tort a comparative backwater alongside human rights claims in these contexts, and the ways in which tort keeps breaking through cosy assumptions about its innate conservatism.

Channelling Litigation Away from Tort

Even as twentieth century tort law in England and Wales embraced a general duty of care in negligence applicable to foreseeable harms, the 'timorous' courts maintained in place policy justifications which in many cases negatived public authority liability for what would otherwise amount to foreseeable harms.[5] This indulgence operated to shield state agents, and particularly the police, from a range of liabilities.[6] As a result, civil actions which have exposed police malpractice, such as *Brooks v Commissioner of Police for the Metropolis*,[7] in which the House of Lords found repeated failings in the treatment of a witness to Stephen Lawrence's murder, all-too-often result in the courts providing no substantive remedy.[8] In light of the strict limitations upon legal aid in civil cases and the risks of a costs order associated with an unsuccessful claim,[9] the limited possibility of substantive remedies makes for a trifecta sufficient to discourage all but the doughtiest of claimants. And even if the claimant is not discouraged, their claim will, in these circumstances, have to provide a sufficiently attractive prospect for one of a very small pool of law firms to offer a conditional or discounted fee arrangement.

With the development of positive obligations in human rights law, and particularly with regard to Articles 2, 3 and 8 ECHR, leading

---

of governmental accountability under tort in England and Wales can be seen in Carol Harlow, *State Liability: Tort Law Beyond* (OUP, 2004) p. 49.

5. Jane Wright, *Tort Law and Human Rights* (Hart, 2001) p. 3.
6. See Claire McIvor, 'Getting Defensive about Police Negligence: The *Hill* Principle, the Human Rights Act 1998 and the House of Lords' (2010) 69 Cambridge Law Journal 133, 133.
7. *Brooks v Commissioner of Police of the Metropolis* [2005] UKHL 24; [2005] 1 WLR 1495.
8. *Brooks v Commissioner of Police* [1]-[3] (Lord Bingham). See R. Hyde, 'The Role of Civil Liability in Ensuring Police Responsibility for Failures to Act after *Michael* and *DSD*' (2016) 22 European Journal of Current Legal Issues.
9. For discussion of these restrictions in light of the Article 6 right to a fair hearing, see *Steel and Morris v United Kingdom* (2005) 41 EHRR 403.

judgments have sought to further ringfence police liability in tort. In *Michael v Chief Constable of South Wales*,[10] Lord Toulson gave a leading judgment against the police owing a duty of care in negligence over a failure to prioritise an emergency call from a woman who was subsequently murdered, citing concern that police practices might be shaped by concerns over tort actions.[11] Whatever force there may be in this argument, and Lord Kerr saw little basis to displace 'the fundamental principle that legal wrongs should be remedied',[12] it made little sense in light of the Court unanimously accepting that the claimant could pursue a Human Rights Act challenge. Defensive police practice would be shaped by potential litigation from either avenue; this outcome simply excluded the possibility of broader damages being available through a negligence action.

Tort is thus, all too often, a closed avenue where state actors are the prospective defendant, at least beyond claims involving the direct infliction of personal injury.[13] Even claims which seem, on first sight, to involve claims in tort, have thus been reconceived as human rights claims in recent decades. The claims relating to the beating to death of Baha Mousa and mistreatment of other detainees in the custody of UK Armed Forces in Basra in September 2003 ultimately saw the UK Government admit 'substantive breaches' Articles 2 and 3 ECHR and reach a settlement of nearly £3 million.[14] As the ongoing case of Saifullah Yar, relating to allegations of extra-judicial killings by members of the Special Air Service in Afghanistan in 2011, demonstrates, where there is insufficient evidence to mount a substantive legal challenge, Article 2 ECHR provides the means to challenge inadequate investigations into deaths caused by agents of the state.[15] The multiple barriers erected within tort have contributed to Human Rights Act claims displacing tort actions, a deliberate channelling of litigation which is exemplified by Lord Toulson's approach in *Michael*, but one

---

10. *Michael v Chief Constable of South Wales* [2015] UKSC 2; [2015] 2 WLR 343.
11. *Michael v Chief Constable of South Wales*, [121].
12. *Michael v Chief Constable of South Wales*, [186].
13. Contrast the rejection of damages for wrongful detention without evidence of harm in *Cullen v Chief Constable of the Royal Ulster Constabulary* [2003] UKHL 39; [2003] 1 WLR 1763, with the treatment of personal injury for a police shooting in *Ashley v Chief Constable of Sussex Police* [2008] UKHL 25; (2008) 2 WLR 975. See Philip Palmer and Jenny Steele, 'Police Shootings and the Role of Tort' (2008) 71 Modern Law Review 801.
14. D. Browne MP, HC Deb, vol. 474, col. 14WS (27 March 2008).
15. See Mqtt Bardo and Hannah O'Grady, 'Did UK Special Forces execute unarmed civilians?' *BBC News* (1 August 2020). Available at: https://www.bbc.co.uk/news/uk-53597137.

which has perhaps served to heap official antipathy upon the Human Rights Act as the primary source of unwelcome litigation, when tort could also be playing a role in vindicating these rights.

This hollowing out of tort is also reshaping judicial review. Cross examination of witnesses was long all-but absent from the jurisdiction. Where human rights claims are at issue, judges have now had to affirm that 'a court conducting a judicial review has all the powers it requires, including the power to hear oral evidence and to order cross-examination of witnesses, to enable it to substitute its own judgment for that of the decision maker, if that is what Article 6 requires'.[16] This receptiveness towards oral evidence is seeping into judicial review cases that have no connect to human rights.[17] So perhaps the story is as much about judicial review becoming more like tort actions, as about it displacing tort. In any event, there remain cases in which human rights have not displaced tort. For example, much as the ECHR's 'underlying values' might have provided a basis for the imposition of investigative duties upon the state in right to life cases, this has been of no help to claimants where the events in question predate the adoption of the ECHR[18] (and/or occurred in contexts beyond its jurisdictional ambit[19]). Such cases continue to provide part of tort's radical fringe.

Repurposing; Empowering?

Tort law can sometimes provide an outlet where people feel let down by the criminal justice system. Although the purpose of the civil actions and criminal prosecutions are often presented as being very different, and the provision of criminal injuries compensation negates the need for many victims to contemplate this possibility, the facts of many cases provide overlapping bases for prosecutions and civil claims.[20] Beyond

---

16. *Secretary of State for the Home Department v MB* [2006] EWCA Civ 1140; [2006] 3 WLR 829, [48] (Lord Phillips).
17. See, for example, *R (Save Britain's Heritage) v Liverpool City Council* [2016] EWHC 48 (Admin).
18. *Keyu v Secretary of State for Foreign and Commonwealth Affairs* [2015] UKSC 69; [2016] AC 1355, [72] (Lord Neuberger). See Brice Dickson, 'The Limitations of a Criminal Law Approach in a Transitional Justice Context' in Laurens Lavrysen and Natasa Mavronicola (eds), *Coercive Human Rights: Positive Duties to Mobilise the Criminal Law Under the ECHR* (Hart, 2020) 223, p. 235.
19. *Al-Skeini v United Kingdom* (2011) 53 EHRR 18. See J. Rooney, 'The relationship between jurisdiction and attribution after *Jaloud v. Netherlands*' (2015) 62 Netherlands International Law Review 407.
20. See Allan Beever, 'Justice and Punishment in Tort: A Comparative Theoretical

cases which seek to hold state agents to account (which might therefore involve limited prospect of prosecutions, but is an issue addressed in other sections of this contribution), such uses of tort have received most attention in the context of the persistently low conviction rates in cases of sexual offences and as a response to failures to prosecute or secure convictions in cases involving the Northern Ireland conflict. Tort is not always an ideal fit in such cases. Negligence, after all, has developed under the influence of accounts of corrective justice to compensate for harms caused in breach of a duty, and the courts have actively restricted the scope of exemplary/punitive damages.[21] The absurdity of the phrase the 'negligent terrorist' has also been noted by the Northern Ireland courts,[22] and conceiving of cases of deliberate harms inflicted in this way as negligence does require the sort of sophistry associated in centuries past with accommodating novel claims within the strictures which had developed as part of action on the case.

The structural commonalities between tort and criminal law nonetheless create an outlet for claimants willing accept the limitations of tort's version of corrective justice (counter-balanced by its lower standard of proof compared to criminal law) when no other avenue to achieve any sort of justice exists. These commonalities are so pronounced that they can even occlude the torts in question in such cases. In *Lawson v Executor of the Estate of Dawes (Deceased)*,[23] for example, Eady J framed the harms inflicted upon the claimant terms of rape and attempted rape, without ever discussing this in terms of the intentional torts.[24] The claimant was nonetheless ultimately successful in her claim for damages, and some commentators have identified such civil claims as an avenue by which survivors can feel empowered.[25] In *Young v Downey*,[26] criminal proceedings against John Downey over the 1982 Hyde Park bombing had collapsed when it was disclosed at trial that he had been given official assurances that he was not under

---

Analysis' in CEF. Rickett (ed.), *Justifying Private Law Remedies* (Hart, 2008) 249, pp. 275-277.

21. *Rookes v Barnard* [1964] AC 1129. See also Peter Jaffey,'The Law Commission report on aggravated, exemplary and restitutionary damages' (1998) 61 Modern Law Review 860.
22. *Breslin v McKevitt* [2011] NICA 33, [14].
23. *Lawson v Executor of the Estate of Dawes (Deceased)* [2006] EWHC 2865 (QB).
24. *Lawson* [2]. See Nikki Godden, 'Claims in Tort for Rape: A Valuable Remedy or Damaging Strategy?' (2011) 22 King's Law Journal 157, 160-163.
25. For discussion, see Godden, 'Claims in Tort for Rape', 179.
26. *Young v Downey* [2019] EWHC 3508 (QB).

investigation for any crimes related to the Northern Ireland conflict. The daughter of one of the victims thus proceeded against Downey on the basis of the tort of trespass to the person, and Yip J concluded that in the circumstance of this case standard time limits should be waived and that, on the balance of probabilities, Downey was involved in the bombing.[27] Martin Spencer J, in calculating damages, explicitly noted that '[p]art of the motivation for the bringing of this claim is therefore to achieve vindication where the State is perceived to have failed the Claimant in relation to the more usual channels'.[28] Notwithstanding his exclusion of exemplary damages[29] and damages for psychiatric harm,[30] Martin Spencer J awarded over £700,000 in damages.

These developments should not be surprising; retributive justice remains close to the surface of common law tort.[31] They moreover illustrate that claimants do not always need to rely on negligence. *Young v Downey*, in particular, illustrates that the intentional torts have not necessarily been relegated to being 'a shrinking and little loved island of private law in constant danger of being completely submerged under the rising seas of the more openly public negligence law'.[32] This repurposing of tort to address the shortcomings of the criminal justice system is not, however, without its costs. In civil actions relating to rape and sexual assault, in particular, claimants do not benefit from the restrictions on cross-examination which apply within criminal law.[33]

Recycling; Upcycling?

Some elements of civil actions have been shown to be remarkably adaptable. *Norwich Pharmacal*[34] was a case about maintaining the profitability of a poultry feed additive, with the claimant company seeking to discover from the customs authorities the identity of others importing 'pirate' versions of the additive into the UK. The customs authorities were not responsible for the harm done to Norwich

---

27. *Young v Downey* [2019] [87](x).
28. *Young v Downey* [2020] EWHC 3457 (QB), [5].
29. *Young v Downey* [2020] [33].
30. *Young v Downey* [2020] [38].
31. Allan Beever, 'The Structure of Aggravated and Exemplary Damages' (2003) 23 Oxford Journal of Legal Studies 87, 105-110.
32. Priel, 'A Public Role for the Intentional Torts', 187; although it should be noted that Priel still sees considerable value in the intentional torts.
33. Godden, 'Claims in Tort for Rape'. xxiv, 177.
34. *Norwich Pharmacal v Customs and Excise Commissioners* [1974] AC 133.

Pharmacal, they were not infringing the company's patent, but they did hold information about those who were. This does not seem like fertile subject matter for providing a protection which would later be relied upon by an individual caught up in the War on Terror. In imposing a discovery obligation upon the customs authorities, however, Lord Reid cast the obligation in such terms as to be recyclable across the whole spectrum of torts:

> If through no fault of his own a person gets mixed up in the tortious acts of others so as to facilitate their wrongdoing he may incur no personal liability but he comes under a duty to assist the person who has been wronged by giving him full information and disclosing the identity of the wrongdoers.[35]

Binyam Mohamed, a UK resident, was held by the United States (US) military at Guantánamo Bay between September 2004 and February 2009, having been detained in Pakistan and turned over to US custody. During his time in US custody he was tortured. The UK's security agencies knew of this treatment, having received information about it from their US counterparts, but continued to supply questions about Mohamed for US interrogators to pursue. With little opportunity to challenge his ongoing detention, Mohamed's lawyers alighted upon the Norwich Pharmacal principle and 'sought to apply this principle to novel circumstances'[36] to expose his treatment to public scrutiny and apply maximum pressure to the US-UK relationship in an effort to secure his release.[37]

This upcycling of the *Norwich Pharmacal* principle to protect the individual ran headlong into the UK Government's assertion of Public Interest Immunity to block the release of information on the basis that it was harm the US-UK intelligence partnership for documentation provided by US agencies to be subject to discovery in the courts of England and Wales.[38] The Court of Appeal, however, maintained that even 'a real risk of serious damage to national security, of whatever degree, should not automatically trump a public interest in open justice',

---

35. *Norwich Pharmacal*, 175 (Lord Reid).
36. *R (Binyam Mohamed) v Secretary of State for Foreign and Commonwealth Affairs* [2008] EWHC 2048 (Admin); [2009] WLR 2579, [64] (Thomas LJ).
37. Colin Murray, 'Out of the Shadows: The Courts and the United Kingdom's Malfunctioning International Counter-Terrorism Partnerships' (2013) 18 Journal of Conflict & Security Law 193, 219-222.
38. See *R (Binyam Mohamed) v Secretary of State for Foreign and Commonwealth Affairs* [2010] EWCA Civ 65, [232] (Sir Anthony May).

especially in a case in which UK officials were facilitating 'interrogation by US officials using unlawful techniques which may amount to torture or cruel, inhuman or degrading treatment'.[39] Given that the information had already entered the public domain through US court cases,[40] Lord Neuberger was wholly unconvinced 'that the US intelligence services would really reduce the supply of information'.[41]

This outcome was acutely embarrassing for the UK security and intelligence services.[42] Indeed, the US and UK authorities were so eager to see the whole episode disappear that Mohamed was released while the litigation was ongoing, doubtless in the hope that he would withdraw his claim. Following the Court of Appeal decision, the UK Government moved swiftly to stamp out this innovation. Parliament enacted the Justice and Security Act 2013, which prevented the courts from using the *Norwich Pharmacal* principle to order the release of 'sensitive information', thereby providing a blanket exclusion covering any material linked to the workings of the security and intelligence services.[43] There was to be no repetition of this embarrassment; at least, not without the *deus ex machina* of the *Belhaj* case, in which details of secret UK involvement in US rendition flights were revealed in the wreckage of Libyan intelligence buildings 'following the fall of the Gaddafi regime'.[44] The domestic courts can no longer be used as a route by which to gain such materials.

Discovery; Recovery?

Discussion of tort actions is often be driven by what damages are recoverable in a given case. On the radical fringes of tort law, however, damages are often incidental. In the cases we have considered above,

---

39. *Binyam Mohamed*, [290] (Sir Anthony May).
40. See Adam Tomkins and Tom Hickman, 'National security law and the creep of secrecy: A transatlantic tale' in Liora Lazarus, Christopher McCrudden, and Nigel Bowles (eds.), Reasoning Rights: Comparative Judicial Engagement (Hart, 2014) 135, pp 141-142.
41. *Binyam Mohamed*, [172] (Lord Neuberger).
42. See Eva Nanopoulos, 'Extraordinary rendition, secrecy and the UK Security Constitution' in Elspeth Guild, Didier Bigo and Mark Gibney (ed.), Extraordinary Rendition: Addressing the Challenges of Accountability (Routledge, 2018).
43. Justice and Security Act 2013, s. 17.
44. *Belhaj v Straw* [2017] EWHC 1861 (QB), [4] (Popplewell J). This case led to a settlement including a formal apology to the claimants in Parliament on the basis that the 'UK Government's actions contributed to your detention, rendition and suffering'; J. Wright MP, HC Deb., vol. 640, col. 927 (10 May 2018).

compensation is either being pursued as a proxy for punishing the defendant (in a case like *Young v Downey*) or was all-but irrelevant to the claimant (*Binyam Mohamed*). Sometimes, moreover, and particularly where claims against the state are at issue, compensation is just a way for public bodies to make a problem go away without having the issue probed too deeply.

In the aftermath of the Irish War of Independence, for example, the UK and Irish Governments agreed to address claims arising out of the conflict through the establishment of the Compensation (Ireland) Commission (also known as the Shaw/Wood-Renton Commission). Between 1922 and 1925, the Commission would deal with some 40,000 claims relating to property damage and personal injury arising out of the conflict in place of civil litigation.[45] Lord Arnold, the minister responsible for the scheme within the UK's Colonial Office as part of the 1924 Labour Government, enthused that 'no Governments in the course of history have made more generous provision to compensate those who have suffered from damage in civil strife than have been made during the last two years by the Free State Government and the British Government'.[46] The Commission, however, in addressing these claims informally, was neither engaged in some form of truth recovery or an adversarial court process. It was an effort to draw a line under the conflict with the minimal possible fuss.[47]

For the UK Government, this compensation scheme brushed the legacies of a conflict under the table without further awkward questions having to be answered about whether the authorities within a liberal democracy upheld the values embodied by such a governance order in their response to political violence.[48] In later 'end-of-Empire' episodes, such as the so-called Malaya Emergency, the Cyprus Emergency and the Kenya Emergency, there was so little attention given to the UK's colonial administrations at the time of the conflicts that there was

---

45. See Michael Noone, 'Tort Claims in Counterinsurgency Operations: The British Experience in Ireland, 1919–21' (1993) 57 Journal of Military History 89, 108.
46. Lord Arnold, HL Deb., vol. 62, col. 89-90 (15 July 1925).
47. Opponents of the scheme in the UK Parliament complained bitterly about this lack of transparency: 'We want to know whether the claims were made by rebels who had no right to compensation whatever, or whether they were made by persons who had a right to compensation under conditions which gave them that right'; Lord Danesfort, HL Deb., vol. 61, col. 646 (17 June 1925).
48. This is not to say that tort law, as it operated in the 1920s, would have provided a more effective means of remedying many of these claims, but to emphasise that finding a way to deal with these cases discretely was as important to both Governments as addressing the claims.

no need for comparable schemes to brush their activities under the carpet. Successive UK Governments agreed to draw a line under the UK's liabilities with newly independent states,[49] and actively promoted the narrative that the British Empire had been wound up without the bloodshed that accompanied the collapse of other European empires.[50]

That reputation has been challenged through a series of tort actions which gained widespread attention after the events surrounding *Mutua v Foreign and Commonwealth Office*.[51] Mutua was not the first such action in the courts of England and Wales, it drew heavily upon earlier efforts by the Chagos Islanders to bring attention to how 'shamefully' they were treated in their expulsion from their home islands, which make up the British Indian Ocean Territory, during the 1960s and 1970s.[52] In post-independence Kenya the Mau Mau movement remained banned for many decades. Only after this ban was lifted were those who remained alive from the era of the independence struggle able to organise and launch a civil action against the UK Government for London's management of the counter-insurgency in the 1950s and the activities of the UK Armed Forces in carrying out that counter-insurgency.

There are numerous problems with using tort to address wrongs committed more than half a century previously. Individuals accused at such a remove in time might not be able to amount an effective defence, evidence will be unavailable and witnesses will have died.[53] Against such a backdrop, it is very difficult for claimants to persuade a court of the fairness of using their power to waive the standard limitation period where personal injury claims are at issue under the Limitation Act 1980.[54] Indeed, there is every likelihood that the *Mutua* litigation would not have led to success in court for the claimants had it been argued to its conclusion.[55] Fixating upon these shortcomings, however, misses the fact that tort is the only show in town; in providing a forum

---

49. See Devoka Hovell, 'The Gulf Between Tortious and Torturous: UK responsibility for mistreatment of the Mau Mau in colonial Kenya' (2013) 11 *Journal of International Criminal Justice* 223, 237.
50. On the myth of '"orderly" decolonialization', see P. Gopal, *Insurgent Empire: Anticolonial Resistance and British Dissent* (Verso, 2019) p. 436.
51. *Mutua and Others v Foreign and Commonwealth Office* [2012] EWHC 2678 (QB).
52. *Chagos Islanders v Attorney General* [2003] EWHC 2222 (QB), [154] (Ouseley J).
53. See Jeremy Waldron, 'Superseding Historical Injustice' (1992) 103 Ethics 4, 16.
54. Limitation Act 1980, s.33.
55. See Colin Murray, 'Back to the Future: Tort's Capacity to Remedy Historic Human Rights Abuses' (2019) 30 King's Law Journal 426.

for these claims, tort offered an avenue for reparative justice where no other legal route existed.[56] And in *Mutua*, providing such a forum made a dramatic difference. During the discovery process as part of the litigation a hitherto undisclosed archive of papers relating to both the Kenya counter-insurgency and similar episodes elsewhere in the British Empire was uncovered.[57] Such was the official embarrassment over the irregular storage of these files and the information contained therein about London's management of the counter-insurgency campaign, the UK Government promptly sought to settle the claims.

The resultant apology in Parliament by the UK's Foreign Secretary, in and of itself, was significant.[58] But official apologies have their own way of trying to terminate the discussion upon issues a Government finds awkward.[59] It was the disclosures obliged by this litigation which changed the historical narrative around events in Kenya in the last decade of colonial rule.[60] As for the compensation settlement, it was rather modest, especially once litigation costs are taken into account and the fact that many potential claimants did not join the *Mutua* action.[61] The particular strength of tort which was demonstrated by this response to historic abuses lies in its ability to explore facts in an adversarial setting, and to bring to light facts which were concealed in the colonial context. Indeed, the subsequent *Kimathi* litigation related to events in Kenya in the 1950s had a diminishing return in regard to discovery, and fell foul of multiple legal barriers to the substantive claims.[62] And the high drama of the secret archive being uncovered

---

56. Mayo Moran, 'The problem of the past: How historic wrongs became legal problems' (2019) 69 University of Toronto Law Journal 421, 428.
57. See *Mutua*, [48]-[54] (McCombe J).
58. W. Hague MP, HC Deb., vol. 563, col. 1692 (6 June 2013).
59. Generalised apologies in the context of mass abuses, of themselves, can often distract from the explanation of the specific wrongs which are the subject of the apology; see Michael Marrus, 'Official apologies and the quest for historical justice' (2007) 6 Journal of Human Rights 75, 90-92. See also Melissa Nobles, *The Politics of Official Apologies* (CUP, 2008) pp. 140-149.
60. On the impact of these disclosures on discourse over the Mau Mau, see David Anderson, 'Mau Mau in the High Court and the "Lost" British Empire Archives: Colonial Conspiracy or Bureaucratic Bungle?' (2011) 39 Journal of Imperial and Commonwealth History 699.
61. See Eric Yamamoto and Susan Serrano, 'Reparations Theory and Practice Then and Now: Mau Mau Redress Litigation and the British High Court' (2012) 18 UCLA Asian Pacific American Law Journal 71, 101 and Moran, Moran, 'The problem of the past', 469-470.
62. *Kimathi and Others v Foreign & Commonwealth Office* [2018] EWHC 2066 (QB); *Kimathi and Others v Foreign & Commonwealth Office* [2018] EWHC 3144 (QB).

through the *Mutua* litigation was not to be repeated in the *Sophocleous* claims arising out of the coterminous suppression of independence movements in Cyprus.[63] Those outcomes notwithstanding, where no public inquiry into events is likely to be forthcoming, civil actions might well be the only way to challenge both these harms and the pernicious effects for a society of silencing or suppressing discussion of them.[64]

Schedule 2 of the Overseas Operations (Service Personnel and Veterans) Act 2021 restricts a court's discretion, under the Limitation Act 1980, to disapply time limits for civil actions in respect of personal injuries or death which relate to overseas operations of the armed forces. For all that ministers like Johnny Mercer, introducing the Bill, talked in florid terms of a need 'to lance the boil of lawfare and to protect our people from the relentless cycle of reinvestigations against our armed forces',[65] the reality is that end-of-Empire claims which had been heard in full, including *Kimathi* and *Sophocleous*, were dealt with as entirely documentary processes.[66] These provisions of the Overseas Operations Act therefore exist primarily to prevent any more embarrassing reminders of Empire resurfacing in the courts. This statutory intervention, however, has not entirely neutralised such uses of tort against the UK Government. The Northern Ireland conflict, unable to be parcelled off as an 'overseas operation' or dealt with summarily by the UK Government without destabilising its peace process, continues to generate cases which are primarily focused on discovery.[67]

Conclusion

Tort does, therefore, have a radical edge. Its assertion of general obligations owed by all to all and its focus on compensation for harms done in breach of those obligations allow for potential causes of action where other legal avenues, and notably human rights law, provide none.[68] In

---

63. *Sophocleous v Secretary of State for Foreign and Commonwealth Affairs* [2018] EWCA Civ 2167.
64. See Ruth Houghton and Aoife O'Donoghue, '"Ourworld": A feminist approach to Global Constitutionalism' (2020) 9 Global Constitutionalism 38, 70-73.
65. J. Mercer MP, HC Deb., vol. 678, col. 1671 (16 July 2020).
66. See *Mutua*, [86] (McCombe J).
67. See Conall Mallory, Sean Molloy and Colin Murray, 'Tort, Truth Recovery and the Northern Ireland Conflict' [2020] European Human Rights Law Review 244.
68. For accounts of how extensions to the categories of actionable damage in negligence are reshaping the broader role of tort law, see Donal Nolan, 'New Forms of Damage in Negligence' (2007) 70 Modern Law Review 59.

many of the cases discussed above, and notably *Mohamed*, *Mutua* and *Belhaj*, the law firm Leigh Day has played a leading role in exploiting this potential within the law of tort in England and Wales.[69] This concentration of activity, however, makes these developments precarious, for the bounded reality of tort is not immune to external influence. Leigh Day has found itself vilified by the UK Government and some of its most high-profile solicitors have been pursued, unsuccessfully, by the Solicitors Regulation Authority for alleged breaches of professional conduct.[70] As for these landmark cases, they will make little long-term imprint on tort. Indeed, if anything radical has happened within tort jurisprudence in England and Wales in recent years, from *Mohamed* to *Mutua*, the best marker of its transformative potential is that it subsequently been overridden by statute.

It is possible to bemoan the ill fit of tort to some of these cases.[71] Or to look askance at the impact of conditional fee agreements on the value of settlements in successful actions.[72] And there is undoubtedly frustration with cases seeking engagement with historic wrongs amongst the judiciary. The *Keyu* claims might not have been a tort case, but Lord Neuberger and Baroness Hale's assertions that the Article 2 ECHR investigative duty could never be applied in a case in which the claimants are not seeking the imposition of civil or criminal liability but pursuing historical truth, can be interpreted as attempting cordon off a range of potential civil actions.[73] A desire exists for these legacies of empire and state orchestrated violence to be relegated to historical debate. Writing about or teaching about these events from a carefully constructed position of epistemic deference potentially has deep societal benefits. But, for all its shortcomings, tort has emerged as the only

---

69. This short contribution has not done justice to all of Leigh Day's involvement in pushing the boundaries of tort, including the £30 million settlement achieved in *Yao Esaie Motto v Trafigura* for residents of the Ivory Coast affected by the discharge of chemical waste from a tanker.
70. For a summary of the action amid subsequent disputes over costs, see *Solicitors Regulation Authority v Day & Others* [2018] EWHC 2726 (Admin). See also Andrew Williams, 'The Iraq abuse allegations and the limits of UK Law' [2018] Public Law 461.
71. See Nathan Miller, 'Human Rights Abuses as Tort Harms: Losses in Translation' (2016) 46 Seaton Hall Law Review 505, 547.
72. There is also the suggestion that much of the attention devoted to claims dissipates upon settlement. In a more traditional application of tort law, one of the Ivorian claimants in the *Trafigura* litigation was successful in a professional negligence action against Leigh Day when her share of the settlement was misappropriated; *Agouman v Leigh Day* [2016] EWHC 1324 (QB).
73. *Keyu*, [110] (Lord Neuberger); [300] (Baroness Hale).

means by which those impacted by these wrongs and their pernicious legacies can actively challenge them.

FURTHER READINGS

- Nikki Godden, 'Claims in Tort for Rape: A Valuable Remedy or Damaging Strategy?' (2011) 22 *King's Law Journal* 157-182.
- Mari J Matsuda, 'Looking to the Bottom: Critical Legal Studies and Reparations' (1987) 22 *Harvard Civil Rights-Civil Liberties Law Review* 323-400.
- Mayo Moran, 'The problem of the past: How historic wrongs became legal problems' (2019) 69 *University of Toronto Law Journal* 421-472.
- Donal Nolan, 'New Forms of Damage in Negligence' (2007) 70 *Modern Law Review* 59-88.

Concept: Colonial Modernity

Sahar Shah

When we think of the term 'modern', 'we' might think of ourselves, our lives, our surroundings. This imaginary might have specific aesthetic overtones: gleaming white interiors, glittering metropolitan cities with fast food and corporate logos shining like beacons. Alternatively, the word might conjure a vague set of ethics: notions of inherent equality amongst people, notions of sexual 'liberty', individual freedom, etc. But for a critical account of modernity there are actually two crucial elements of these imaginaries that tend to fade into the background: the *We* that we imagine as the subject of modernity (which is really an *I*) and the *now* that we imagine constituting modernity (which is both *now* and *from now on*).

The notion of the 'modern' is dependent upon historical 'periodisation'—a linear sequentialisation of human history, and a compartmentalisation of this history into 'eras' with each era defined by particular characteristics. This approach to history and time dominates Western historiography, but not other historiographic traditions. The epistemological beginning of modernity can be marked by the Renaissance and Enlightenment eras, during which European thinking was transformed by the scientific revolution. Man (and particularly, Man's mind, endowed with the ability to reason) came to be seen as the source of all truth and knowledge. Modernity, through periodisation, is defined in opposition to What Came Before - both the 'status-ridden, oppressive medieval or feudal age[s]' of Europe and 'various 'non-Christian', barbaric or savage peoples excluded from a universalized civility'.[1] Because the idea of Man's mind, and its ability to discern ultimate and universal truth through reasoning, is attributed solely to *modernity*, What Came Before becomes a time during which genuine knowledge acquisition could not have occurred.

Crucially, modernity is spatialized and racialized[2] - the subject of modernity (capable of knowing and reasoning) is European; non-Europeans are amongst its objects (to be known and acted upon/against).[3] While 'modernity' may seem like a term that is purely about time, what is relegated to 'pre-modernity' in the modern/colonial imagination actually exists *contemporaneously* with the European modern man. Indigenous peoples and subaltern peoples remain 'pre-modern' within modernity's racialized and colonial configurations.[4] It is precisely this contemporaneous/racialized pre-modernity, Fitzpatrick argues (drawing on Foucault), that gives modernity its linear, teleological temporality.[5] The co-existence of the 'pre-modern' with the modern gives modernity a *project*—societies and individuals to 'fix', to integrate, to 'civilise'. And as modernity trains its violent gaze upon subaltern peoples, it also (in different ways) works upon the 'subjects' of the Global North—in addition to the Other, Global Northerners must endlessly scrutinize *themselves*, engaging in a ceaseless project of alignment and perfection. There is always, in modernity, progress to be made—Global North subjects are thus continuously primping with nowhere to go, because we can never truly 'arrive' at an end destination of modernity. Modernity's 'end' goal is progress itself, which requires us to be (or seem) in flux, in constant motion, progressing and progressing *ad infinitum*. The Global North must be perpetually agitated. Meanwhile, modernity relegates the rest of humanity to a proverbial prehistory, objectified until such time as they become modern—if they ever can (spoiler: they cannot).

---

1. Fitzpatrick, Peter. 2013. 'Marking Time: Temporality and the Imperial Cast of Occidental Law'. *Birkbeck Law Review*, 1: 67
2. Dube, Saurabh (ed.). 2009. *Enchantments of Modernity: Empire, Nation, Globalization.* Routledge.
3. Quijano, Anibal. (2007) Coloniality and Modernity/Rationality. *Cultural Studies*, 21(2-3): 168-178.
4. Mignolo, Walter. 2011. *The Darker Side of Western Modernity: Global Futures, Decolonial Options.* Duke University Press.
5. Fitzpatrick, 'Marking Time'

If we are to ever look past the 'enchantments'[6] and 'mythologies'[7] of modernity, then it is imperative that we recognize modernity as exactly this—a series of narratives and mythologies mired in enchantment.

---

6. Dube, *Enchantments of Modernity*
7. Fitzpatrick, Peter. 1992. The Mythology of Modern Law. Routledge.

21

Concept: Power

Alex Sharpe

There are a huge number of different concepts of power, but in the last three decades, Michel Foucault's ideas surrounding it have been particularly influential. In order to grasp Foucault's concept of power we need to grasp the relationship it bears to two other concepts in Foucault's body of work: *knowledge* and the *subject* (what liberals refer to as the individual). However, before turning to an understanding of Foucault's concept of power through the prism of these other related concepts, it is helpful to begin by thinking about a more familiar idea of power, one that might seem to provide, at least at first glance, a more accurate description of the phenomenon. This conception of power, one Foucault set himself against, is familiar to us because it is endlessly replicated within liberal legal orders. This type of power, which Foucault described as 'juridical'—coercive, repressive, censorious, something negative—imagines power to be embodied in the figure of the sovereign. Here power is understood as residing in a set of monarchical, or more recently, liberal democratic institutions. According to this view, power is seen as concentrated and static and thought to be exercised by individuals and/or institutions who in some sense possess it. This view of power has encouraged forms of resistance that aim to cut off the king's head, either literally or metaphorically.

By contrast, Foucault, thought of power quite differently. While he recognised 'juridical' power to be something real (and often violent/terrifying), he took the view it has been superseded, or at least supplemented, by a new form of power emerging in the eighteenth century, which he termed 'disciplinary' power.[1] What is interesting about this new kind of power is, rather than being concentrated in the personage of the king or in some other set of (liberal democratic) institutions, it is considered to be located 'everywhere.' In saying power is everywhere, Foucault should not be understood as suggesting a world without freedom, a totalitarian nightmare. Indeed, Foucault distinguished power, which, for him, always implies the possibility of resistance, from what he described as 'force relations,' which do not. Rather, what is important to recognise is Foucault conceived of power as existing in every relationship: interpersonal, familial, institutional, corporate, national. For this reason, he was always suspicious of revolutionaries who sought to deliver a decisive blow against 'it.'

Moreover, disciplinary power was something Foucault saw as positive, productive or generative rather than negative or juridical. Thus, in addition to understanding power in relational terms—as dynamic and contingent—Foucault reconceptualised how we think about the relationship between power and the subject. While power, understood in liberal terms, is exercised by autonomous individuals who act in and on the world, for Foucault, the opposite is true. That is, on his account, power comes first and constitutes 'us' as subjects. We do not exercise power, but rather are the effects of its prior workings and, in this sense, are socially constructed. And because Foucault thought about the subject/power relationship in this way, he necessarily thought of knowledge as anything but disinterested. Indeed, he saw power and knowledge as utterly inseparable (a debt he owed to Friedrich Nietzsche). Foucault developed this idea of power/knowledge through studies of the institution of the prison (and the attendant discourse of criminology) and the institution of the asylum (and the attendant discourses of sexology/psychoanalysis), which converted criminal acts, acts lying beyond reason, and sodomy into 'criminal man,' the 'madman' and the 'homosexual' respectively. As Foucault observed in relation to the latter, where there had been only sodomy we witness the 'birth of a species.'[2] As Foucault's work developed, he articulated the concept of 'biopower.'[3] While disciplinary power focused on, and constituted,

---

1. Michel Foucault, *Discipline and Punish: The Birth of the Prison* (London: Penguin, 1977).
2. Michel Foucault, *History of Sexuality* (London: Penguin, 1981).
3. Michel Foucault, *The Birth of Biopolitics: Lectures at the College of France 1978-1979* (London: Palgrave MacMillan, 2010).

particular types of subject, the term 'biopower' captures how power's object gradually came to encompass, not merely 'abnormal' individuals/groups, who it simultaneously constituted, but the population as a whole—a biological species. Foucault also articulated the concept of 'governmentality.'[4] In this regard, and while his view 'power is everywhere' persisted, he began to focus more on the state and the ways in which it governs populations. At the heart of Foucault's work, lies an understanding of power as inseparable from knowledge and the production of subjects. Indeed, we might think of power and knowledge as a helix, dancing through time and ourselves as the product of this dance.

---

4. Michael Foucault, *Security, Territory, Population: Lectures at the College of France 1977-1978* (London: Palgrave MacMillan, 2007).

22

The Biopolitics of Environmental Law

Environmental Law, Legal Theory

Vito De Lucia

Biopolitics is one of two modes of operation of a new form of power that seizes life under its purview: biopower. Biopower is a concept conceived by French historian and philosopher, Michel Foucault, who used it to describe the way that 'life' became the object-target of power in the 19th century. By claiming to manage or protect 'life', power can be intensified and rendered immune from particular forms of criticism. But as Foucault notes, while this biopower 'exerts a positive influence on life', it does so by 'subjecting it to precise controls and comprehensive regulations'.[1] Biopower is further distinguished in power over individual bodies, which Foucault calls anathamopolitics—and power over entire populations, which Foucault calls biopolitics. In this chapter, I want to show you how biopolitics can be mobilized to articulate a radical critique of environmental law.

Environmental law is a specialized branch of public law. In general terms, its central goal is the protection of the natural environment from the negative consequences of human activities. Environmental law, in what is characterized as its modern phase, emerged in the late 1960s and early 1970s and has since enjoyed sweeping success, at least if judged by the growth of environmental legislation at both domestic and international level.[2] However, while environmental law has successfully mitigated many discrete problems, the overall state of

---

1. Michel Foucault, *The Will to Knowledge: History of Sexuality, Vol I*. (1976) 137
2. Jane Holder, 'New Age: Rediscovering Natural Law,' *Current Legal Problems* 53/1 (2000), 165–7.

the environment is deteriorating.[3] The key reason for this fundamental discrepancy is what some have called a 'deep contradiction' affecting environmental law.[4] Environmental law, it is suggested, is trying to find solutions while being simultaneously deeply imbricated with the prevailing philosophical and legal paradigm that is creating the problem in the first place. The result of this contradiction is that environmental law 'extends, rather than resolves' the pervasiveness and intensity of environmental problems as it helps to reproduce key elements of this prevailing paradigm.[5] For example, the very adjective *environmental* in fact signals the 'malaise' that affects it.[6] Indeed the environment—as that which surrounds us—already contains two crucial assumptions that environmental law internalizes and then operationalizes: the separation between man and nature (that is, its environment); and the modern obsession with the centre, and in particular with a *human* centre. Additionally, environmental law has been aptly described as 'hot', in the sense of being situated at the crossroads of many value conflicts and operational uncertainties.[7] As such, positivist and doctrinal approaches to environmental law prove insufficient, and have very early been accompanied by contextual, socio-legal and critical approaches to the study of environment law. In this respect, there have been urgent calls for methodological pluralism, that is for the utilization of a variety of methods exceeding doctrinal approaches, and a significant amount of alternative scholarship has developed in the last decade alone.[8]

---

3. IPBES, *Global assessment report on biodiversity and ecosystem services of the Intergovernmental Science-Policy Platform on Biodiversity and Ecosystem Services*, eds., Eduardo S. Brondízio, Josef Settele, Sandra Díaz, and Hien T. Ngo. (Bonn, Germany: IPBES secretariat, 2019); IPCC, *Special Report on the Ocean and Cryosphere in a Changing Climate*, 2019.
4. Michael M'Gonigle and Louise Takeda, 'The Liberal Limits of Environmental Law: A Green Legal Critique,' *Pace Environmental Law Review* 30/3 (2013), 1005–15.
5. M'Gonigle and Takeda, Liberal Limits of Environmental Law, 1005.
6. Andreas Philippopoulos-Mihalopoulos, ed., *Law and Ecology. New Environmental Foundations* (New York: Routledge, 2011), p. 159.
7. Elizabeth Fisher, 'Environmental Law as 'Hot' Law,' *Journal of Environmental Law* 25/3 (2013), 347.
8. On Methodological pluralism, see Elizabeth Fisher, Bettina Lange, Eloise Scotford and Cinnamon Carlarne, 'Maturity and Methodology: Starting a Debate about Environmental Law Scholarship,' *Journal of Environmental Law* 21/2 (2009), 213–50. For alternative scholarship developed in the last decade see e.g., Mariachiara Tallacchini, 'A Legal Framework from Ecology,' *Biodiversity and Conservation* 9/8 (2000), 1085–1098; Cormac Cullinan, *Wild Law: A Manifesto for Earth Justice* (South Africa: Siber Ink, 2002); Klaus Bosselmann, *The Principle of Sustainability: Transforming Law and Governance* (Aldershot: Ashgate 2008); Peter D. Burdon, 'Wild Law: The Philosophy

Many of these trajectories focused on the intertwined questions of value and of the subject.

The reason is that he foundation of environmental law, reflected in most of its concepts, principles, and rules, is based on an anthropocentric value system which places the human subject at the centre, and considers nature valuable, and therefore worthy of protection, *only* if useful to the human subject. The very notion of environment already contains two crucial assumptions that environmental law internalizes and then operationalizes: the separation between man and nature (that is, its environment); and a fundamental obsession with the centre, and in particular with a *human* centre, that is the human subject, the only capable of bearing moral and, crucially, legal rights, while nature and non-human entities remain, for law, mere objects, primarily susceptible of extractive or consumptive use and appropriation.

Biopolitics & Critical Environmental Law

Critical environmental law can be described as 'an enquiry into the theoretical and institutional apparatus of both environmental law and the rationality of environmentalism'.[9] An important aim of a critical legal approach to environmental law is to *open up* the field of analysis, rather than producing the types of closures we find in more conventional legal scholarship. Drawing on Foucault, one way of producing these openings is to employ his method of genealogy. If one understands environmental law as 'hot', as mentioned above, genealogy appears as a suitable method of inquiry since the aim of genealogy is the reconstruction of the contingencies and contestations constituting the complex history of (legal) concepts. Genealogy, as Foucault illustrates, is a history that does not search for a single point of origin; it does not attempt to find the true essence, or original identity, of concepts and phenomena; it rejects a linear understanding of history where 'values unravel inexorably towards their perfection'.[10] In a genealogical approach, everything is the result of a 'play of forces'.[11] It follows that

---

of Earth Jurisprudence,' *Alternative Law Journal* 35/2 (2010), 58.
9. Andreas Kotsakis and Vito De Lucia, 'Searching for Critical Environmental Law: Theories, Methods, Critiques,' *Critical Legal Thinking*, 22 March 2018, accessed 28 March 2021, https://criticallegalthinking.com/2018/03/22/cfp-searching-for-critical-environmental-law-workshop-oxford-11-may-2018/.
10. Costas Douzinas and Adam Gearey, *Critical Jurisprudence. The Political Philosophy of Justice* (Oxford and Portland, Oregon: Hart Publishing, 2005), 54.
11. Douzinas and Gearey, Philosophy of Justice, 49.

every concept, understood genealogically, is the result of an ensemble of competing forces, each trying to assert hegemony. Every concept is thus also susceptible to many possible, and conflicting, interpretations. Environmental law is, in light of its 'hot' character, a privileged point of emergence of such conflicts and contestations.

However, if genealogy provides a broad methodological framework to be applied to the reconstruction and deconstruction of contingencies and contestations that affect environmental law, in a second, more focused sense, genealogy underlies and enables a *biopolitical* critique of environmental law. One of the reasons why biopolitics is particularly helpful is that, unlike polarizing critiques, such as those based on ecocentrism–an idea and value proposition antithetical yet commensurate to anthropocentrism, both remaining dependent on a centre—is that biopolitics avoids righteous closures. In other words, analysing, or even critiquing environmental law on the basis of the binary anthropocentrism-ecocentrism produces sharp thresholds and a linearization that unduly simplifies environmental law, which is by contrast complex, non-linear, utterly conflictual and ultimately irreducibly genealogical. A biopolitical analysis, by contrast, allows to explore all relevant ambiguities and to highlight the lacerations implicated in the critical history of every legal concept and, importantly, on its operationalization.

While the history of biopolitics, with its multiple lines of elaboration, is complex to trace, a usual starting point is the work of Michel Foucault.[12] Biopolitics is one of two modes of operation of a new form of power that seizes life under its purview: biopower. Biopower reflects a shift in discursive and operative emphasis. Power no longer operates in term of a sovereign command over life and death but takes life under its care. Unlike sovereign power, biopower, aided by the development of new forms of knowledge, qualifies, measures, appraises, and hierarchizes, with the ultimate aim of fostering life. This is achieved at two levels. At the level of the individual body, through disciplinary interventions; and at the level of populations, through interventions aimed at controlling life as a set of biological processes.

The goal of biopolitics is thus to foster life, insofar as it can be regularized, and its processes predicted and optimized. With particular respect to the environment, nature is no longer simply an object of sovereign exploitation, but becomes subjected to a series of positive

---

12. See e.g., Michel Foucault, *The History of Sexuality. Volume I: An Introduction* (New York: Pantheon Books, 1978); Michel Foucault, *'Society Must be Defended'. Lectures at the Collège de France 1975–1976*, (London: Penguin Books, 2004).

interventions that aim at its care, at fostering and optimizing its processes, and at the same time at the enhancement of its productive forces. Biopolitics enfolds nature in its logic in two distinct but complementary ways: first as a set of processes central to human well-being, to the extent that human populations are affected in multiple ways by the environment they live in and by natural processes; secondly, as the immediate focus of concern. From this second perspective, biopolitics aims at the protection, regularization, and optimization of *nature itself*.

Furthermore, and in line with Foucault's insight of the co-implicated relation between power and forms of knowledge, the expansion of biopolitical regimes to the natural environment is historically contingent on the development of a number of scientific disciplines such as biology and ecology, on key conservation concepts such as biodiversity, as well as on a number of technologies and techniques that allow the continuous monitoring of ecosystem processes. Ecology in particular plays a crucial part, as it 'provided the political technology for new forms of regulatory intervention in the management of the population and resources'.[13]

Environmental law, from this perspective, becomes a crucial juncture where knowledge and power intersect and coalesce into a regulatory framework aimed precisely at protecting, regularizing, and optimizing nature, particularly through the double goal of conservation and sustainable use of biological diversity. This framework, where genealogy and biopolitics intersect, is but a starting point, and much work remains to be done, but it has proven, arguably, a useful way to illustrate the complexities and dilemmas of environmental law, and the ambiguity and potential danger, to recall the initial quote by Michel Foucault, that can hide even in the most 'progressive' environmental legal concepts.

Conclusions

The biopolitical framework presented in the previous section represents only one possibility for a critical theoretical analysis of environmental law, and many other trajectories can be traced. Biopolitics has proven particularly fruitful for discovering ambiguities, contradictions, and dilemmas that all inevitably reproduce the internal tension of environmental legal regimes. However, the crucial point to make is that environmental law, because it is traversed by many fundamental value

---

13. Paul Rutherford, 'The Problem of Nature in Contemporary Social Theory' (PhD thesis, The Australian National University, 2000), 4

conflicts, and because it is so central in terms of its goals in a time when the human presence has become a geological force, and in a time of multiple environmental crises (climate change and biodiversity loss, for example). It is then paramount that environmental law is the subject of sharp critical inquiries through the use of a multiplicity of methodological and theoretical approaches.

23

Law at the Intersection

FEMINIST LEGAL THEORY, CRITICAL RACE THEORY

Carolina Alonso Bejarano

You have probably heard somebody use the term 'intersectionality' to refer to the rejection of single-axis analyses of identity and oppression, and the necessary connections between different efforts for liberation. What you may not know is that this concept comes from feminist legal theory and in specific Kimberlé Crenshaw, a critical race theorist who coined the term in an essay evidencing how the needs, claims and rights of Black women (and other differently marginalized people) are rendered invisible within a legal system that is white supremacist and patriarchal.

For lawyers in particular (given that the law engages with heterogenous groups of people at the local, national and international levels) and for critical thinkers especially (who understand the law as a tool for marginalization and dehumanization but also as a means for social justice and transformation) it is key to engage with theories of liberation that recognize intersectional approaches to identity and oppression. This chapter will discuss the importance of intersectionality for legal scholars as a methodological tool for research and political intervention, while positioning it as a significant part of the US Third World Feminist tradition.

In the year 2000, Chela Sandoval published *Methodology of the Oppressed*, introducing the term 'US Third World Feminism' to refer to a deliberate political project, signalling a denunciation of geographic, economic, and cultural borders in the interest of the creation of a new feminist internationalist consciousness and location.[1] Both in spite

---

1. Chela Sandoval, *Methodology of the Oppressed* (Minneapolis: Minnesota UP,

of and because they were situated within different internally colonized communities, US women of colour in the 1970s and '80s generated a common discourse, a theoretical structure lingering outside the limits of dominant male, white, middle class, Eurocentric theories of the subject.

It was in this context that Kimberlé Crenshaw coined the term 'intersectionality' in 1989, pointing to the intersections between race and gender and their effects on the lived experiences of Black women in the US. The concept's oppositional force had already been at the heart of various intellectual projects by Black people who were thinking and writing about–and against–both white supremacy and white normativity. For instance, the canonized 1851 speech *Ain't I a Woman?* ostensibly delivered by former slave Sojourner Truth, challenges the liberal feminist discourse on womanhood of the US suffragist movement (which claimed to fight for 'women's equality' while only representing the interests and viewpoints of middle-class white women), and is often used as a starting point for historical accounts of Black feminist cosmologies in the United States.[2] Moreover, as argued by Anthony Bogues in *Black Heretics, Black Prophets*, the existence of slave memoirs and oral traditions serve as evidence that a fundamental departure from liberal constructions of subjectivity and difference is a cornerstone of US Black radical thought dating back to the Atlantic slave trade.[3] In this regard, in *Black Feminist Thought*, Patricia Hill Collins points to slave memoirs as the first written renditions of Black female oppositional theory,[4] and identifies teacher and journalist Maria Stewart (1803-1879) as the first Black intellectual to leave a record of her work, examining the experiences of Black women: 'How long shall the fair daughters of Africa be compelled to bury their minds and talents beneath a load of iron pots and kettles?'[5]

In *Living for the Revolution*, Kimberly Springer writes about Black activist organizations of the 1970s that specifically used feminist theory to develop their projects, and she claims that due to the subtle and not subtle racism and homophobia of many white feminist groups, Black women often formed their own organizations–which included lesbians and other women of colour–such as the National Black Feminist

---

2000).
2. Sojourner Truth, 'Ain't I a Woman?' in *The Norton Anthology of Literature by Women*, ed. Sandra Gilbert and Susan Gubar (New York: WW Norton, 1985), 252-253.
3. Anthony Bogues, *Black Heretics, Black Prophets* (New York: Routledge, 2003).
4. Patricia Hill Collins, *Black Feminist Thought* (Boston: Unwin Hyman, 1990).
5. Maria Stewart, *America's First Black Woman Political Writer: Essays and Speeches*, ed. Marilyn Richardson, (Bloomington: Indiana UP, 1987), 38.

Organization (1973) and the Combahee River Collective (1974).[6] In the 1980s US women of colour advanced their presence in mainstream academia through the publication of a number of anthologies that called into question notions of 'universal sisterhood' by arguing that race, ethnicity, class and sexuality (that is, racism, ethnocentrism, capitalism and heteronormativity) crucially influence and complicate female experiences of patriarchal oppression. Among these, *This Bridge Called My Back* edited in 1981 by activist poets Cherríe Moraga and Gloria Anzaldúa, publishing work by women of colour,[7] and *All the Women Are White, All the Blacks Are Men, But Some of Us Are Brave*, edited in 1983 by Gloria Hull, Patricia Bell Scott and Barbara Smith, featuring work exclusively by Black women.[8]

Drawing from her intersectional identity ('a 49-year old Black, socialist, lesbian, mother of two in an interracial couple'), Audre Lorde's ground-breaking 1977 essay *Age, Race, Class, and Sex: Women Redefining Difference* points to the history of Western philosophy and claims that white women's fear of difference is rooted in the assumption underlying modern thought that 'difference' necessarily means 'hierarchical difference.'[9] Lorde calls for the embrace of different differences as the only means for women to 'dismantle the master's house' of its patriarchal economies of oppression. In her 1978 *Disloyal to Civilization: Feminism, Racism, Gynophobia*, Adrienne Rich addresses the universal voice associated with most European theories of modernity.[10] She argues that this voice is constituted around a colonial, middle class, male subjectivity concealed as non-racial, non-gendered objectivity, whose viewpoint is confused with the 'neutral' point of view (which is passed on to white women who, but for gender, share many of these same cultural, economic and social characteristics). Rich refers to this universalist tendency as 'white solipsism,' the propensity

---

6. Kimberly Springer, *Living for the Revolution: Black Feminist Organizations, 1968-1980* (Durham: Duke UP, 2005).
7. Cherríe Moraga and Gloria Anzaldúa, *This Bridge Called My Back* (Watertown: Persephone Press, 1981).
8. Gloria Hull, Patricia Bell Scott, and Barbara Smith, ed. *All the Women Are White, All the Blacks Are Men, But Some of Us Are Brave* (New York: Feminist Press, 1983).
9. Audre Lorde, 'Age, Race, Class, and Sex: Women Redefining Difference' (1984) in *Let Nobody Turn Us Around: Voices of Resistance, Reform, and Renewal: An African American Anthology*, ed. Manning Marable and Leith Mullings (New York: Bowman & Littlefield, 2000), 538.
10. Adrienne Rich, 'Disloyal to Civilization: Feminism, Racism, Gynophobia.' In *On Lies, Secrets and Silence: Selected Prose 1966-1978*. (New York: Norton, 1979).

to 'think, imagine and speak as if whiteness described the world,'[11] a 'tunnel vision' that does not conceive of non-white experience or existence as significant, that in 'guilt-reflexes' claims to recognize such existence in a way that nevertheless negates its continuing momentum and political usefulness.

In her 1982 book *Ain't I a Woman?* bell hooks problematizes the common practice of the US feminist movement of comparing the situation of oppression of women with that of Black people. She argues that underlying such practices is the assumption that all women are white, and all Blacks are men, thus silencing the voices of Black women and rendering their experiences of oppression invisible.[12] In her 1982 *Theories of Race and Gender: The Social Construction of Whiteness*, Elizabeth Spelman argues that these 'additive approaches' understand different subject positions as placed within a stable and fixed 'background' to which it is possible to add layers of oppression.[13] The additive analysis of oppression implies that a woman's racial identity can be subtracted from her combined racial and gender identity because in the end 'we are all women.' This approach fails to recognize the fact that different women may look to different forms of liberation on the basis of their multiple and intersecting experiences as other-than-white. In this regard, Gloria Anzaldúa's celebrated 1987 *Borderlands/La Frontera* traces the historical and personal journey of the people who inhabit the border between Mexico and the United States, elucidating the socioeconomic, political and spiritual impact of the European conquest on indigenous peoples.[14] She signals the emergence of 'mestiza consciousness,' rooted in the borderlands, in the breaking down of cultural boundaries and the synthesis of different cultures, races, and languages; an 'amalgamation' that results in a new awareness that subverts traditional perspectives on 'pure' cultural identities.

It was building on this legacy of feminism, and in particular Black radical thought, that Kimberlé Crenshaw wrote her 1989 seminal piece *Demarginalizing the Intersection of Race and Sex: A Black Feminist Critique of Antidiscrimination Doctrine, Feminist Theory, and*

---

11. Rich, 'Disloyal to Civilization,' 299.
12. bell hooks, *Ain't I a Woman?: Black Women and Feminism* (London: Pluto Press, 1982).
13. Elizabeth Spelman, 'Theories of Race and Gender: The Social Construction of Whiteness, *Quest: A Feminist Quarterly* 5/4 (1982), 36-62.
14. Gloria Anzaldúa, *Borderlands/La Frontera* (San Francisco: Aunt Lute Books, 1987).

Antiracist Politics,[15] which, along with her 1991 *Mapping the Margins: Intersectionality, Identity Politics, and Violence against Women of Color*,[16] went on to become the formative text that solidified as a feminist heuristic the theorization of the intersections of differences. The term 'intersectionality' was introduced through Crenshaw's analysis of US antidiscrimination legal doctrine, specifically, the jurisprudence on Title VII of the Civil Rights Act of 1964, a federal law that prohibits employers from discriminating against employees on the basis of sex, race, colour, national origin and religion.

Crenshaw examines 1976 Title VII case *DeGraffenreid v General Motors* along with two other cases to explore how courts frame and interpret the stories of Black women plaintiffs. In *DeGraffenreid*, five Black women brought suit against General Motors, alleging that the employer's seniority system perpetuated the effects of past discrimination against Black women. Evidence presented at trial revealed that General Motors did not hire Black women prior to 1964 and that all Black women hired after 1970 lost their jobs in a seniority-based layoff during the following recession. The district court granted summary judgment for the defendant, rejecting the plaintiffs' attempt to bring a suit not on behalf of Blacks or women, but specifically on behalf of Black women. The court said: 'This lawsuit must be examined to see if it states a cause of action for race discrimination, sex discrimination, or alternatively either, but not a combination of both...The legislative history surrounding Title VII does not indicate that the goal of the statute was to create a new classification of "black women" who would have greater standing than, for example, a black male.'[17] In other words, the judge dismissed the suit because the employer did not fire all Black employees or all women. However, all the Black people fired were women and all women fired were Black.

What this means, Crenshaw argues, is that the boundaries of sex and race discrimination in legal doctrine are defined by white women's and Black men's experiences, respectively. Under this view, Black women are protected only to the extent that their experiences coincide with those of either of the two groups. For white women, claiming sex discrimination is a statement that but for gender, they would not have

---

15. Kimberlé Crenshaw 'Demarginalizing the Intersection of Race and Sex: A Black Feminist Critique of Antidiscrimination Doctrine, Feminist Theory, and Antiracist Politics.' in *Feminist Legal Theory* 1st ed. (Routledge, 1989), 57-80.
16. Kimberlé Crenshaw, 'Mapping the Margins: Intersectionality, Identity Politics, and Violence against Women of Color.' In *Stanford Law Review* 43 (1991), 1241-1299.
17. Crenshaw, 'Demarginalizing the Intersection of Race and Sex,' 141.

been disadvantaged. There is no need to specify discrimination as *white* women because their race does not contribute to the disadvantage for which they seek redress. The view of discrimination that is derived from this grounding takes race privilege as a given. The case is the same for Black men: for them claiming racial discrimination is a statement that but for race, they would not have been disadvantaged. Their gender doesn't contribute to the disadvantage, and gender privilege is taken as a given. Discrimination against white women is thus the standard sex discrimination claim and discrimination against Black men is the standard race discrimination claim. The single-axis frame used by the court to define discrimination is therefore partial. This structure leaves Black women with no legal mechanism to prove that they have been discriminated against either as Blacks who are women or as women who are Black.

After explaining this situation, Crenshaw proposes intersectionality as a prism that allows us to see Black women through the cracks in the law. She argues that the analogy of the intersection better permits judges to grasp the dilemma of *DeGraffenreid*. She proposes that we imagine two roads that intersect. Each one represents the ways in which the workforce is structured by race and by gender, respectively. Traffic in those roads is the hiring policies of the company. Emma DeGraffenreid and the other plaintiffs, being Black and female, were situated at the intersection of the two roads, and they were hit there, both by the gender traffic and the race traffic. In this example we cannot understand gender as distinct from race. Because the intersectional experience is greater than the sum of racism and sexism, any analysis that does not take intersectionality into account cannot sufficiently address the particular manner in which Black women are subordinated.

As Jennifer Nash claims in *Black Feminism Reimagined*, the word intersectionality has since migrated from the pages of the Chicago Legal Forum (where Crenshaw published her article), through Women's Studies journals and conference keynotes, into daily conversation, and (at times misused and misunderstood) everyday hashtags.[18] It was added to the Oxford English Dictionary in 2015 and has been used by organizers around the world to signal that we must recognize the multiple axes of oppression that operate in our daily lives, and determine the positions from which we can organize and build solidarity across differences. In her essay *My Name is This Story* poet Aurora Levins Morales reflects upon the relationship between intersectional identity

---

18. Jennifer Nash, *Black Feminism Reimagined* (Durham: Duke UP, 2019).

and world-changing practices: 'This tribe called 'Women of Color' is not an ethnicity. It is one of the inventions of solidarity, an alliance, a political necessity that is not the given name of every female with dark skin and a colonized tongue, but rather a choice about how to resist and with whom.'[19]

A framework for community organizing, intersectionality is also useful as a methodological tool for the study of how agendas are established, and which knowledges and experiences are taken into account when making policy, laws, and history. Indeed, intersectional analyses, by focusing on marginalized people, are used to call into question the quality of substantive representation for historically oppressed groups and to understand complex inequalities and public identities. For instance, in her essay *Aren't Poor Single Mothers Women?* Gwendolyn Mink conducts an intersectional analysis on The Personal Responsibility Act implemented in the United States in 1996, arguing that the Act effectively and disproportionately violates poor women of colour's rights to reproductive choice and sexual privacy, to rearing their own children, and to occupational freedom.[20] These accounts of oppression and agency challenge both additive and analogical (being x is like being y) analyses of difference.

When reflecting upon intersectionality it is crucial to remember that in specific historical circumstances and geographical locations there are particular social divisions that determine an individual's positioning—for instance, differences in how religion, gender, ability, race, and sexuality are conceived. Chandra Mohanty's *Under Western Eyes* articulates a transnational feminist response to Western scholarship that emphasizes the unacknowledged colonial division of labour that permits the circulation of some ideas across intellectual, disciplinary and national borders, and specifically points to US-centred intersectional analyses as an example of this.[21] Nira Yuval-Davis' *Intersectionality and Feminist Politics* follows Mohanty and argues that the point of intersectional research is to examine the differential ways in which various social divisions are concretely entangled and construed by each other, and how they relate to subjective and political constructions of

---

19. Aurora Levins Morales, 'My Name is This Story.' In *Telling to Live: Latina Feminist Testimonios*, ed. Luz del Alba Acevedo (Durham: Duke UP, 2001), 22.
20. Gwendolyn Mink, 'Aren't Poor Single Mothers Women?' In *Whose Welfare?* ed. Gwendolyn Mink (Cornell University Press, 1999), 171-188.
21. Chandra Mohanty, 'Under Western Eyes: Feminist scholarship and colonial discourses.' In *Third World Women and the Politics of Feminism*, eds. Chandra Mohanty, Ann Russo, and Lourdes Torres (Bloomington: Indiana UP, 1991).

identities.[22] Similarly, Alice Ludvig's *Differences Between Women?*[23] and María Lugones' *Heterosexualism and the Colonial/Modern Gender System* maintain that the particularities of gender can only be understood by taking into consideration the specificity of time and place of the production of structural differences between women (and between men and women), viewing colonialism as a primary mechanism for this production.[24] This method of contextualizing categories as a recognition of conceptual instabilities is also proposed by Gudrun-Axeli Knapp's *Race, Class, Gender: Reclaiming Baggage in Fast Traveling Theories* when addressing the problem of the geographical differentiation of the social meaning of ideas: categories have histories and they do not travel well.[25] This means that in order to make use of them, it is imperative to rethink and adapt them, taking into account the sociological context within which they will be applied.

To sum up, intersectionality as a critical legal analytical tool grew out of a long tradition of both Black and US Third World Feminist thought that rejects the notion of independent identity categories and single-axis analyses of oppression. Such categories are mutually constituted and cannot be added together or separated out into discrete and pure strands, as they are always relational and never fixed. In the context of national and international policy and legislation that erases women's complex identities, intersectionality informs our critical approaches to the law by focusing our attention on differently marginalized peoples and their struggles for freedom from oppression. How do multiple axes of identity (cultural, political, psychic, subjective, economic, and phenomenological) interconnect in specific hierarchical systems of differentiation? What is the role of the law in shaping—and dismantling—the latter? And, how can we use the learnings from intersectionality's history along with the tools it offers to further our collective liberation?

---

22. Nira Yuval-Davis, 'Intersectionality and Feminist Politics' *European Journal of Women's Studies* 13/3 (2006), 193-209.
23. Alice Ludvig, 'Differences Between Women? Intersecting Voices in a Female Narrative,' *European Journal of Women's Studies* 13/3 (2006), 245-58.
24. María Lugones, 'Heterosexualism and the Colonial/Modern Gender System,' *Hypatia* 22/1 (2007), 186–209.
25. Gudrun-Axeli Knapp, 'Race, Class, Gender: Reclaiming Baggage in Fast Traveling Theories,' *European Journal of Women's Studies* 12/3 (2005), 249-265.

FURTHER READINGS

- Kimberlé Crenshaw, 'The Urgency of Intersectionality.' TED Talk (2016). Available at: https://www.ted.com/talks/kimberle_crenshaw_the_urgency_of_intersectionality?language=en
- Patricia Hill Collins, 'Intersectionality's Definitional Dilemmas.' In *Annual Review of Sociology* 41 (2015), 1–20.
- María Lugones, 'Intersectionality.' Decolonial Summer School Middleburg (2018). Available at: https://vimeo.com/335967759

Concept: Care and Vulnerability

Vanessa Munro

In 1982, Carol Gilligan's *In a Different Voice* identified a gendered dynamic within moral reasoning.[1] Drawing on experiments—most famously with two 11 year olds, Jake and Amy—Gilligan observed that women gravitate towards an ethic of care that prioritises relationships, context, and compromise, whilst men gravitate towards an ethic of justice that prioritises competition, self-interest and abstract rights. While such binaries are over-simplistic, the claim that legal methods have privileged the latter values at the expense of the former has continued to influence critical scholarship, which has often pushed for more communitarian, relational and contextual understandings of law and life. We can see traces of this ethics of care, for example, in the greater use of mediation over adversarial justice, or in tests for consent constructed around the freedom and capacity to exercise choice.

At the same time, this attention to context and connection—advocated as an antidote to law's propensity towards masculinist modes of disembodied and disembedded rationality—has emerged as a precarious critical friend. In a world in which power is unevenly distributed, it is not difficult to imagine why care for more privileged others might bring instrumental benefits; and it may be hard to disentangle a valorising of care from a valuing of those dividends. Care may emerge, in other

---

1. Carol Gilligan, *In a Different Voice: Psychological Theory and Women's Development* (Harvard University Press 1982)

words, as a survival strategy. So too, it can be commodified or celebrated in ways that are disempowering and self-destructive.

Care and vulnerability can become part of a conceptual pairing. But when they do, the need to handle care *with* care becomes increasingly apparent. Martha Fineman has insisted the state must be responsive to the reality that vulnerability is universal and inherent in the human condition.[2] And yet, as Stålsett has observed, the fact that vulnerability is shared does not entail that it is mutual or symmetrical.[3] A politics of vulnerability emerges regarding who is, and is not, recognised as vulnerable in a relevant way for the purposes of legal redress or policy intervention, and why. Being labelled as vulnerable (often by virtue of context and connection) can serve progressive ends (for example, trial protections afforded to 'vulnerable witnesses'). But it can also infantilise or 'other' recipients in ways that justify regressive interventions on their bodies and agency (for example, the rescue and return of 'vulnerable migrants' within domestic immigration policies).

---

2. Martha Fineman, 'The Vulnerable Subject: Anchoring Equality in the Human Condition' 20 *Yale Journal of Law and Feminism* (2008) 1-23
3. Sturla Stålsett, 'Ethical Dimensions of Vulnerability and Struggles for Social Inclusion in Latin America' 23 *Urbe et Ius Newsletter* (2006) 1-21

Concept: Social Reproduction

Serena Natile

In the 1970s the International Feminist Collective started a movement called Wages for Housework Campaign, they claimed that families and communities are places of social reproduction and women should be rewarded for the unpaid work they do.[1] The movement sought to challenge dominant understandings about socio-economic relations and obtain recognition that unpaid labour, such as care and sexual, emotional and affective services, is the foundation of productive work and necessary for the functioning of society. The movement considered wage as a direct expression of hierarchies of power in society and one of the most tangible objects of struggle over its terms. While historically the concept of social reproduction originated in the context of bourgeois economics to indicate the processes by which a social system reproduces itself, this idea was used by Wages for Housework campaigners to denounce an area of exploitation, the unwaged economy, that until then was unrecognised even by Marxist and unorthodox thinkers.[2] Feminist economics, feminist political economy scholars and gender and development scholars have furthered this analysis highlighting the

---

1. Mariarosa Dalla Costa, and Selma James *The Power of Women and the Subversion of the Community* (Falling Wall, 1972); for the history see Louise Toupin, *Wages for Housework: A History of an International Movement 1972-1977*, (Pluto Press, 2018)
2. Silvia Federici, 'Social Reproduction Theory: History, Issues and present Challenges', Radical Philosophy https://www.radicalphilosophy.com/article/social-reproduction-theory-2 (2019) (accessed 16/06/2021)

importance of redistributive policies, public social infrastructure and labour regulation necessary to recognise, support and reward social reproduction work.³

In feminist analyses social reproduction refers to the social relations, processes and labour that go into the daily and generational maintenance of the population.⁴ It includes 'the provisioning of material resources (food, clothing, housing, transport) and the training of individual capabilities necessary for interaction in the social context of a particular time and place',⁵ as well as community work,⁶ activism and solidarity work. Social reproduction can be organised by and through households, communities, grassroots groups and non-profit organisations, and facilitated by the state through socio-economic rights and welfare policies. Social reproduction work is disproportionately sustained by women and unequally distributed across race, class, disability, sexuality, gender identity, legal status (e.g. migration), coloniality and geopolitical location.

This unequal distribution is the result of capitalist structures and logics of value extraction, and of neoliberal policies of privatisation and marketisation. However, capitalist relations that exploit social reproduction work are also intertwined with colonial histories. This consideration is important not only because the capitalist accumulation of wealth in Western countries relied on resources and work from former colonies,⁷ but also because capitalist rules of production and reproduction were exported and globalised via colonialism. These rules include the commodification of land, the introduction of property rights and the wage economy⁸ characterised by gender norms such

---

3. Lourdes Beneria, *Gender, Development and Globalisation: Economics As If All People Mattered*, (Routledge, 2003). See also Lourdes Beneria and Gita Sen, 'Accumulation, Reproduction and Women's Role in Economic Development: Boserup Revisited'. *Signs* 7(2) (1981), 279–298; Shirin Rai and Georgina Waylen, *New Frontiers in Feminist Political Economy*. (Routledge, 2014), 189–212
4. Isabella Bakker and Stephen Gill 'Introduction: Social Reproduction and Global Transformations—from the Everyday to the Global' in Isabella Bakker and Rachael Silvey (eds) *Beyond States and Markets: The Challenges of Social Reproduction*, (Routledge, 2008).
5. Antonella Picchio, *Unpaid Work and the Economy: A Gender Analysis of the Standards of Living*, (Routledge, 2003) 2
6. Nina Banks 'Black Women in the United States and Unpaid Collective Work: Theorizing the Community as a Site of Production' in *The Review of Black Political Economy* 47(4) (2020), 343-362.
7. Adom Getachew *Worldmaking After Empire*. (Princeton University Press, 2019)
8. Barbara Rogers, *The Domestication of Women: Discrimination in Developing*

as male breadwinner and household head.[9] These norms have been institutionalised and reproduced via legal instruments, but they could also, possibly, be transformed through the law. The concept of social reproduction is important for any analysis of law in context as it allows to understand where gendered inequalities lie in society and reflect on how to bring about social change.

Societies, (Kogan Page: 1980), Maria Mies, *Patriarchy and Accumulation on a World Scale: Women in the International Division of Labour*. (Zed Books, 1986)
9. Diane Elson, 'The Economic, the Political and the Domestic: Businesses, States and Households in the Organisation of Production' *New Political Economy* 3(2), (1998) 189-208; Diane Elson and Nilufer Cagatay, 'The Social Content of Macroeconomic Policies' *World Development* 28(7), (2000) 1347–1364

26

Criminal Injustice

CRIMINAL LAW, CRIMINOLOGY

Yvette Russell

I have always loved the criminal law and I am frankly incredulous to hear that there are law students out there who don't enjoy studying it. The cases are mostly sensational, the doctrine is fascinating and ludicrous, and the stakes don't really get any higher. It is to the criminal law, after all, that one has to come to see the individual confront the full force of the state and its monopoly on punishment. In this chapter, I want to focus on the uneasy relationship between criminal law and what we call justice. I interrogate the key principles upon which our system of criminal law and justice proceeds and argue, with reference to the insights of queer, feminist and anti-racist scholars, that a critical approach to criminal law leads us inexorably to question much of what the criminal law tells us about justice, and that this is no bad thing.

What is Justice?

What do we mean when we talk about justice? In the first year of the law degree students will spend a lot of their time coming to terms with the notion of procedural justice; the idea that if the procedure is just or followed faithfully, the outcome will necessarily be just. This idea of procedural justice is very much at the heart of what we learn in criminal law, in evidence or in sentencing law. As we proceed through our degree we should, if we are being taught to think critically, become aware of the limits to procedural justice. Procedural justice only works if the procedure and those implementing it are completely free from bias. Because the exercise of discretion is often a key aspect of procedural justice, it is virtually impossible to guarantee that the law will be applied free from discrimination or prejudice. This is where justice as fairness or equality brushes up against procedural justice and students are forced to confront just one example of the conceptual messiness of law.

In the criminal law we often talk about criminal justice as both a concept (or set of principles) and a system. First year criminal law students will learn to reel off and explain criminal justice as deterrence, as retribution, as rehabilitation, incapacitation, restitution or denunciation. The system refers to the arms of the state from police, to prosecutors, to the judiciary, and prisons and probation, which are responsible for implementing the aims and goals of criminal justice. Those aims and goals include insuring and maintaining public order, social control and personal safety, vindicating individual autonomy and protecting property. What necessarily underpins the conceptual and institutional understandings of criminal justice are: first, an agreement that the goals of criminal justice are valid and accurately capture the notion of 'justice'; second, a societal acceptance that it is legitimate for the system to pursue and implement those goals on our behalf and; third, a faith in the capacity of the system to deliver these goals. Queer, feminist and anti-racist scholars and activists however, fundamentally challenge these presumptions.

The Validity of Criminal Justice Goals

Critical scholars challenge the very values upon which criminal justice goals are based and claim their validity. Criminal justice principles and goals reflect a hierarchy of values that are, more often than not, designed to protect existing structures of power and the status quo. The legal fiction of 'joint enterprise' is an oft-cited example of how criminal justice goals are selectively deployed in ways that entrench existing inequalities, often with discriminatory and unjust outcomes.

The doctrine of secondary (or accessory) liability is used in criminal law to deal with cases in which groups of people are involved in criminal activity and where responsibility for a particular criminal consequence is shared. Prior to 1985, the law in England and Wales operated on the basis of principles that had been law for at least 120 years,[1] in which secondary liability was based on proof that a defendant had 'aided, abetted, counselled or procured' the commission of the principal offence. The accompanying mens rea required proof of an accomplice's intent to do those acts of assistance or encouragement,

---

1. Accessories and Abettors Act 1861, section 8.

with the awareness of their ability to assist or encourage the principal in committing a criminal offence.[2]

In 1985 the Privy Council heard a case that profoundly changed the law in respect of secondary liability in cases of joint enterprise.[3] These are cases in which two or more people agree to commit one crime (crime A) but during the commission of that crime, one of them goes on to commit another offence (crime B). What happens, for example, when two or more people agree to commit a burglary, but during the course of that burglary a murder is committed? The legal problem in these cases of joint enterprise is ascertaining the liability of those accomplices *to* crime A *for* crime B. In *Chan Wing-Siu* the Privy Council held that, in cases of joint enterprise, an accessory to crime B will be guilty of that crime if he had foreseen the possibility that the principal actor might act as he did. An accessory's foresight of that possibility, plus his continuation in the enterprise to commit crime A, were held sufficient in law to bring crime B within the scope of the conduct for which he was criminally liable. The law, therefore, no longer required proof of intent on the part of the accessory for liability for crime B.

The consequences of this change in law were significant. Because secondary parties are convicted of the same offence as the principal offender, one glaring implication of *Chan Wing-Siu* was that a lower threshold of mens rea was now required to convict a secondary party (who may not have even been at the scene of a crime) of an offence like murder, than the principal who actually committed the actus reus. The House of Lords adopted the reasoning in *Chan Wing-Siu* in *Powell and English* in 1999,[4] endorsing and developing the policy basis for the Privy Council's departure from settled doctrine. In the words of Lord Steyn: 'The criminal justice system exists to control crime. The prime function of that system must be to deal justly but effectively with those who join with others in criminal enterprises... In order to deal with this important social problem the accessory principle is needed and cannot be abolished or relaxed.'[5]

The cases of *Chan Wing-Siu* and *Powell and English* met immediately with robust scholarly criticism and as the effects of the law became

---

2. See *Johnson v Youden* [1950] 1 KB 544; *Bainbridge* [1960] 1 QB 129; *Maxwell v DPP for Northern Ireland* [1978] 3 All ER 1140.
3. *Chan Wing-Siu v The Queen* [1985] AC 168.
4. [1999] 1 AC 1.
5. per Lord Steyn in *Powell and English* [1999] 1 AC 1, 14.

more widely publicly known, popular dissent followed.[6] It was not until 2016 in *Jogee* that the Supreme Court overturned its own precedent, stating that the Court had taken a 'wrong turn' in *Chan Wing-Siu*, and the law of joint enterprise should revert to its previous doctrinal status as a species of secondary liability proper, in which foresight was not equivalent to intent but was instead only relevant as evidence of that intent.[7]

It is important for us to think about the political and policy context in which this 'wrong turn' took place, among the consequences of which were the mass imprisonment of, disproportionately, young men of colour, many of whom were subject to life sentences.[8] In 1997, the New Labour Government of Tony Blair swept into power with a flagship policy called 'Tough on Crime, Tough on the Causes of Crime', which was designed to rival the Conservative's monopoly as the party of law and order.[9] That policy relied on bullish crime control rhetoric and gave way to the Crime and Disorder Act 1998, which ushered in a new agenda of 'authoritarianism, communitarianism, remoralization [and] managerialism' in criminal justice administration in the UK, much of which was explicitly targeted at young people.[10] The moral panic of the time was heavily focused on the spectre of marauding gangs of youths, wantonly committing crime with no accountability, parental or otherwise.[11]

As a number of criminal justice scholars have pointed out, the rhetoric that supported this shift took a highly racialised tone that bled through to its implementation.[12] There is a documented link between

---

6. See, for example, 'Jengba', formed in 2010 to campaign against the law of joint enterprise. 'Joint Enterprise,' accessed 16 June 2021, https://jointenterprise.co.
7. *R v Jogee* [2016] UKSC 8; *Ruddock v The Queen* [2016] UKPC 7.
8. A survey of prisoners in 2014 suggested that up to half of those imprisoned pursuant to joint enterprise laws identified as 'BAME'. Patrick Williams and Becky Clarke, *Dangerous Associations: Joint Enterprise, Gangs and Racism* (Centre for Crime and Justice Studies, 2016), accessed 16 June 2021, https://www.crimeandjustice.org.uk/sites/crimeandjustice.org.uk/files/Dangerous%20assocations%20Joint%20Enterprise%20gangs%20and%20racism.pdf.
9. Fran Abrams, 'Election '97: Blair Promises Bill to Tackle Youth Crime,' *The Independent*, 25 April 1997, accessed 16 June 2021, https://www.independent.co.uk/news/election-97-blair-promises-bill-to-tackle-youth-crime-1269277.html.
10. John Muncie, 'Institutionalized intolerance: Youth Justice and the 1998 Crime and Disorder Act,' *Critical Social Policy* 19/2 (1999), 147.
11. See the comments of Jack Straw, former Home Secretary, cited in *Guardian*, 28 November 1997, cited in Muncie, 'Institutionalized Intolerance', 148.
12. Claire Alexander, '(Re)thinking "Gangs."', *Runnymede*, 2008, accessed 16 June 2021, https://www.runnymedetrust.org/uploads/publications/pdfs/RethinkingGangs-2008.pdf;

the criminalisation of young Black men in particular with the 'gangs discourse' that accompanied these broad legal and policy changes.[13] The Met Police's 'Trident Matrix', for example, includes a database of those subject to surveillance pursuant to 'gangs' policing, 86% of which were revealed in 2019 to be Black, Asian or minority ethnicities.[14] These changes occurred too at a time when crime rates were declining and there existed no credible data to suggest gang violence was a growing or especially acute problem in the UK.[15] Indeed, and as the Supreme Court pointed out in *Jogee*, there was no 'objective evidence' that the law prior to *Chan Wing-Siu* or *Powell and English* failed to provide adequate protection from 'gang' crime.[16] Instead, the departure from precedent was justified with reference to 'weighty and important' practical policy considerations, which 'prevailed over strict logic.'[17]

It is in contexts like these then that critical scholars call the validity of criminal justice goals into question, and where it can seem that criminal justice rhetoric and infrastructure is being used as a shroud to control and discipline specific populations. Or where the principle of public order is relied upon to trump that of individual autonomy, though it is the autonomy of a few that is most heavily impacted.

As critical criminal lawyers we should be clear that decisions like those taken by the Courts in rewriting the doctrine of joint enterprise involve value judgments that can't be artificially extricated from the political context in which they sit by a veneer of legal positivism. Thus, although the principles and goals of criminal justice are supposed to vindicate our shared values critical scholars argue that in practice,

---

Patrick Williams, 'Criminalising the Other: Challenging the Race-Gang Nexus.' *Race & Class* 56/3 (2015), 18–35.
13. Williams and Clarke, *Dangerous Associations*; Amnesty International. *Trapped in the Matrix: Secrecy, Stigma, and bias in the Met's Gangs Database* (London: Amnesty International UK, 2018). Accessed 16 June 2021, https://www. amnesty.org.uk/files/reports/Trapped%20in%20the%20Matrix%20Amnesty%20report.pdf
14. Met Police, 'Current list of people listed on the Gang Matrix,' March 2019, accessed 16 June 2021 https://www.met.police.uk/foi-ai/metropolitan-police/disclosure-2019/march/current-list-people-gang-matrix/
15. Juanjo Medina and Jon Shute, '"Utterly Appalling": Why Official Review of UK Gang Policy is Barely Credible,' Manchester Policy Blogs, 16 December 2013, accessed 16 June 2021, http://blog.policy.manchester.ac.uk/featured/2013/12/utterly-appalling-why-official-review-of-uk-gang-policy-is-barely-credible/; Hannah Smithson, Rob Ralphs and Patrick Williams, 'Used and abused: the problematic usage of gang terminology in the United Kingdom and its implications for ethnic minority youth,' *British Journal of Criminology*, 53/1 (2013) 113-28.
16. *Jogee*, 75.
17. *Jogee*, 55-56.

criminal justice is often mobilized to perpetuate class, race and other inequalities.[18]

The Legitimacy of the System

Closely related to our discussion of the validity of criminal justice goals, above, is a critical concern with the legitimacy of the criminal justice system in its pursuit and implementation of criminal justice principles and goals. Our recognition of the state's right to determine and implement criminal justice policies on our behalf is grounded fundamentally in the social contract, or the idea that we cede some of our freedom to the state in exchange for its protection. However, some argue that not everyone is included in this contract, or that the contractual benefits do not accrue equally.[19]

One way in which the system lacks legitimacy is that the use of state force is disproportionately applied. Above I discussed the troubled doctrinal history of joint enterprise as an example of criminal law and policy that has more severely impacted some communities over others, calling us to question the validity of the criminal justice goals upon which such laws are based. In fact, there is evidence of the disproportionate application of state force to racialized and minoritized communities at every point of the criminal justice system. This is true of police use of stop and search powers, arrest and prosecution rates, conviction and imprisonment rates and disproportionate rates of deaths in custody or following police contact.[20] Between the years 1991—2014, 509 people from BAME, refugee and migrant communities died in suspicious circumstances after coming into contact with the police, prison authorities or immigration detention officers.[21] There has never been a successful prosecution of a criminal justice actor for the unlawful

---

18. For an approach to criminology that centres class and gender see: James W. Messerschmidt, *Capitalism, Patriarchy, and Crime: Toward a Socialist Feminist Criminology* (Totowa, NJ: Rowman & Littlefield, 1986).
19. Charles Mills, *The Racial Contract* (Ithaca: Cornell University Press, 1997). See also Carol Pateman, *The Sexual Contract* (Stanford: Stanford University Press, 1988).
20. See: David Lammy, *The Lammy Review: An Independent Review into the Treatment of, and Outcomes for, Black, Asian and Minority Ethnic Individuals in the Criminal Justice System* (London: Lammy Review, 2017), accessed 16 June 2021, https://assets.publishing.service.gov.uk/government/uploads/system/uploads/attachment_data/file/643001/lammy-review-final-report.pdf.
21. Harmit Athwal and Jenny Bourne, eds, *Dying for Justice* (London: Institute of Race Relations, 2015), accessed 16 June 2021, https://irr.org.uk/app/uploads/2015/03/Dying_for_Justice_web.pdf

killing or otherwise of a person of colour while in state custody in the United Kingdom.

The system faces a crisis of legitimacy, then, among those communities who bear the brunt of its surveillance and application of force and for whom the dissonance between the promise of criminal law and justice and the lived reality is most stark. A wave of Black Lives Matter protests across Britain over the summer of 2016 and again in 2020 saw thousands of young people on the street protesting racist policing, and police violence. There is little evidence today of any change in the conditions in which that unrest germinated. Black people continue to be stopped and searched by police at a rate nines times greater than that of white people.[22] The onset of the COVID-19 pandemic saw lockdown regulations imposed in racially discriminatory ways[23] as well as exposing, again, the ways that the consequences of crises are disproportionately borne by poor people and people of colour.[24] An investigation of the policing of the Black Lives Matter protests found that police disproportionately used excessive force at Black-led protests, and against Black protesters in particular.[25] It also found that police regularly neglected their duty of care to anti-racist protestors, both in terms of welfare support and in failing to facilitate the right to peaceful protest and assembly.[26]

The consistent dissonance then between what the criminal law and justice system says it will do for us, and the hard reality, leads to a crisis of legitimacy, which is only added to by its lack of capacity.

---

22. Home Office, 'Police Powers and Procedures, England and Wales, Year Ending 31 March 2020 Second Edition,' *Gov.UK*, 16 November 2020, accessed 16 June 2021, https://www.gov.uk/government/statistics/police-powers-and-procedures-england-and-wales-year-ending-31-march-2020. Searches of all 'BAME' groups were four times higher than those of white people.
23. Adam Elliot-Cooper, *'Britain Is Not Innocent' A Netpol report on the policing of Black Lives Matter protests in Britain's towns and cities in 2020* (London: Netpol, 2020), 12-13, accessed 16 June 2021, https://secureservercdn.net/50.62.198.70/561.6fe.myftpupload.com/wp-content/uploads/2020/11/Britain-is-not-innocent-web-version.pdf.
24. Public Health England, 'Disparities in the Risk and Outcomes of COVID-19,' *Gov.uk*, 2 June 2020, accessed 16 June 2021, https://assets.publishing.service.gov.uk/government/uploads/system/uploads/attachment_data/file/908434/Disparities_in_the_risk_and_outcomes_of_COVID_August_2020_update.pdf.
25. Elliot-Cooper, *'Britain is Not Innocent'*, 18-25.
26. Elliot-Cooper, *'Britain is Not Innocent'*, 25-28.

The Capacity of the System

As to the third presumption underpinning the logic of criminal justice, our faith in the capacity of the criminal justice system to deliver on its stated goals, critical scholars are skeptical. Even if we did accept the validity of criminal justice goals and the legitimacy of the system, that system often fails to deliver on what it says it is trying to do. There is an immediate tension, for example, between criminal justice principles like retribution and rehabilitation. There is a substantial body of literature attesting to the brutalizing effects of imprisonment, even for those who serve short sentences,[27] and an eye-wateringly high rate of reoffending among those who have previously been sentenced to imprisonment.[28] Surveys of public opinion towards punishment shows that people see rehabilitation as a key goal of imprisonment, however, few people seem to have faith that rehabilitation is ultimately possible in prison.[29] The literature on the effectiveness of rehabilitative initiatives in prison environments, coupled with reoffending data, would seem to bear out that skepticism.[30] It's important, therefore, for critical scholars and students to have an honest discussion in the classroom about the limits

---

27. Seena Fazel et al., 'Mental Health of Prisoners: Prevalence, Adverse Outcomes, and Interventions.' *Lancet Psychiatry* 3/9 (2016), 871-881; Zoe Cutcher et al. 'Poor Health and Social Outcomes for Ex-Prisoners with a History of Mental Disorder: A Longitudinal Study,' *Australian and New Zealand Journal of Public Health* 38/5 (2014), 424-429; Tyson Whitten et al., 'Parental Offending and Child Physical Health, Mental Health, and Drug Use Outcomes: A Systematic Literature Review,' *Journal of Child and Family Studies* 28/5 (2019), 1155–1168; Lucius Couloute, 'Nowhere To Go: Homelessness Among Formerly Incarcerated People,' *Prison Policy Initiative* (2018).
28. A large-scale study in the United States, for example, showed that around two-thirds of ex-detainees were rearrested within three years, and three-quarters within five years. Matthew Durose, Alexia D. Cooper, and Howard N. Snyder, *Recidivism of Prisoners Released in 30 States in 2005: Patterns from 2005 to 2010* (Washington, DC: Bureau of Justice Statistics, 2014). For recent data showing rates of recidivism year-to-year in the UK see: Gov.uk, 'Reoffending', *Gov.uk*, 19 April 2021, accessed 16 June 2021, https://www.ethnicity-facts-figures.service.gov.uk/crime-justice-and-the-law/crime-and-reoffending/proven-reoffending/latest#full-page-history.
29. Julian V. Roberts and Mike Hough, 'The State of the Prisons: Exploring Public Knowledge and Opinion,' *The Howard Journal of Criminal Justice* 44/3 (2005), 286, 296-298.
30. M. Keith Chen and Jesse M. Shapiro, 'Do Harsher Prison Conditions Reduce Recidivism? A Discontinuity-Based Approach,' *American Law and Economics Review* 9/1 (2007), 1-29; Patrick Bayer, Randi Hjalmarsson and David Pozen, 'Building Criminal Capital Behind Bars: Peer Effects in Juvenile Corrections,' *The Quarterly Journal of Economics* 124/1 (2009), 105-147.

of the criminal justice system and its bluntness as a tool for social engineering. It is unlikely, for example, that the criminal justice system is going to be capable of fixing legal and policy failure in the areas of employment, health care, and education where this leads to criminality, particularly in retrospect.

Alongside conceptual tensions like those between retribution and rehabilitation lie very real material concerns about the capacity of criminal justice to deliver on its goals. The Chair of the Criminal Bar Association in the UK recently described the criminal justice system as 'on its knees' due to a crisis in funding.[31] Cuts to funding over the last 10 years have impacted at almost every point in the system. The under resourcing of the police, prosecution services and courts have meant that, against the system's own measures of success in rates of prosecutions and convictions, many seriously offences are accurately described as having been decriminalized.[32] Cuts to legal aid for those who can't afford representation when charged with a criminal offence have had serious implications for equality of access to justice.[33] A lack of support for those being released from prison and on probation only adds to high recidivism rates among ex-detainees.[34]

Reflecting on the foregoing discussion calling into question the validity, legitimacy and capacity of the system and its underlying rationale then, there is an immediate conundrum for the critical scholar teaching the criminal law: How do we navigate the contradictions that the criminal law presents for us in the classroom and in our work? What does it mean to teach the doctrine of the criminal law, which is underpinned by and proceeds on the basis of these presumptions above, when all the while we believe them to be almost entirely fictitious? In a

---

31. Owen Bowcott, 'Criminal Justice System is 'On Its Knees', Says Top English Lawyer,' *The Guardian*, 19 November 2020, accessed 16 June 2021, https://www.theguardian.com/law/2020/nov/19/criminal-justice-system-is-on-its-knees-says-top-english-lawyer.
32. A stark example of this kind of failure can be seen in sexual offences. See: Centre for Women's Justice, End Violence Against Women Coalition, Imkaan and Rape Crisis England and Wales, 'The Decriminalisation of Rape: Why the Justice System is Failing Rape Survivors and What needs to Change,' *indd*, November 2020, accessed 16 June 2021, https://indd.adobe.com/view/4453b960-41a2-4eff-8aea-1839ec0aa2a5.
33. Dominic Gilbert, 'Legal Aid Advice Network 'Decimated' by Funding Cuts', *BBC*, 10 December 2018, accessed 21 June 2021, https://www.bbc.com/news/uk-46357169.
34. Robert Wright, 'England's probation service at risk from cash squeeze, watchdog warns', *Financial Times*, 28 September 2020, accessed 21 June 2021. https://www.ft.com/content/526fec7a-6537-4979-a45c-606d1f168372; 'London Prisons Mission' accessed 16 June 2021, https://www.londonprisonsmission.org/safe-homes-for-women-leaving-prison

final reflection below I want to suggest that while a critical lens on the criminal law might lead us to question the foundations of the criminal law and the criminal justice system this doesn't need to end in nihilism (if we don't want it to!)

The Cost of Criminal Justice or an Alternative Horizon

It is a familiar criticism of the critical perspective that it can lead us to a dead end, in which a productive escape from real and material inequality and injustice are all but impossible. There is a paradox at the heart of our study of the criminal law for the critical scholar or student that might not necessarily be readily apparent through a liberal or 'mainstream' account of criminal law, and that appears when we consider what we must give up to accept the coherence of the criminal justice system in its totality. In other words, some of the aims we might have as queer, feminist and anti-racist scholars and activists are simply at odds with what criminal law offers us as justice. How do we reconcile our support, for example, for calls to defund the police or to abolish prisons with a concept of justice that has carceral responses at its apex?[35] We want the state to take crime seriously and to protect us, but we don't want to be used as a cover for increasing the power of the state, knowing what we know about how that power is unevenly distributed and applied.[36]

Our wariness about the validity, legitimacy and capacity of criminal law and justice means that we are also concerned with the way in which criminal justice goals are used to justify other forms of state violence like deportations,[37] or unequal access to state services like healthcare,[38]

---

35. see further: 'Abolitionist Futures', accessed 21 June 2021, https://abolitionistfutures.com; Adam Elliot-Cooper, 'Defund the Police' is not Nonsense. Here's What It Really Means', *The Guardian*, 2 July 2020, accessed 16 June 2021, https://www.theguardian.com/commentisfree/2020/jul/02/britain-defund-the-police-black-lives-matter.
36. See further on this point: Sarah Lamble, 'Queer Necropolitics and the Expanding Carceral State: Interrogating Sexual Investments in Punishment,' *Law and Critique* 24/3 (2013), 229-253; Yvette Russell, 'Criminal Law to the Rescue? 'Wolf-Whistling' as Hate Crime,' *Critical Legal Thinking*, 20 July 2016, accessed 21 June 2021, https://criticallegalthinking.com/2016/07/20/wolf-whistling-as-hate-crime/
37. Luke de Noronha, *Deporting Black Britons: Portraits of Deportation to Jamaica* (Manchester: Manchester University Press, 2020).
38. Medact, Migrants Organise, New Economics Foundation, 'Patients Not Passports: Migrants' Access to Healthcare During the Coronavirus Crisis,' *New Economics*, June 2020, accessed 21 June 2021, https://neweconomics.org/uploads/files/Patients-Not-Passports-Migrants-Access-to-Healthcare-During-the-Coronavirus-Crisis.

or just the everyday violence of being constantly subjected to humiliating harassment by state agents who seem to face little accountability for their actions.[39] In many ways, the cost of entry into the realm of criminal justice may just be too high to pay, both personally and politically.[40] Alternatively, our awareness of the paradox at the heart of criminal law may lead us to get to work rethinking the basis upon which we demand criminal justice and the animating principles and concepts upon which the system is based.

There is a long history in queer, feminist and anti-racist communities of mutual support and protection, and in some cases, of generating alternatives to current systems of criminal law and justice.[41] These groups emphasize the need to transform the meaning of justice as we currently understand it through the narrow lens of criminal law controlled by the state, and to build towards a future by harnessing the power of collective solidarity. Dean Spade calls this type of survival work 'mutual aid', when it is done in collaboration with social movements demanding transformative change.[42] Mutual aid is a good way of describing a move towards social justice and away from criminal justice.[43] Social justice seeks individual accountability alongside a conscious politics of

---

pdf ; Mattha Busby, Rhi Storer and Eric Allison, 'They're Going Grey in The Face': How Covid-19 Restrictions Are Affecting UK Inmates,' *The Guardian*, 20 October 2020, accessed 21 June 2021, https://www.theguardian.com/society/2020/oct/20/covid-19-prison-staff-say-restrictions-creating-a-mental-health-timebomb.

39. Lewis, Paul et al. *Reading the Riots: Investigating England's Summer of Disorder* (London: London School of Economics and Political Science and The Guardian, 2011). Accessed 21 June 2021. http://eprints.lse.ac.uk/46297/1/Reading%20the%20riots%28published%29.pdf, 19.

40. See further on this point: Yvette Russell, 'The Cost of "Justice": Sexual Offence Complainants and Access to Personal Data,' *Critical Legal Thinking*, 7 May 2019, accessed 21 June 2021, https://criticallegalthinking.com/2019/05/07/the-cost-of-justice-sexual-offence-complainants-and-access-to-personal-data/.

41. For example, see the long history of Black and Asian grass roots organising in Britain, much of which promoted its own progressive political and social vision: Jasbinder S. Nijjar, 'Building From the Base, Starting From The Streets,' *Institute of Race Relations*, 22 October 2020, accessed 21 June 2021, https://irr.org.uk/article/building-from-the-base-starting-from-the-streets/; Anandi Ramamurthy, 'Racism, Self Defence and the Asian Youth Movements,' *Discover Society*, 3 April 2019, accessed 21 June 2021, https://discoversociety.org/2019/04/03/racism-self-defence-and-the-asian-youth-movements/; Our Migration Story, 'Resisting Racism: the Bradford 12 Defence Campaign,' *Our Migration Story*, accessed 21 June 2021, https://www.ourmigrationstory.org.uk/oms/resisting-racism-the-bradford-12-defence-campaign.

42. Dean Spade, *Mutual Aid: Building Solidarity during this Crisis (and the Next)* (London & New York: Verso Books, 2020).

43. 'Abolitionist Futures.'

building and mobilizing collective action to address harm and foster wellbeing, while resisting neoliberal cooption.[44]

A key aspect of this work is about an acknowledgement that the systems that are in place do not meet many peoples' needs and an unwillingness to rely on the law or the various arms of the state to act as saviour. Mutual aid focuses on building capacity within communities to enable them to respond to the needs of their members with their own resources, as well as building a shared understanding of why it is that people don't have what they need.[45] Part of this work might involve, for example, generating discussion about alternatives to imprisonment, or promoting contextual understandings of crime and what is owed to each person as 'fairness' 'tak[ing] into account someone's upbringing, health and social background in thinking about how the justice system should deal with them'.[46] There may well still be a place for criminal law in such an alternative, but that place is likely to be strategic or tactical rather than central.[47]

Many mutual aid and community groups organizing an alternative to criminal justice emphasize the need for 'care not cops'.[48] That invocation of care as a central organizing concept for this type of work attempts to shift the focus away from punitiveness as the animating rationale for so much of what passes currently for criminal justice, and towards holistic responses focused on harm reduction, safety, health and well-being. Activists who work together toward a future without prisons, police and punishment urge their members and supporters to 'practice everyday abolition'[49] by drawing on shared resources to '[build] the future from the present'.[50] This involves working to address the conditions under which prison and police are considered to be

---

44. Rickke Mananzala and Dean Spade, 'The Nonprofit Industrial Complex and Trans Resistance,' *Sexuality Research & Social Policy* 5/1 (2008), 53.
45. Spade, *Mutual Aid*.
46. 'Reframing,' *Transform Justice*, accessed 21 June 2021, https://www.transformjustice.org.uk/reframing/.
47. Dean Spade, 'Laws as Tactics,' Columbia Journal of Gender and Law 21/2 (2011), 40-71.
48. See, for example, this community group organizing in Portland, Oregon: 'Care Not Cops,' https://www.carenotcops.org.
49. Sarah Lamble, 'Practising Everyday Abolition,' in *Abolishing the Police*, Koshka Duff ed. (London: Dog Section Press, 2021) 147-160.
50. Ruth Wilson Gilmore, 'Making Abolition Geography in California's Central Valley,' *The Funambulist*, 20 December 2018, accessed 21 June 2021, https://thefunambulist.net/making-abolition-geography-in-californias-central-valley-with-ruth-wilson-gilmore.

the best option for us to deal with social problems, and by undoing the naturalness of carceral logic. Abolitionist practice can mean, for example, demanding police out of schools,[51] campaigning against educational exclusion,[52] or advocating for universal health care and housing. Working towards abolition is an ongoing process of everyday practice, both personal and political, and one that decentres criminal justice and asks different questions of and about the law.

Conclusion

What does it mean to demand accountability for criminal behaviour, while also being profoundly wary of the state's approach to criminal justice? These are difficult questions but ones that we need to ask ourselves from the beginning of our study of the law. In this chapter I've offered a critical perspective on some of the key elements that scaffold what we learn in criminal law early on in our degrees. Those elements include the concepts and principles that underlie criminal law, and some of the key aims and goals of the criminal justice system. The critical perspective requires us to think about the doctrine in context and to maintain, perhaps, a healthy skepticism towards what the criminal law says about itself.

Our critical skepticism of the cohering logic behind our study of criminal law and criminal justice doesn't need to lead us to abandon the social contract all together. It might instead direct us to more creative thinking about what social solidarity means and what accountability and responsibility requires under conditions of profound social, economic and political inequality. We might take to seeing the criminal law as 'tactics' to both deconstruct and deploy as necessary,[53] rather than as a coherent whole the rules of which we need to internalize and memorize to pass our law degree successfully. However we perceive it, learning the tools to think critically for ourselves remains crucial.

---

51. Vik Chechi-Ribeiro, 'Why the Police Have No Place in Schools,' *The Guardian*, 5 September 2020, accessed 21 June 2021, https://www.theguardian.com/commentisfree/2020/sep/05/police-schools-manchester.
52. Berni Graham et al., *School Exclusion: A Literature Review on the Continued Disproportionate Exclusion of Certain Children* (UK Department of Education, 2019).
53. Spade, 'Laws as Tactics.'

Further Readings

- Kaba, Mariame. *We Do This 'til We Free Us: Abolitionist Organizing and Transforming Justice*. Chicago: Haymarket Books, 2021.
- Lamble, Sarah. 'Queer investments in punitiveness.' In, *Queer Necropolitics*. Jin Haritaworn, Adi Kuntsman and Silvia Posocco eds. London: Routledge, 2014.
- Naffine, Ngaire. *Criminal Law and the Man Problem*. Oxford: Hart Publishing, 2019.
- Norrie, Alan. *Crime, Reason and History: A Critical Introduction to Criminal Law* Cambridge: Cambridge University Press, 2014.
- Shankley, William and Patrick Williams. 'Minority ethnic groups, policing and the criminal justice system in Britain.' In *Ethnicity and Race in the UK: State of the Nation*. Bridget Byrne, Claire Alexander, Omar Khan, James Nazro, William Shankley eds. Bristol: Policy Press, 2020.

27

Making and Br(e)aking Power

CONSTITUTIONAL LAW

Angus McDonald

The challenges facing a critique of the theory and practice of constitution in the UK focus on quite specific features that make the UK constitutional tradition markedly different from those of other countries. Indeed, this is quite often the first thing that students of constitution learn—that the UK has a singular, if not unique, position as regards constitution compared with other countries. Sometimes, this is summarised by the provocative claim that 'we don't have a constitution'; a claim in part true, in part misleading, as students on a course on this supposedly non-existent thing quickly work out. The confusion arises not because of the content, which is pretty standard, but because of the form, which is unusual. In the terms made famous by Deleuze and Guattari, while most constitutions are arborescent, that of the UK is rhizomatic[1]. Instead of a root, a trunk and branches, a unity, we find a multiplicity, in which any point can be connected to any other, not a single fabric but a patchwork.

The Uncodified Constitution

Constitution, as a field of study, embraces public law, but also history and politics. It is, for better or worse, an amalgam of impure elements from which it is impossible to extract a purified legal essence. Although

---

1. Gilles Deleuze and Felix Guattari, *A Thousand Plateaus* (London: Athlone Press, 1988), 9. 'The point is that a rhizome or multiplicity never allows itself to be overcoded, never has available a supplementary dimension over and above its number of lines.' This is precisely the status of the UK constitution, unlike others.

all legal topics benefit from being situated in social, political and historical contexts, with constitution contextualisation is not only desirable, but unavoidable. This arises from the famously peculiar nature of constitution in the UK, its 'unwritten' status, or as it would be better called, its *uncodified* status. Most countries have a single constitutional document, emergent from a historical rupture, wherein the legal system gives to itself definition, form and rule book. This rupture may be a revolution, a war of independence, a coup, or any regime change. What counts is that the rupture draws a line, one side of which is before and the other after, and the constitutional document is produced to announce how 'after' will proceed legally. This document is necessary because the way in which law proceeded 'before' is now discredited, denounced as tyrannical or disorderly, and the new must define its values and rules by way of contrast. The new, in order to emphasise its difference from the old, in order to insist on the rupture, makes the constitution it produces a *codified* document, a law operating at a deeper level than ordinary law, an entrenched law.

The UK claims to be different. There is no constitutional document, no codification, no entrenchment, no special constitutional procedures. The UK claims this is because there is no line between old and new in the UK's history, no rupture. Just as a sceptical attitude in other countries might start by questioning the claim of a radical rupture—perhaps by finding unexpected continuities between old and new regimes—in the case of the UK, as the claim is that there is no rupture, we look for signs of rupture being denied, continuities being used to paper over the cracks. There are in fact several moments when these breaks could be located, when a rupture that could have given rise to a moment of constitution formation happened—the English Civil War, the Restoration, the Union of Scotland and England, and others.

If History Never Breaks?

Our interest lies in the consequences of a mindset that sees only continuity and never a radical break in British history. The key consequence is that it is used to justify the lack of a codified constitution. No revolution, so no constitution. This can be put another way. In systems with a clear break, there is a moment of constituting power, after which there is constituted power in place. This might be a revolution or coup or 'regime change', but it is some (usually violent) action which ruptures constitutional continuity. This can happen more than once. Without any rupture, however, it might be thought that in the UK the moment of constituting power never arrives. Actually, it is more the case that the moment of constituting power never ends. The power structured by constitutional tradition in the UK never stops constituting and re-constituting itself; it never becomes an achieved constituted power.

Another consequence follows. Where power is constituted in an achieved constitution, that itself constitutes a break. But it is not just a temporal break between past and future (the ancient regime and the new constitutional order), it is also a conceptual break between the pre-conditions for law and the existence of law. We might think of the historical, political, societal, economic contexts out of which law emerges. For many countries the formation of a constitution is explained by these factors—pre-eminently in the situation where a revolution explains the moment of constitution building. A revolution which gives birth to a constitution is a completed project. The sequence is: Social Conditions produce Revolution produces Constitution produces Legal System. Thereafter the existence and functioning of the legal system is explained purely by reference to the constitution. You need look no further than, nor behind, the constitution, to explain any facet of the legal system. The constitution is the foundation. Historians can explain why the revolution happened. Lawyers can then explain the reason for any law by reference to the constitution alone, as any answers to questions about the law will be found in the constitution. This will also be true not only for students, but for all officials of the legal system—the constitution will be the document the judges of the Supreme Court look to for answers too.[2] The break is a barrier to otherwise endless sequences of cause and effect, of reasoning. One simply cannot, *legally*, ask, why obey the constitution? Kelsen's theory of the *grundnorm* acknowledges this.[3] This creates both problems and opportunities for the critical study of law in these countries.

But we must investigate what problems and opportunities arise for the critical study of constitution in the UK, where different conditions persist. The first advantage of constitutional critique in the UK is that there is no break between history and politics on one side, and the constitution and the legal system on the other. It is always about history and politics, and never stops being so. In an incomplete constitutional

---

2. Literally any case would do, but, from the USA, see Taylor v Riojas 592 US (decided November 2, 2020) concerning the detention of a prisoner in a 'shockingly unsanitary' prison cell. The question is posed as a question whether 'any reasonable officer should have realized that Taylor's conditions of confinement offended the Constitution.'

3. Hans Kelsen, *The Pure Theory of Law* (Berkeley: University of California Press 1970)

process, there is nothing where there should be something, or more precisely, where there would be a document. Instead there is only a tradition of discussion around the topic of constitution. Rather than asking the question, 'how do we interpret our constitutional document?' in the UK, we have to ask, 'how do we construct our constitutional tradition, in the absence of a document?' This means that, unlike the tradition of codified constitutions, where the ultimate point of reference is the constitution, in the UK, the common law system of binding precedent means that, to make a legal decision, any one case can be connected to any other case in a chain of reasoning which is in principle endless (this is the Deleuzian rhizomatic logic referred to in the opening comments). The sequence is briefer: in the UK, Social Conditions produce Legal System directly, whose content resides in the case law, which is where the question, 'which interpretation of the rule must we obey?' will be answered. No conceptual break, no Revolution, and no Constitution standing above ordinary law, just Legal System. This is the sense in which Constitutional Law is ordinary law in the UK, no hierarchy of higher and lower law, no Basic law. Notice that this means, as said before, that constitutional tradition in the UK is permanently in the process of being constructed; the question of its contents is never definitively settled. It lacks a central point of reference, instead principles circulate. A conservative interpretation might not even want to concede that this tradition is 'constructed', that being too active a concept; what happens is the discovery of our tradition, or even better, the relaying of it from one generation keeping it in safekeeping to the next.

The present-day Conservative government under Boris Johnson gives the lie to this. Since coming to power, it has taken an explicitly destructive approach to many of the assumptions as to what is in the constitutional tradition. It has attempted to prorogue Parliament, until told by the Supreme Court that it could not.[4] It has proposed a law in breach of international treaty obligations entered into by itself less

---

4. *R (on the Application of Miller) v The Prime Minister; Cherry and others v Advocate General for Scotland* [2019] UKSC 41, [2019] 4 All ER 299 At para 18: 'The United Kingdom does not have a constitution to be found entirely in a written document. This does not mean there is an absence of a constitution or constitutional law. On the contrary, the United Kingdom has its own form of *constitutional* law.' The crucial difference is between the appeal in the USA to 'the Constitution', and the appeal in the UK to 'constitutional law' (which turns out to be not so much law as principle, such as Parliamentary Sovereignty).

than a year ago[5]. These moves to test the boundaries of the constitution follow on from its most singular constitutional innovation, the decision to take the outcome of a referendum on membership of the EU as a higher power binding on the Government and Parliament, which the latter were duty-bound to deliver.[6] These examples are mentioned here to illustrate the point that, in other countries, the question, 'can they do that?' would be answered by way of reference to the constitution, and its interpretation by the judiciary. Here, even with the Supreme Court's prorogation decision, the situation is less clear. The government takes the view that their *opinion* that they can act in these ways is sufficient to empower them to do so. Are they right? In a system without a break in power, are there any brakes on power?

A Constitutional Tradition (1): Three Institutions

Having spent so long saying what the UK constitution is not, let us try to summarise what we do know about it. The UK constitutional tradition consists of a set of institutions animated by a complementary set of principles. The institutions are a way of slicing up the power of the state in a way that ought to operate to avoid the concentration of too much power in one place, on the democratic assumption that the state needs power to implement the policies governments are voted into power to deliver, but also it should not have too much power lest it become an unchecked tyranny. That power is needed is justified by Hobbes,[7] that it must be subject to limits by Locke.[8] This is part of the meaning of the much used phrase, 'checks and balances'.

There are three key institutions. The first is Parliament. Parliament is made up of two groups of people, the House of Commons, the elected MPs, and the House of Lords, the unelected part. It is also known as the legislature, as it makes the laws, under the direction of the executive. The second key institution is the executive, or the government,

---

5. Brandon Lewis, Hansard, Vol 679 Col 509 8 September 2020: 'Yes, this does break international law in a very specific and limited way. We are taking the power to disapply the EU law concept of direct effect, required by article 4, in certain very tightly defined circumstances.'. In the event, the breach did not occur.
6. This was a political choice, not a constitutional requirement. Constitutionally, the referendum was advisory.
7. Thomas Hobbes, *Leviathan* (Penguin, 1980) 227
8. John Locke, *An essay concerning the true original, extent and end of civil government*, in *Social Contract*, ed Ernest Barker (Oxford University Press, 1962) 143.

in plain language. The Prime Minister and the Cabinet are the key elements. As its name suggests, it is in place to execute the policies of the day. It is closely linked to Parliament, in that its members are also members of Parliament, they sit in Parliament, and are scrutinized by Parliament. The third key institution is the judiciary. The judges in the courts enforce the laws proposed by the executive and passed by Parliament, and also operate on occasion to constrain the government by ensuring compliance with the law, particularly by the use of judicial review, to ensure that the executive is not exceeding the powers given to it by Parliament. These are the simplest definitions of the three key institutions that can be given. They also summarise the liberal theory of government, in the values that underlie them. Liberalism as a political philosophy seeks to empower government 'enough but not too much'. This means both building power and limiting it—making and braking, as my title says. Making enough power to provide peace and security, particularly to property and its owners, while putting the brakes on to avoid tyranny, excessive power which would infringe liberty.

A Constitutional Tradition (2): Three Guiding Principles

To go a little further, each of these institutions can be understood by reference to a guiding principle which informs their purpose.

The guiding principle for Parliament is 'sovereignty'. This means (the classic definition comes from Dicey) that Parliament is sovereign in the specific sense of 'legislative sovereignty': it can 'make and unmake any law', and no power is recognised by law as having the right to set aside Parliament's legislation[9]. This is a consequence of the absence of a higher constitutional law. Where the latter could draw a line between the matters Parliament has the power to legislate upon and those that are beyond its powers, in the absence of such a higher constitutional law, Parliament is sovereign, and recognises no limits on its law-making powers.

The guiding principle for the judiciary is the idea of the 'Rule of Law'. In other jurisdictions, this might be called 'constitutionality', but not in the UK, for reasons that are hopefully becoming obvious. The idea of the Rule of Law is the idea that power—by which we mean executive power—cannot be arbitrary or discretionary, but must be

---

9. Albert Venn Dicey, *Introduction to the Study of the Law of the Constitution* (London: Macmillan, 1924), 38.

grounded in the laws passed by parliamentary sovereignty. The judiciary should enforce this.

The third guiding principle, which informs how the executive functions, is a little more complicated, as it is the rejection of a principle common to many constitutions—the principle of separation of powers. The separation of powers establishes clear distances between the three state institutions, whereas in the UK, we have fusion of powers between the executive (the Government) and legislature (Parliament)[10]. In practice, separation of powers in the UK comes to mean the more limited notion of the 'independence of the judiciary'.

Conclusion: Critique

With these definitions we can see that our study of constitution is essentially a study of institutions and their practices, and principles and their definitions. Noting that institutional practice contradicts animating principle is just the beginning of critique. Principles are always in part uncertain, contradictory in themselves, in their relation to the other principles and in their application to the institutions. Working out whether there is any consistency in a principle is a work of critical theory. Working out how three principles work or don't work together, likewise. Working out how this combination of three principles applies to the interactions of three institutions is, again, the work of critique. Whether one is engaged in the critical study of the law, or instead the opposite, which would be a study affirming that the law is a seamless whole, making perfect, consistent sense, is really a matter of emphasis. If one ends up finding seams, unpicking them, seeing gaps, seeing a patchwork of various materials sometimes pulling against each other, then one has engaged in critique. Such gaps, once seen, are harder to ignore than to acknowledge.[11]

Critique, then, is a demystifying project. We might conclude by distinguishing the liberal approach to constitution, which *makes* and applies the *brakes* to power, from the radical critique of constitution, which, in its unpicking of the apparent and ideological unity of constitution, ultimately also *breaks* power (breaks constitution, breaks

---

10. Walter Bagehot, *The English Constitution* (London: Collins Fontana, 1968) 68. 'A Cabinet is a combining committee—a *hyphen* which joins, a *buckle* which fastens the legislative part ... to the executive part.'
11. That a constitution not made all at once in a moment of rupture, but accumulated during a tradition of centuries will contain inconsistencies and contradictions is however both undeniable and widely denied.

history), opening up anew the question of if, and, if so, how, we should live with power.

FURTHER READINGS

- Walter Bagehot, *The English Constitution* (London: Collins Fontana, 1968). Bagehot's 1867 guide to his middle class readership on how to retain power in the face of an extending franchise, turning on a distinction between the 'dignified and the 'efficient' parts of the constitution. If you can find an edition with Richard Crossman's 1963 introduction, even better.
- I discuss his work in Angus McDonald, 'The Noble Lie: Critical Constitutionalism, Criticised' in *Polycentricity, The Multiple Scenes of Law*, ed. Ari Hirvonen (London: Pluto Press, 1998), 61-96.
- Albert Venn Dicey, *Introduction to the Study of the Law of the Constitution* (London: Macmillan, 1924) From the first edition in 1885, Dicey's study of 'two or three guiding principles' is unavoidable.
- I discuss his work in Angus McDonald, 'Dicey Dissected: Dominant, Dormant, Displaced' in *Feminist Perspectives on Public Law*, eds. Susan Millns & Noel Whitty (London: Cavendish, 1999) 107-128.

28

Constitutional Justice

PUBLIC LAW, POVERTY LAW

Karen Ashton

This is a public law practitioner's-eye view of our legal system. That system is based, in large part, on the idea that justice can be delivered by a one-on-one dispute resolution system. But can it? More particularly, is it fit for purpose in the delivery of *administrative* justice where the context is the exercise of state power and the purpose goes beyond justice for those affected and extends to the health of our constitutional settlement? For a public law practitioner in the social welfare field, it very quickly becomes clear that, when the delivery of justice is experienced in its context of systemic inequalities, discrimination and unfairness, a narrow individualistic dispute resolution model is a form of justice riddled with the same structural deficits.

Access to justice in the real world requires so much more than a theoretical right to 'go to court'. As a starting point, it requires both parties to the process to have sufficient knowledge and personal resources (financial and otherwise) to utilise the system of legal contestation and litigation. The availability of sufficient state support (a legal aid scheme) which helps with the costs of specialist legal advice and representation and truly effective, culturally embedded, public legal education are vital, and neither, currently, are properly fit for the 'justice' purpose they should serve. But improving an individual's access to the current dispute resolution process is not be enough, important though it is. That process itself needs to change and that need is at its most pressing in the public law field where one of the parties to the dispute is the state and the issue at stake is often one with significant implications for the quality of life and life chances of the other.

More often than not, if one person is subject to a particular incidence of unlawful state decision-making and action, they are one of many. Experience suggests illegality, unfairness and unreasonableness are very often not a random consequence of poor-quality decision-making by a rogue official. It is more often the product of some underlying systemic cause, ranging from the application of regulations which breach the Human Rights Act, to an unlawful practice which has become embedded because it is consistent with the interests of the state. For example, an unlawful time limit restriction on the availability of vital discretionary payments used to meet basic housing costs, irrespective of the indefinite nature of the need, delivers savings in the (never-ending) period of austerity. Some will be able to use the current system successfully to challenge and remedy the wrong for themselves, but for every individual who is able to do so, how many are not? And those who make up that 'excluded' group are (again) unlikely to be a random selection of individuals but are more likely to be the most powerless, however that is measured.

Court rulings on any dispute will apply across the board, so the wider impact should be felt by everyone affected. But whilst this is true, this fails to eliminate the 'real world' justice gap. We can identify three common hindrances.

The case settlement problem

Research has found about 60% of potential judicial review challenges settle following the sending of a formal pre-action letter to the public authority under challenge[1] and settlement is often in favour of the individual who is making the challenge. At the Law Centre, in some fields, such as social care, we find the percentage to be even higher—in the region of 80%. There is also a relatively high rate of settlement after judicial review proceedings have been issued.[2] Settlements (even those achieved after issue of proceedings which will have the benefit of some kind of court order bringing the proceedings to an end) will not necessarily include a provision which ensures that all those affected will take the benefit.

---

1 Varda Bondy and Maurice Sunkin,) *The Dynamics of Judicial Review Litigation: The resolution of public law challenges before final hearing* (The Public Law Project, 2009).
2. Robert Thomas, 'Mapping immigration judicial review litigation: an empirical legal analysis,' . *Public Law* (2015).

For example, a Clinical Commissioning Group (CCG) has a policy of funding only 20 nights of residential respite care away from home for adults with disabilities for whom they have responsibility. Jo is a young woman with learning disabilities and challenging behaviour who lives with her family, who are her main carers. When the local social services authority was responsible for providing support services, they funded 40 nights of residential respite for her. As her behaviour deteriorated, responsibility passed from social services to the NHS. The CCG took over the commissioning responsibility and reduced this respite provision by half, failing to consider her individual needs and the willingness and the ability of the family carers to continue in that role. In response to the formal pre-action protocol letter warning of an imminent judicial review challenge, the previous level of respite care was reinstated. But the unlawful blanket policy remained in place, to be used again for others who might not find their way to specialist legal help, risking the breakdown of family caring arrangements. The failure to correct underlying wrongs cannot be explained away as mere oversight; it is important to recognise its systemic underpinnings; its relationship to the interests of the state.

This kind of problem arises even in cases which would be thought to be immune. For example, if the challenge is to the lawfulness of regulations which cause the unlawful action as a direct result of their application, it might be thought that a successful settlement would necessarily require an amendment to those regulations to cure the legal wrong whereupon all of those who have been affected would benefit from that success. However, in recent times, the Law Centre has had experience, on more than one occasion, of a government department delaying the necessary amendment to regulations which it had conceded were unlawfully discriminatory. Although accompanied by an agreed mechanism to try and ensure that others would not continue to be affected, that has proved not to provide a failproof guarantee. Two of the six projects to date undertaken by the Strategic Public Law Clinic (a joint initiative between Warwick Law in the Community and Central England Law Centre) have worked on ensuring implementation of an outcome in two such cases: the availability of free nursery education for two years olds to certain migrant families and of student finance for students with the benefit of humanitarian protection.[3]

---

3. 'New Toolkit launched to help students with humanitarian protection access home fees and student finance' Central England Law Centre.

The Practicalities of 'Pure' Public Interest Litigation

There are any number of barriers to 'pure' public interest litigation -litigation which carries no personal benefit to the person bringing the case. A court will sometimes agree to hear a case which has become academic for the individual bringing the challenge because it has wider implications. But, even if the individual wants to continue to pursue a case of no real further interest for them, the availability of legal aid to fund that continued action in these circumstances is very limited; there has to be *some* potential benefit for the individual, for example, securing a declaration that there has been a breach of the rights protected by the Human Rights Act 1998.

'Pure' public interest litigation is possible but difficult. Such actions are usually brought (when they are) by NGOs. Although a court may be satisfied as to the organisation's 'standing' to do so because of its policy interests or charitable objectives, legal aid funding is only available to individuals. The issue of resourcing such an action is a significant barrier and such cases will tend to be limited to ones raising very high profile issues with serious national implications. It is very unlikely to be the answer to the 'everyday' systemic unlawfulness of, for example, local policies.

Identifying the Underlying Systemic Cause

The third issue to consider is the visibility, or rather the invisibility, of underlying systemic causes. As the courts have noted, a public law challenge is one which starts with *"the vast majority of the cards ... in the* [public] *authority's hands"*.[4] Judicial review is not a form of public inquiry—the court does not have an investigative function and so a less obvious underlying systemic cause of the individual decision or action is not always revealed. The developing ground of systemic unfairness in judicial review is helpful.[5] Matters that might have been seen as purely mal-administrative, and therefore a subject for complaint rather than litigation, may now be characterised as issues of lawfulness.

But, in order to make a 'systems' challenge, significant work is

---

4. *R v Lancashire County Council ex parte Huddleston* [1986] 2 All ER 941 [945] (Sir John D)..
5. See the principles set out in *R(Refugee Legal Centre) v Secretary of State for the Home Department* [2004] EWCA Civ 1481; [2005] 1 WLR 2219, and summarized by the Divisional Court in *R(Woolcock) v Secretary of State for Communities and Local Government and others* [2018] EWHC 17 (Admin).

often required to obtain the evidence. Judicial review is a front-loaded process—it is for the claimant to establish there is an arguable case if the court is to grant permission for it to proceed to full consideration. The Legal Aid Agency may grant funding for substantial investigative work, but preliminary research will be required to establish that the case meets the gatekeeping criteria.

Ombudsman schemes do have investigative functions. The two main statutory schemes in England are the Local Government and Social Care Ombudsman [LGSCO][6], dealing with complaints against local government, and the Parliamentary and Health Service Ombudsman dealing with complaints against central government and the NHS.[7] In its Annual Review 2018-19, the LGSCO acknowledged the increase in cases they see with systemic problems:

> Where we identify common themes in the complaints we investigate we may publish a focus report or guidance note to help authorities avoid similar problems.... With more of the clear-cut problems often resolved before coming to us, *we are seeing more cases showing underlying problems with systems, policies and the way procedures are being applied.*[8]

One of the cases referenced in this report was summarised as follows:

> Our investigation found that Wiltshire Council was setting maximum budgets when calculating the cost of people's care. A complaint about a man's care being cut revealed that the council was using an outdated matrix tool to calculate personal budget amounts. The tool was contrary to the Care Act 2014 and we reminded all councils that eligible care needs must be based on assessed needs not on capped-costs. *The council agreed to stop using the tool and to review all similar cases to ensure no other service users had been similarly affected. This review resulted in revised provision for 13 other service users.*[9]

---

6. 'The Local Government & Social Care Ombudsman', accessed 22 December 2020, https://www.lgo.org.uk/.
7. 'Welcome to the Parliamentary and Health Service Ombudsman', accessed 22 December 2020, https://www.ombudsman.org.uk/.
8. Local Government & Social Care Ombudsman, Review of Local Government Complaints 2018-19. Coventry: Local Government & Social Care Ombudsman, 2019. Accessed 24 February 2021. https://www.lgo.org.uk/assets/attach/5655/LG-Review-FINAL.pdf. [Emphasis added.]
9. Local Government & Social Care Ombudsman, Review of Local Government Complaints 2018-19. Coventry: Local Government & Social Care Ombudsman, 2019. Accessed 24 February 2021. https://www.lgo.org.uk/assets/attach/5655/LG-Review-FINAL.pdf. 6 [Emphasis added.]

Clearly this was a case where the local authority's decision-making was unlawful (it was contrary to the Care Act 2014), and systemic, and the Ombudsman crafted a remedy with the aim of reaching all those affected. But the Ombudsman scheme is not, in and of itself, the magic answer:

- The Ombudsman can only investigate if a complaint is brought and complaints cases are also subject to aspects of the 'early settlement' problem.
- The Ombudsman is not allowed to investigate a case where an individual has a remedy in court unless it is not reasonable to expect that course of action to be taken.
- It can take a long time from the start of using the complaints procedure to the point of publication of an Ombudsman report and the Ombudsman, unlike the court, does not have the power to grant an interim remedy pending the outcome.

In any event the Ombudsman is, generally, not the appropriate place to resolve contentious questions of lawfulness, such as the correct interpretation of a legislative provision.

If access to justice is to be more than theoretical in the public law sphere, we need a radical shift away from the largely individualistic 'dispute resolution' system. We need holistic administrative justice which recognises that injustice will persist for those least able to make use of whatever system is in place unless that system takes every opportunity to identify and right systemic wrongs. Although a government is currently contemplating reform to judicial review[10], it is it is not with this aim in mind. Its purpose is to consider *"whether the right balance is being struck between the rights of citizens to challenge executive decisions and the need for effective and efficient government"*[11] in a context where the view of Government is that the balance has shifted too far in favour of the citizen. In those circumstances, any reform is very unlikely to tackle questions of inequality and exclusion. But if, at some time in the future, a review is launched which is driven by these concerns, the following are some of the ideas that might be worth some attention:

---

10. 'Judicial Review Reform', GOV.UK, accessed 21 March 2021. https://www.gov.uk/government/consultations/judicial-review-reform.
11. 'Government launches independent panel to look at judicial review', accessed 22 December 2020, https://www.gov.uk/government/news/government-launches-independent-panel-to-look-at-judicial-review.

- A legal aid scheme which funds interest groups (whether in the form of an established NGO or not) to bring cases to address systemic issues at a local or national level;
- Public sector ombudsman schemes with own-initiative powers to investigate issues which appear to have systemic causes without having to wait for an individual complaint to be made or reach the Ombudsman stage;
- An integrated court and ombudsman system with flexible cross-referral powers so that the court can have the benefit of the ombudsman's investigative function but can also rule on points of law and unlawfulness by reason of systemic unfairness;
- An administrative court able and willing to proactively supervise final orders following settlement or trial in order to ensure all those who should benefit do so;
- The availability of penalties that can be imposed on public authorities (and perhaps even senior public officials) who knowingly allow unlawful practices to continue.

But we may have some time to wait for that opportunity to arise. In the meantime, a public law practitioner who is concerned about social and constitutional justice will continue to feel the frustrations of their role within the current repeat 'case by case' system. The most immediate answer is not only to make use of whatever tools there are to hand to maximise the impact of each case (whenever compatible with the interests and wishes of the individual client), but also to develop new ones (such as the Strategic Public Law Clinic[12]) wherever possible within the current framework.

---

12. 'Strategic Public Law Clinic', accessed 22 December 2020, https://warwick.ac.uk/fac/soc/law/applying/linc/projects/.

Concept: The State

Illan rua Wall

In *The Nervous System*, Michael Taussig points out that we habitually identify the state as a thing, which then becomes 'animated with a will and mind of its own.'[1] The state looks after health and welfare; it defends the territory from incursion, manages the flows of people across borders; it regulates economic activity; and manages the legal system. The state is a thing which acts (for better or worse) on the population. At the level of common sense this all seems fairly straight-forward. But what is it, in each of those functions, that *is* the state? What is the additional element that makes these functions into 'the state'.

One of the primary activities of the state is identifying its state-actors. It gives people jobs, and responsibilities, uniforms, codes of conduct, and health-and-safety training. It gives them a sense of themselves *as state actors*. So when a Department of Work & Pensions caseworker sanctions a family on social welfare, he might feel the state's desire to 'protect tax-payers' money'; Or when a police officer raises her truncheon against a protestor, she might feel the state's aim to 'protect the public's order'. In these moments, the state is a set of ideas and feelings that helps these people make sense of their actions.

In an interview on Taussig's book *The Magic of the State*, Daniel Levi Strauss asks: 'How much of the magic of the state is manipulation by state operators, and how much is projection from the people onto those

---

1. Michael Taussig, *The Nervous System* (Routledge, 1992) 112

operators and operations'? Taussig responds very simply. He says, 'It's a circle.'[2] By this he means that it is not enough to understand how the state functions through its actors, but also to see that the populace must take part in this magic. They must be enchanted by the state, convinced on an ideological and affective level of the pre-eminent power of the state to protect and change society. Force alone will not get millions of people to comply willingly, most will have to be enchanted. Those that remain can be 'managed'—stop and search, racialised policing, disciplinary social welfare rules, precarious employment. The magic of the state enchants the majority in such a way that the force exercised on the minority becomes invisible. It is a circle, Taussig says. The state is a thing because, everyday, we make it so. This is the magic of the state.

---

2. Michael Taussig, 'The Magic of the State: An Interview With Michael Taussig' Cabinet Magazine, (2005) https://www.cabinetmagazine.org/issues/18/strauss_taussig.php (accessed on 15/06/2021)

Concept: Ideology

Tor Krever

The richest strand of thinking about ideology can be found in the Marxist tradition. Marx insisted that our ideas about the world and consciousness of social problems are rooted in actual social relations—what he called 'material conditions'.[1] But they are not simply a reflection of material conditions, in fact, they often distort or mystify those material conditions, distracting us from our oppression and exploitation. In this way ideology can protect structures of power. Importantly then, on this view, to say an idea is 'ideological' is not simply to call it false or an illusion, but to insist on a direct relationship between consciousness and power.[2] Ideology, can be found in the ideas, but also the discursive strategies and rhetorical practices, that serve to constitute and stabilise relations of power. In John Thompson's formulation, ideology points us to how 'the meaning constructed and conveyed by symbolic forms serves, in particular circumstances, to establish and sustain structured social relations from which some individuals and groups benefit more than others'.[3]

---

1. Karl Marx and Friedrich Engels, *The German Ideology* (Lawrence & Wishart, 1942)
2. Terry Eagleton, Introduction to *Ideology* (Routledge, 1994) 7.
3. John Thompson, *Ideology and Modern Culture: Critical Social Theory in the Era of Mass Communication* (Stanford University Press, 1990) 72-73.

In this sense, ideology is a really powerful way of thinking about law and legal discourse. In the sphere of exchange, individuals are understood legally as juridical equals meeting in the marketplace to engage in acts freely of their own will.[4] This legal construction of abstract equality, however, obscures the unequal power of capitalist and worker—namely the economic need of the worker to sell his labour. That need lies behind and animates the inequality of the exchange relationship. But this inequality has no bearing under the rule of law: however unequal they may be, 'parties to the exchange transaction appear as equal persons who just happen to own different things'.[5] The power that capitalists exert over workers, as well as broader questions about the distribution of and access to material and cultural resources in society, recedes from view. We may recognise that labour relations are not in reality equal, but the law treats them as though they were. The focus on formal equality under the rule of law thus serves to deflect attention from the real social relations. Cloaked in the rule of law's garbs of equality and freedom, inequalities of capitalist social relations appear not only legitimate but fair.

Marx's analysis points to the need for critical scholars to look beyond the neutral façade of law to how legal discourse operates ideologically to sustain constellations of power. Indeed today there exists a rich body of critical legal scholarship showing how the claim of the rule of law to neutrality is, at best, a sleight of hand. At heart it reflects and reproduces political relations of power.[6] It is precisely in acting *as though* law were neutral that legal discourse operates *ideologically*, not merely making those inequalities appear a natural, even inevitable, part of a neutral and impartial legal order.

---

4. See Karl Marx, *Capital* Vol 1 (Vintage Books, 1977) 272, 280.
5. Jeffrey Reiman, 'The Marxian Critique of Criminal Justice', (1987) 6 Crim Justice Ethics 30, 38.
6. See, e.g., Diane Polon, 'Toward a Theory of Law and Patriarchy' in David Kairys (ed), *The Politics of Law: A Progressive Critique* (Pantheon, 1982) 294. For an important example of ideology critique in international law, see Susan Marks, *The Riddle of All Constitutions: International Law, Democracy & the Critique of Ideology* (Oxford University Press, 2000).

31

Witnessing Health Law

MEDICAL LAW, HEALTH LAW

Ruth Fletcher

Medical law has given a lot of space to the witness as an external source of knowledge, knowledge which law needs but cannot generate by itself.[1] This witness is conventionally perceived as an outsider, a third party to legal process and an independent source of expertise about what counts in people's lives before the law. Through these witnesses, legal audiences have their imaginations shaped by the evidence they receive. Law sees the specialist experts are the ones who know the significance of injury, decision-making, illness, and other lived phenomena. Psychiatric evidence of personal 'insight' becomes the ground on which legal decision-making capacity is granted or denied.[2] Statistical probabilities limit the legal threshold for compensatable harm.

Medical law scholars have raised concerns about the contribution of such witnessing to hidden law-making,[3] medicalised hierarchies of knowledge,[4] and 'dangerous liaisons' between psychiatry and law.[5]

---

1. John Harrington *Towards a Rhetoric of Medical Law* (Abingdon: Routledge, 2018); John Harrington, 'Elective affinities: The art of medicine and the common law' 55 *Northern Ireland Legal Quarterly* (2004), 259.
2. Paula Case, 'Dangerous Liaisons? Psychiatry and Law in the Court of Protection—Expert Discourses of 'Insight' (and 'Compliance')' 24.3 *Medical Law Review* (2016), 360.
3. Jonathan Montgomery, Caroline Jones and Hazel Biggs, 'Hidden Law-Making and Medical Jurisprudence' 77 *Modern Law Review* (2014), 343
4. Beverly Clough, 'People Like That: Realising the Social Model in Mental Capacity Jurisprudence' 23.1 *Medical Law Review* (2015), 53; Jaime Lindsey, 'Competing Professional Knowledge Claims About Mental Capacity in the Court of Protection' 28.1 *Medical Law Review*, (2020), 1.
5. Paula Case, 'Dangerous Liaisons?'

Here I want to pick up on that concern and propose a way of thinking about witnessing which takes these processes seriously, but invests in them from a critical feminist perspective. Rather than seek a counter to hidden and hierarchical knowledge-making via more transparency in legal witnessing processes, I offer a way of working with witnessing that improvises[6] with legal consciousness[7] and engages with partial, half-hidden meanings. If criticism is to work reparatively,[8] we need to find ways of occupying and repurposing existing legal terrain for building worlds anew.[9] Here I ask what would it mean to take law's witnessing practices seriously, if also playfully, as processes which move across porous boundaries and enable legal reproduction?[10] How might we refigure legal witnessing in more partial, popular and participatory terms?

In answering these questions, this piece looks towards scholarship which works with situated and embodied witnessing[11] to build a critical concept of legal witnessing that is mixed, reproductive, and comforting. Secondly, it thinks about how such witnessing makes it possible to see different dimensions of the key commitments that drive medical law along. Whether we pay attention to the reduction of harm and illness, or the reproduction of power and privilege, or even to the promotion of choice, critical scholars and students of medical law need concepts and methods which allow us to see harm/illness/power/privilege/choice as they actually work in people's lives. Understanding how witnesses and witnessing practices gather together to make a case for medical

---

6. Sara Ramshaw, *Justice as Improvisation: The Law of the Extempore.* (Abingdon: Routledge, 2013)
7. Simon Halliday and Bronwen Morgan 'I fought the law and the law won? Legal Consciousness and the Critical Imagination' 66.1 *Current Legal Problems* (2013), 1.
8. Eve Kosofsky Sedgwick, 'Paranoid Reading and Reparative Reading; or, You're So Paranoid, You Probably Think This Introduction is About You in *Novel Gazing: Queer Readings in Fiction* (Durham: Duke University Press, 1997).
9. Davina Cooper, *Everyday Utopias: The Conceptual Life of Promising Spaces* (Durham: Duke University Press, 2013); Davina Cooper and Didi Herman 'Doing activism like a state: Progressive municipal government, Israel/Palestine and BDS', 38.1 *Environment and Planning C: Politics and Space* (2020), 40-59.
10. Ruth Fletcher, 'Entangled rights and reproductive temporality: Legal form, continuous improvement of living conditions, and social reproduction' in Jessie Hohmann and Beth Goldblatt *The Right to the Continuous Improvement of Living Conditions: Responding to Complex Global Challenges* (London: Bloomsbury, 2021)
11. Donna Haraway, *Modest_Witness@Second Millennium. FemaleMan_Meets_OncoMouse* (Abingdon: Routledge, 2018); Michelle Murphy, *Seizing the Means of Reproduction: Entanglements of Feminism, Health and Technoscience* (Durham: Duke University Press, 2012).

law to move along, could reveal concepts which may have liberalism in their lineage, but in a lineage that is mixed and inclusive. As Hill Collins has shown us, watching how knowledge of individual autonomy is actually built by racialised domestic labourers may reveal a concept of choice that is not liberal.[12] Rather witnesses of (reproductive) choice could be more invested in the kind of 'self-definition' that is created in relation with others and by generating alternative ways of living in an unjust world, a practice like the one Hill Collins found in the double-consciousness of Black feminist thought.

If we turn to critical theorising on witnessing we gain a collection of curious practices to inform and animate critical approaches to medical law and medico-legal studies. Such a collection pulls feminist and critical concern in medical law beyond calls for the appreciation of care[13] and embodiment[14] as sites of medical law. In building a collection of witnessing practices, we also make available a set of knowledges which work with the partiality and incompleteness of legal knowledge, and provide stimulation and sustenance in the struggle for justice. Critique of medical law, and indeed law more generally, could benefit from a critical repertoire of witnessing practices that looks at how partial, compositional[15] knowledges are built in particular sites, but stay open and ongoing.[16] Such witnessing reaches out across borders and has the potential to assemble into some kind of multi-dimensional, moving whole that makes a just world possible.

Critical Witnessing

Feminist science and technology scholars have provided an important touchstone for thinking about witnessing through their elaboration of the techniques of scientific observation as partial and participatory processes of knowledge generation. Haraway's critique of the modest

---

12. Patricia Hill Collins, *Black Feminist Thought: Knowledge, Consciousness and the Politics of Empowerment* (Abingdon: Routledge, 2009); on non-liberal approaches to freedom and rights, see further Ratna Kapur, *Gender, Alterity and Human Rights: Freedom in a Fishbowl* (Edward Elgar Publishing, 2020).
13. Sally Sheldon and Michael Thomson, *Feminist Perspectives on Health Care Law* (Abingdon: Routledge, 1998)
14. Ruth Fletcher, Marie Fox and Julie McCandless 'Legal Embodiment: Analysing the Body of Healthcare Law' 16.3 *Medical Law Review* (2008), 231.
15. Denise Ferreira da Silva, 'Fractal Thinking' 2 *Accessions* (2016)
16. Veronica Gago, *Feminist International: How to change everything* (London: Verso, 2020).

witness of scientific investigation is a key intervention in the feminist science and technology studies approach to knowledge production, an approach which speaks to concerns in medical law.[17] Haraway recuperates an idea of the modest witness, away from the neutral 'culture of no culture' of self-invisible technoscientists, and towards a yearning for knowledge projects as freedom projects. This a relentlessly polyglot, material and practical yearning which she associates with feminist sciences studies. For her 'valid witness depends not only on modesty but also on nurturing and acknowledging alliances with a lively array of others, who are like and unlike, human and not, inside and outside what have been the defended boundaries of hegemonic selves and powerful places'.[18]

Murphy has built on Haraway's critique of the neutral scientific witness as a knower who leaves context and motivation out of knowledge.[19] By theorising the knowledge-generating practices of US feminist self-help groups as they develop protocols for observing vaginas and acquiring gynaecological knowledge, Murphy elaborates an account of immodest witnessing. These techniques of assembled knowledge production were important in challenging gynaecological control of women's reproductive bodies. But they also provide a way of thinking epistemologically which makes three, at least, theoretical contributions. In developing its own protocols and blueprints for acquiring, documenting and sharing gynaecological knowledge, 'protocol feminism', relies on an agency that is both the subject and object of knowledge creation (e.g. the self-examining woman). Second protocol feminism combines experimentation *and* repetition as protocols for vagina examination are developed as DIY experiments and then repeated, adapted and adjusted with different audiences. Third, protocol feminism is always gathering the whole together by bringing different partial perspectives into conversation with each.

I see 'cheeky witnessing' as an example of how art-activists perform this kind of situated and embodied witnessing, and make another contribution to the moving repertoire of practices that observe medico-legal problems from multiple sides.[20] In thinking with Speaking of IMELDA as a particularly irreverent, playful and dissenting group of activists,[21]

---

17. Haraway, *Modest Witness*.
18. Haraway, *Modest Witness*, 269
19. Murphy, *Seizing the Means of Reproduction*
20. Ruth Fletcher 'Cheeky Witnessing' 124.1 *Feminist Review* (2020) 124.
21. Speaking of I.M.E.L.D.A. 'Dirty work still to be done: Retrieving and activating

that contributed to making a call for legal change persuasive, cheeky witnessing showed how this 'least respectable' of practices has something to contribute to a critical account of legal witnessing. Speaking of IMELDA engaged in actions which crashed important public events, including a fundraising dinner with the Taoiseach of Ireland, entertained other feminist activists at marches for reproductive rights, and generated a living archive of reproductive injustice (including through the Knickers for Choice campaign discussed below). Between 2013 and 2018 they organised as a London-based group of feminist Irish migrants and became a small but regular feature in the moving collection of activities that produced repeal of the eighth amendment and the constitutional restriction of abortion. In this way, a critical legal approach to witnessing brings Murphy's concept of alternative scientific witnessing into conversation with feminist art-activism in legal reform campaigns.[22]

Cheeky witnessing practices move a concern for partial and participatory perspectives into the realm of challenging state and legal control of pregnancy, abortion and reproduction, as they improvise with legal consciousness. Such witnessing is affective in its messiness as it mixes different sources of incomplete knowledge together and mocks a law which denies reproductive choice. It is itself a form of reproductive labour which synthesises the contributions of other reproductive labourers such as migrant cleaners, domestic labourers and pregnant people into a call for legal action. These witnesses reach out to occupy public places and make them more comfortable for sexual and reproductive bodies by connecting different places up with each other.[23] This is a witnessing which joins with other witnesses in facing down a care-less state, much like feminist strikers who withdraw their care labour in calling for public care of the one body with all bodies.[24] They divest from the state's legal infrastructure in order to invest their resources elsewhere.

---

feminist acts of resistance' *Contemporary Theatre Review* (2015) online at: http://www.contemporarytheatrereview.org/2015/margaretta-darcy/

22. Fletcher 'Cheeky Witnessing'
23. Fletcher 'Cheeky Witnessing' 127
24. Gago, *Feminist International*, 9.

Witnessing Choice

Cheeky witnessing was one among many forms of witnessing that contributed to critical and constructive repair of medico-legal worlds as the Irish public voted in favour of abortion rights and reproductive choice in 2018.[25] Legal consciousness of other witnesses, of one's body as a 'body that never depends solely on itself',[26] was evident in campaigns which proudly and loudly called for choice along the way. The Knickers for Choice campaign provides one example of a migrant led kind of witnessing which made the case for reproductive choice not just by disrupting an Irish state's response to global relations of reproduction, but also by foregrounding international solidarity among sexual and reproductive agents as the wearers of knickers. The campaign called on people everywhere to hang their knickers in a public place, photograph them and share the photographs on social media with the hashtag #KnickersForChoice. As carefully placed knickers appeared on a laundry line across the façades of public buildings such as a rural post office, they joined up interested parties from around the globe with feminist activists campaigning for constitutional change in Ireland. But they also reproduced solidarity with the Indian feminists whose chaddis or knickers had participated in the pink chaddi campaign as women objected to their public presence being policed for modesty.[27]

The social media campaign was launched with the sharing of a video of 'The Quiet Woman?',[28] a performance action which they improvised and filmed.[29] The video follows the actions of a group of women dressed in red, wearing headscarves, as they 'clean up' the Irish Embassy in London and hang knickers for choice on its façade. The women call for reproductive choice and abortion rights. They refuse to be quiet and appear as a curious collection of happy housewives and glamorous migrant cleaners. As they hang laundry and clean up public buildings,

---

25. Ruth Fletcher, '#Repealedthe8th: Translating travesty, global conversation, and the Irish abortion referendum' 26.3 *Feminist Legal Studies* (2018), 233; Kath Browne and Sydney Calkin *After Repeal: Rethinking Abortion Politics* (London: Zed, 2020).
26. Gago, *Feminist International*, 55.
27. Hemangini Gupta, 'Taking Action: The Desiring Subjects of Neoliberal Feminism in India' 17.1 *Journal of International Women's Studies* (2016), 152.
28. Speaking of I.M.E.L.D.A. 'The Quiet Woman?', 23 September 2014, available to view here: https://www.youtube.com/watch?time_continue=8&v=cEkD_cWgxaE (film credit Kevin Biderman) [last accessed 14 August 2019]
29. See Speaking of I.M.E.L.D.A., Knickers for Choice https://www.speakingofimelda.org/knickers-for-choice.

they connect different kinds of sexual and reproductive labour and make these connections the basis of their knowing call for choice. They are migrant cleaners, domestic goddesses, glamorous sexual beings, and feminist activists dressed in trade-mark red, all at the same time.

As Walsh explains,[30] the action is knowing in its use of the washer woman figure who cleans up around her as she criticizes the Irish state for its neglect of abortion-seeking people. By connecting pregnant people with domestic labourers, these witnesses locate abortion as a moment in social reproduction and reproductive labour. They repurpose 'choice' as one dimension of a global struggle for reproductive justice, a global struggle which draws from feminists in the global south for inspiration and information. They witness in a way that makes the experience of migrants and reproductive labourers central to the call for choice. An action such as Knickers for Choice makes choice a goal of internationalist, materialist and migrant-led feminist struggle, and demedicalises authority over reproduction.

This witnessing of choice as a medico-legal need draws on feminist rather than medical scientific knowledge. It is messy and irreverent, multi-dimensional and fractal, as it provides shelter and comfort for multiple bodies. Those who *use* choice provide the evidence and expertise, as they demand that choice be made available over and over again, often at considerable personal cost. This call for choice materialises a critical feminist internationalism by drawing on a collectivist and cross-generational feminist history. It matters that medico-legal tools such as reproductive rights are held accountable to that material history, rather than positioned as themselves the initiators and agents of legal reproduction.

Conclusion

If critical approaches to medical law are going to be constructive and reparative in building another world, then we need critical knowledge practices which value the stories of those who have found ingenious ways to survive the illnesses and injuries inflicted by poverty, racism and patriarchy. Finding and following different witnesses of medical law as they tell stories or paint pictures of legal effects gives us a way to build on Harrington's call for a reorientation towards the rhetoric of medical

---

30. Helena Walsh, 'Hanging Our Knickers Up: Asserting Autonomy and Cross-Border Solidarity in the #RepealThe8th Campaign' 124.1 *Feminist Review* (2020), 165.

law, and away from the limitations of a normative ethical framework.[31] Witnesses of knicker-objects, that cross borders and comfort the exiled and alienated, stretch space in much the same way that Grabham's activist lawyers expand and contract time for sick clients seeking financial support.[32] They show us how to move medical law beyond jurisdictional and national boundaries[33] and participate in the global not only on the terms of public health concerns but also on the terms of collected individuals. By reproducing with different legal sources and making careful connections, witnessing can also be a conceptual means of drawing on abolitionist and critical race perspectives. Such perspectives seek to make everyday care an alternative to everyday carcerality,[34] and to repair the health and welfare of those who are living with the legacy of colonial theft.[35] Witnessing offers medical law, and law more generally, a repertoire of mixed, reproductive and comforting critical practices that could yet build a careful, multi-dimensional and moving legal infrastructure by gathering together partial, participatory and popular knowledge.

---

31. Harrington, *Towards a Rhetoric of Medical Law*.
32. Emily Grabham, *Brewing Legal Times* (Toronto: University of Toronto Press, 2016).
33. Sharifah Sekalala, *Soft Law and Global Health Problems* (Cambridge: Cambridge University Press, 2017).
34. Sarah Lamble, 'Practising Everyday Abolition', in Koshka Duff ed. *Abolishing the Police: An Illustrated introduction* (Dog Section Press, 2020) 147; Vanessa Thompson, 'Policing in Europe: disability justice and abolitionist intersectional care' 62.3 *Race and Class* (2021), 61.
35. Nadine El Enany, *Bordering Britain* (Manchester: Manchester University Press, 2020).

32

A Living Labour of Law

Employment Law, Labour Law

Anastasia Tataryn

Employment law: the laws regulating the contractual relationships of persons at work. To suggest that, based on this definition, employment law is a simple field of law is a chimera. Employment law, the law that governs, regulates, guides, relations in the workplace, is also often referred to as labour law. The former suggests a clearer delineation and definition of 'employment', discussed below, whereas the latter often suggests a broader scope: 'labour' accounts for work beyond an employment arrangement or contract, and has been theorised as a legal field that is, at its core, constitutional and public/political, as opposed to private and based on a contractual model of relationships and bargaining power.[1] Nevertheless, whether we call it employment law or labour law, as a legal field regulating relations of work, labour/employment exists between private (contracts, obligations), public (social law, welfare law, EU law) and administrative (tribunal processes and industrial relations/human resources regulatory processes and bodies) laws.

Scratching the surface of the claim above that employment law is the law regulating the contractual relationships of persons of work, it is imperative to clarify, what is work? What is the nature of this contractual arrangement, is it individual, personal, sector-specific, or collective? What does it mean to be in employment (an 'employee'), as opposed to a worker or self-employed? Labour/employment law thus begins by asking questions. How we engage with the responses to

---

1. Ruth Dukes, *The Labour Constitution: The Enduring Idea of Labour Law*. Series: Oxford monographs on labour law. (Oxford University Press: Oxford, 2014).

these questions, as well as find relevance in the answers that have been given by scholars, practitioners, and people-at-work, forms the basis of critical thinking in employment law.

Conventionally, UK employment law's boundary is found at the definitions laid out in the Employment Rights Act 1996 (ERA), section 230 (1), which provides a definition of who is an employee. Simply, '"employee" means an individual who has entered into or works under (or, where the employment has ceased, worked under) a contract of employment'. Such an employee is entitled to the rights and protections of the ERA, with some additional provisions depending on ones' continuity of employment (the time requirement often depends on regulations put in place by the government of the day). If one does not meet this s 230 (1) definition, one can be considered a 'worker' (s 230 (3) ERA), and certain, limited, rights apply to 'workers' as well as 'employees'; a worker has access to a lesser category of protections, i.e. minimum wage and working time regulations, and protection against discrimination at work according to the Equality Act 2010. However, the gamut of employment rights is unavailable to s 230 (3) 'workers'. Strictly, employment law begins and ends with the rights and protections granted to those with 'employee' status, those in a contract of employment.

A person in self-employment, also referred to as an independent contractor, has even less recourse under Employment law/ ERA 1996. Employment law traditionally excludes such persons, self-employed, who are assumed to be in contracts individually entered into to provide a direct service (contract for service) versus the employment contract that is a commitment to provide ongoing services (contract of service). It is, furthermore, assumed within traditional definitions in employment law that a contract for service (self-employment) lacks the requisite amount of control held by the employer over the employee in a contract of service (employment). The 'satisfactory' level of control, however, continues to be vague and ambiguously defined in UK employment case law.[2]

---

2. Linda Clarke, 'Mutuality of Obligations and the Contract of Employment: Carmichael and Another v National Power plc,'. *The Modern Law Review* 6/5 (2000), 757-763; Einat Albin, 'The Case of Quashie: Between the Legalisation of Sex Work and the Precariousness of Personal Service Work,' *Industrial Law Journal* 42/ 2 (2013), 180-191. See *Pimlico Plumbers Ltd and Another v Smith* [2018] UKSC 29; *Montgomery v. Johnson Underwood Ltd* [2001] EWCA Civ 318; *Carmichael and Another v National Power plc* [2000] IRLR 43 (HL).

There is no doubt that employment/labour law emerges from practice, from the very experience of work and labour in the world. Currently, headlines bring to light exploitation in gig economy labour, precarious work, the vulnerability and exposure of frontline workers during the Covid-19 pandemic. These are all employment law issues. Seeing employment law in its context[3] sheds light on how the boundaries or parameters of employment law necessarily must stretch beyond traditional definitions of the employment contract and s. 230 of the ERA if employment law is meant to be reflective of people at work. The effects, consequences and challenges of the limited definition of 'employee' in existing employment law surround us in the disconnect between what was seen, pre-Covid-19 as a rise in people-at-work, but also a rise in in-work poverty.[4] Jobs may be available, but not employment.

Employment law's traditional limit at the contract of employment exposes the shortfalls of the contract of employment, and a growing fallacy that self-employment contracts are 'independent' contracts. The notion of independence further assumes that there is some equality of bargaining power between the two contracting parties in self-employment arrangements, completely ignoring a structurally reinforced imbalance of power between those who are giving work and payment, and those who are seeking work and an income. Indeed, the individual standardised contract of employment has gained prominence in employment relations and practice in the past 20 years, in contrast to collective agreements and bargaining models more prevalent in mid 20th century industrial labour.[5] The individualised model of employment relations has further precipitated into increasingly non-standard types of employment, where workers not only have less legal protection due to the definition of their labour contract but lack solidarity with other workers in similar situations as a result of the individualised casual labour arrangements, fixed term contracts, agency work and/or subcontracted labour.[6] Workers, increasingly individual 'contractors'

---

3. David Cabrelli, *Employment Law in Context*, 3rd ed. (Oxford: Oxford University Press, 2018).
4. Helen Barnard, (2018) 'UK Poverty 2018' Joseph Rowantree Foundation [Online] accessed 24th December 2020 https://www.jrf.org.uk/report/uk-poverty-2018
5. Mark Freedland & Nicola Kountouris, *The Legal Construction of Personal Work Relations* (Oxford University Press, 2011).
6. Guy Standing, *The Precariat: The New Dangerous Class*. (Bloomsbury, 2011); Judy Fudge and Kendra Strauss ed. *Temporary work, agencies and unfree labour: insecurity in the new world of work* (Routledge, 2013)

disassociated from a collective sector, are often given a take-it-or-leave-it standardised contract that may specify their independence as self-employed. Employment relations communicate a mirage of freedom and flexibility. Meanwhile, the conditions of the work arrangement may have levels of control and dependency characteristic of worker or employee contracts in addition to circumventing obligations such as providing consistent work, opportunities for advancement and/or leave, or a decent, living wage .[7]

Living and working within a society that is experiencing profound shocks in labour market shifts, opportunities, and shortfalls, case law from employment tribunals up to the UK Supreme Court demonstrate that employment is changing. Case law recognises that there is a pressing need for employment law to catch up. For example, the recent controversial case where Uber appealed a Court of Appeal decision that Uber drivers should be considered as workers of the company and not self-employed contractors.[8] This case has profound ripple effects for the 'gig economy', but the need for employment law to catch up does not end there. The very structures of employment law have yet to allow for sustained discussions about how the law can extend protection towards non-marketised, or unpaid, work, such as care work and work in the home (traditionally gendered work, with gender divisions of labour remaining into the present day) or casual work in online environments. The shifts in digitisation and digital work where ones' employer is an online platform further trouble the standard legal framework employment tribunals and practitioners rely on. The existing legal framework furthermore relies on a citizenship-based model of legal subjectivity, deferring to immigration law to protect the nation-state over protection against exploitative labour practices where a workers' legal right to work in the country is in question. The question is, can the existing framework of employment/labour law extend itself towards these challenges?

The priorities and provisions (regulations) in employment law are unabashedly political. In 2003, Lord Millet stated, 'Work is one of

---

7. Nicola Kountouris "Uses and Misuses of 'Mutuality of Obligations' and the Autonomy of Labour Law" in *The Autonomy of Labour Law*, ed.Alan Bogg, Costello, Davis and Prassl (Oxford University Press, 2015), 169-187; Alan Bogg, 'Sham Self-Employment in the Supreme Court' *Industrial Law Journal* 41/3 (2012), 328-345; Hugh Collins, 'Legal Responses to the Standard Form Contract of Employment' *Industrial Law Journal* 36/1 (2007), 2-18.
8. See see *Uber B.V. ("UBV") & Ors v Aslam & Ors* [2018] EWCA Civ 2748; [2021] UKSC 5

the defining features of people's lives'.[9] And yet employment law, as it exists under the ERA 1996, exists only for a diminishing population considered to be in a recognised 'contract of employment'.[10] For this reason, the study of employment and labour law constantly needs to return to the question: what is employment law? How does it define 'work'? Where does this law come from? What does it concern/Who is it for? And who decides? Case law is, over time, shaping definitions to include more 'atypical' and yet increasingly standard forms of work arrangements.[11] Yet so long as the market economic system, together with an industrial model of labour,[12] remain the driving forces behind political priorities shaping labour and employment law, the legal framework will continue to allow for the profound inequalities experienced between those who work and those who are business owners, employers and profiteers from an increasingly precarious, insecure albeit flexible, labour market.[13] Employment law's gaps, being the persons-who-work who are excluded from the ERA by the nature of their work arrangement and precarity, are perpetuated by the social-political-economic-cultural reality of the United Kingdom. Moreover, the globalised world that is ever-present in any labour market, wage, employment decision or dispute made on the local, national or international level.

Importantly, the employment law regulations in effect in the UK today (e.g. sick pay, leave, unfair dismissal, redundancy, the right to unionise), are largely a consequence the UK's membership in the European Union. Since 1996, and notably in 2008 when the Treaty of the European Union (TEU) was adopted, a plethora of EU Regulations and Directives impacted on UK employment law.[14] Provisions and regulations further implemented by the UK government responded to changes in the UK labour market and employment (such as the Transfers

---

9. *Johnson v Unisys* [2003] at 549
10. While statistics of 'persons at work' in the UK may have been rising pre-Covid 19, the quality of work was decreasing and 'persons at work' does not equal employee status in a stable, secure contract of employment. See Tataryn, *Law, Migration and Precarious Labour: Ecotechnics of the Social.* (Abington: Routledge Taylor-Francis, 2021).
11. Sir Brian Langstaff, 'Changing Times, Changing Relationships At Work...Changing Law?' Industrial Law Journal 45/2 (2016), 131-143.
12. Simon Deakin and Frank Wilkinson, *The Law of the Labour Market: Industrialization, Employment and Legal Evolution* (Oxford University Press, 2005).
13. Brian Langille and Guy Davidov, ed. *The Idea of Labour Law* (Oxford University Press, 2012).
14. Including, among many others, EU Pregnant Workers Directive 1992, Parental Leave Directive implemented in the UK in 2013, Fixed-Term Worker and Part-Time Worker Directives, and the Agency Worker Regulations in 2011.

of Undertakings (Protection of Employment) Regulations 2006 and the Trade Union Act 2016).[15] The Equality Act 2010, revising the previous Race Relations Act 1976, intersects with employment law on issues of discrimination in the workplace, and in the process of hiring/looking for work. Based on EU Directives, many of the existing UK employment laws and regulations can be called into question, or significantly altered if not overturned, following the UK's exit from the EU.[16]

The concept of labour and employment protection in law emerged from struggle: struggle for control over populations to deal with disease, revolt, and migration (Vagrancy Laws[17]), co-existing with a struggle for land and food; then struggle for labourers (slavery, Master and Servant Act); struggle for autonomy, struggle for wages, struggle for representation; struggle for rights and attention to the disparity between owners and workers; struggle for decent wages, struggle for access to legal subjectivity; struggle for food, for money to pay rent and basic living costs, struggle to negotiate care responsibilities and family.[18] In our current reality, whether these struggles manifest as issues of migrant workers and immigration illegality in employment disputes; gig-economy workers and disputes fighting for employee status; care-workers and recognition of atypical, non-standard working arrangements including domestic in-home care in employment law; gender pay gap and gendered divisions of labour; service work and non-marketized labour; zero-hour contracts differentially affecting younger versus aging workers; and the fragmentation in labour sectors shifting traditional modes of organising labour and collective bargaining units, the labour struggle continues. As case law such as *Uber v Aslam* and the UCU strike actions that disrupted teaching across UK Universities in 2017, 2019 and 2021 can attest to, so long as this struggle of work and labour continues, so does the need to continue asking, what is employment

---

15. Michael Ford, 'Legislating for Control: The Trade Union Act 2016' *Industrial Law Journal* 45/3 (2016), 277-298.
16. Linda Medland et al., 'The 'Future' of Work? A call for the recognition of continuities in challenges for conceptualising work and its regulation' Bristol Law Research Paper Series; vol. 2019 (2018), no. 001; Tonia Novitz, 'Collective Bargaining, Equality and Migration: The Journey to and from Brexit,' *Industrial Law Journal* 46/1 (2017), 109-133.
17. See Bridget Anderson, *Us & Them: The Dangerous Politics of Immigration Control* (Cambridge University Press, 2013).
18. Lydia Hayes, *Stories of Care: A Labour of Law Gender and Class at Work* (Palgrave MacMillan, 2017); Judy Fudge, 'Feminist Reflections on the Scope of Labour Law: Domestic Work, Social Reproduction, and Jurisdiction,' *Feminist Legal Studies* 22/1, 1-23.

law? Where does it come from? What does it concern and who is it for? And who decides?

FURTHER READINGS

- Harry Arthurs, 'Labor Law as the Law of Economic Subordination and Resistance: A Thought Experiment.' *Comparative Labor Law and Policy Journal* 34/3 (2013): 585-604.
- Diamond Ashiagbor (ed), *Re-Imagining Labour Law for Development: Informal Work in the Global North and South* (Bloomsbury, 2019).
- Miriam Kullmann, Ania Zbyszewska and Alysia Blackham (eds), *Theorising Labour law in a Changing World* (Bloomsbury, 2019).
- Anastasia Tataryn, *Law, Migration and Precarious Labour* (Routledge, 2021)

33

Human Rights as a Contested Terrain

INTERNATIONAL HUMAN RIGHTS LAW

Raza Saeed

The key to understanding human rights law critically and contextually lies, counterintuitively, outside the confines of the legal paradigm itself. That which we recognise as human rights law, in the conventional sense of the term, is primarily the ordered and structured layer, readily visible but covering a multitude of conceptual issues, ideological struggles, political interests, philosophical debates, and histories of control and resistance. Although the contestation never really diminishes from the practice of human rights law itself, it is nonetheless difficult to understand the discourse of human rights in depth unless we recognise that human rights law is born of and situated in a 'terrain of contestation'.[1]

Recognising human rights as a contested terrain takes us beyond the identification of legal rights or a discussion on their sources and enforcement; rather, we are compelled to equally acknowledge that human rights discourse is chequered with clashes between notions of humanity and in/sub-humanity; between ideas of duties and rights, entitlements and obligations; it is a space where subjectivities of various kinds have been and are created, and destroyed, made dominant or hidden away across the abyssal divide.[2] This serves as the main insight that the current introductory chapter seeks to convey, and we will return to this point later in the course of the discussion. In order to

---
1. Balakrishnan Rajagopal, "The International Human Rights Movement Today," *Maryland Journal of International Law* 24, no. 1 (2009): 56.
2. See José-Manuel Barreto, "Epistemologies of the South and Human Rights: Santos and the Quest for Global and Cognitive Justice," *Indiana Journal of Global Legal Studies* 21, no. 2 (2014).

provide a critical overview of the field, the text that follows is divided into three subsections: the first will provide a brief overview of what is generally meant by human rights law; the second section will return to the idea of contestation, and the final section will highlight some other key conceptual issues affecting human rights, which will then be followed by a conclusion.

A Glance at Human Rights Law

Far from being a monolithic positivist legal structure, contemporary human rights law operates in a space of 'interlegality', whose multiple layers were laid down across different times, moved by various forces, and generated to fulfil a multitude of needs.[3] It exists as an amalgamation of domestic, international and regional legal frameworks, which overlap in terms of some socio-cultural values, languages and modes of enforcement, but also diverge by way of responding to contextual considerations.

One of the more recognisable manifestations of human rights law is within the international realm. International human rights law encompasses a range of instruments which are aimed at protecting human rights within particular geographical or legal jurisdictions, or which are geared towards safeguarding specific groups of people or targeting particular wrongs. The most notable among these instruments is the International Bill of Rights, a label collectively used to refer to the Universal Declaration of Human Rights (UDHR),[4] and the two associated international treaties—the International Covenant on Civil and Political Rights (ICCPR) and the International Covenant on Economic, Social and Cultural Rights (ICESCR).[5] Prepared in the aftermath of World War II and the Holocaust, the UDHR is considered by commentators to have represented a near-universal consensus of the different countries of the world at the time (although it excluded the colonies and protectorates). It lists a multitude of civil, political, social and economic rights and its preamble claims the (re)assertion

---

3. Boaventura De Sousa Santos, *Toward a New Legal Common Sense: Law, Globalization and Emancipation* (Butterworths LexisNexis, 2002), 428-38.
4. Universal Declaration of Human Rights (adopted 10 December 1948 UNGA Res 217 A(III) (UDHR).
5. International Covenant on Civil and Political Rights (adopted 16 December 1966, entered into force 23 March 1976) 999 UNTS 171 (ICCPR); International Covenant on Economic, Social and Cultural Rights (adopted 16 December 1966, entered into force 3 January 1976) 993 UNTS 3 (ICESCR).

of inherent human dignity and equality. While it is a non-binding instrument—which means that it does not create legal obligations on its own as an international agreement would—the UDHR's significance emerges from the supposedly universal moral values it is claimed to encompass, which is why some scholars even consider it to be part of customary international law.[6]

The initial intent behind the UDHR was that it would eventually lead to a legally enforceable international treaty, as the key charter of fundamental rights for the whole world. However, as soon as the world emerged from WWII, it delved into Cold War politics which meant that any notion of a universal and harmonised system of human rights law became secondary to ideological and economic interests.[7] This led to the emergence of two separate covenants, ICCPR and ICESCR, which came into operation a quarter of a century after the UDHR. ICCPR focuses on civil and political rights, such as the right to vote, the privacy of individuals, and so on—rights that we individuals can claim by virtue of their participation in the civic life and political affairs of a state—while the ICESCR focuses on rights to education, healthcare, etc. With some caveats,[8] these two covenants are legally binding on the countries that have signed and ratified them—at this point in time, there is a near universal coverage for ICCPR and ICESCR (although there are some notable absences—for instance, the US has not yet ratified the ICESCR and China has similarly not accepted ICCPR obligations).

International human rights law also includes a multitude of human rights frameworks focussing on addressing either particular categories of wrongs or protecting specific groups of people. By way of example, the former category includes the Convention against Torture and the Convention against Genocide,[9] while the latter includes Convention

---

6. Ed Bates, "International Human Rights Law: History," in *International Human Rights Law*, ed. Daniel Moeckli, Sangeeta Shah, and Sandesh Sivakumaran (Oxford University Press, 2014), 30-32. On customary international law, also see B. S. Chimni, "Customary International Law: A Third World Perspective," *American Journal of International Law* 112, no. 1 (2018).

7. For an historical overview of international human rights law, see Micheline Ishay, *The History of Human Rights: From Ancient times to the Globalization era* (University of California Press, 2004). Especially, see the section on 'The World Wars: The Institutionalisation of International Rights and the Right to Self-Determination', 174-243.

8. See, for instance, Theo Van Boven, "Categories of Rights," in *International Human Rights Law*, ed. Daniel Moeckli, Sangeeta Shah, and Sandesh Sivakumaran (Oxford University Press, 2018).

9. Convention Against Torture and Other Cruel, Inhuman or Degrading Treatment or

on Discrimination against Women (CEDAW) and the Child Rights Convention.[10] These instruments are binding on the countries that have accepted their obligations through signature and ratification of international treaties or their protocols, and the states' performance against human rights benchmarks are periodically monitored and reported on by specific monitoring bodies.[11]

Between the wider international realm and national human rights frameworks, there lies a tier of regional human rights frameworks. These include the African Charter and the American Convention,[12] as well as the European Convention on Human Rights (ECHR).[13] While these instruments are more or less structured along a similar core of civil and political rights, there are differences between them in terms of their approach towards collective values, duties, individualism, and so on. The African Charter and the American Convention highlight the primacy of duties and adopt a more collective lens to look at rights than present in the ECHR.[14] Alongside their associated courts, the African Charter and the American Convention have faced significant difficulties historically with regards to gaining legitimacy within state parties and strengthening their enforceability, legitimacy and operationalisation, although they are gradually gaining more acceptance.[15]

The ECHR is by far the most prominent human rights regime operating at a regional level, partly because of its reach across most of Europe as well as Turkey and Russia, but also because of its impact

---

Punishment (adopted 10 December 1984, entered into force 26 June 1987) 1465 UNTS 85; Convention on the Prevention and Punishment of the Crime of Genocide (adopted 9 December 1948, entered into force 12 January 1951) 78 UNTS 277.
10. Convention on the Elimination of All Forms of Discrimination against Women (adopted 18 December 1979, entered into force 3 September 1981) 1249 UNTS 13; Convention on the Rights of the Child (adopted 20 November 1989, entered into force 2 September 1990) 1577 UNTS 3.
11. See Olivier De Schutter, *International Human Rights Law: Cases, Material, Commentary*, 3rd ed. (Cambridge University Press, 2019). 869-985
12. African Charter on Human and Peoples' Rights (adopted 27 June 1981, entered into force 21 October 1986) (1982) 21 ILM 58 (African Charter); American Convention on Human Rights 'Pact of San José, Costa Rica' (adopted 22 November 1969, entered into force 18 July 1978) 1144 UNTS 123.
13. European Convention for the Protection of Human Rights and Fundamental Freedoms (European Convention on Human Rights, as amended by Protocols Nos. 11 and 14) (ECHR) (adopted 4 November 1950, entered into force 3 September 1953) ETS 5.
14. See, for instance, Chapter II of the African Charter on Duties.
15. For introduction, see Schutter, *International Human Rights Law* 1020-1060.

on the enforcement and shaping of human rights within state parties.[16] While it initially focussed mainly on civil and political rights, its remit has gradually expanded through additional protocols and jurisprudence of the European Court of Human Rights. The ECHR operates under the aegis of the Council of Europe and has a separate yet complementary status with regards to the European Union's rights framework. Within the EU, the Charter of Fundamental Rights (EU CFR) is also a key instrument that is applicable on member countries during the application of European Law (although this regime is likely to change in the UK after the Brexit transition).[17] One significance of the EU CFR lies in the fact that it conceptualises rights differently from most other human rights instruments—rather than dividing rights along the lines of the International Bill of Rights, it divides them into different categories that brings civil and political rights together with economic and social rights.[18] This signals the wider trend within the human rights discourse of a move towards the acknowledgement of indivisibility of rights—it suggests that rights should generally be considered as interlinked and interdependent, and that the direct violation of one may lead to an indirect violation of the other.

Away from the international realm, the most visible manifestation of human rights law is within the national and sub-national legal frameworks that operate at the level of state and local normative orders. This is the space where we find constitutional documents, bills of rights, and charters guaranteeing basic rights for citizens, and these instruments govern the everyday realities for us. The constitutions of many countries enshrine some sort of fundamental rights frameworks within their constitutions, which are then materialised and actualised through a variety of legislations, courts and institutions within different jurisdictions. In the US, fundamental rights (such as the infamous right to bear arms) are included in the first set of amendments within the constitution.[19] In places such as Bangladesh, India, Kenya, Pakistan, and Sri Lanka, their shared colonial history suggests that their constitutional documents

---

16. For an introduction to the history and strengths of, as well as challenges for, ECHR, see Steven Greer, "What's Wrong with the European Convention on Human Rights?," *Human Rights Quarterly* 30, no. 3 (2008): 680-702.
17. For a general introduction to European human rights regimes, see Eleanor Spaventa, "Fundamental Rights in the European Union," in *European Union Law*, ed. Catherine Barnard and Steve Peers (Oxford University Press, 2017).
18. Charter of Fundamental Rights of the European Union [2012] C 326/02.
19. Constitution of the United States (ratified 21 June 1788, entered into force 4 March 1789, amended 15 December 1791), First Amendment.

depict a somewhat common approach towards inclusion of human rights focussing largely on civil and political rights. It should be emphasised, however, that the ambit of these rights differs based on individual legal regimes and developments in common law and jurisprudence (the expansion of the right to life in India to safeguard socio-economic rights is a key example). These domestic frameworks, moreover, do not operate in a vacuum and constantly interact with international and regional regimes, often complementing but at times clashing with each other. In the UK, the Human Rights Act 1998 is an apt example of this move between domestic and international regimes.[20] In the absence of a written constitution and an effective domestic Bill of Rights, the HRA 1998 creates channels for the application of ECHR within UK's domestic legal framework.

Situating Human Rights Law

If international and domestic human rights law can be charted out with such clarity, why is it important to acknowledge the notions of contestation, contextuality, and breadth associated with the human rights discourse? This is because the legal manifestation of human rights does not have the capacity to tell us about the struggles that allowed us to reach this point and which continue to inform and question the practice of law at every juncture. A purely legalistic approach underplays the fact that human rights paradigm and legal instruments are inherently based on struggle, resistance and contestations.[21]

For instance, the mainstream ideas of human rights hold that human rights started life either in one of many ancient religions, or in ancient Greece where the interplay between natural law, justice and law began to be understood.[22] From there it jumped a few centuries, borrowing the notion of individuality and brotherhood from Christianity, which concretised as Europe moved through the Renaissance and the Enlightenment. This movement is then said to have converged in the contemporary human rights law regime. The classic 'legal' story of human rights, similarly, begins with the Magna Carta, and travels through the English Bill of Rights, the American Declaration, the French Declaration, leading up to the Holocaust. The latter is said to have cast

---

20. Human Rights Act 1998 (UK).
21. Costas Douzinas, *The Radical Philosophy of Rights* (Routledge, 2019), 169.
22. Paul Gordon Lauren, *The Evolution of International Human Rights: Visions Seen* (University of Pennsylvania Press, 2011), 6-10.

a shadow over the world so dark that the countries of the world had to come together and not only create the United Nations, but also the UDHR as the main global human rights charter, followed by numerous other instruments since then.

These versions would be acceptable if it were not for the significant jumps over centuries, the concealment of historical and conceptual contradictions, and the veiling of the voices of the excluded and marginalised from such human rights narratives. These accounts do not highlight, for instance, why the Declaration of the Rights of Man and Citizen in France was coupled with a suppression of women's rights, which were voiced in the form of the Declaration of the Rights of Women.[23] These narratives do not speak about why the claims of equality and fraternity were followed by curbing of slave rebellions,[24], or how the claims of inherent and universal human dignity could be reconciled with slavery and colonialism.[25] These versions do not tell us why, if the English Bill of Rights was the precursor of human rights for all, it coincided with the continuation of sectarian conflict and religious marginalisation of some communities within England.[26] They do not question why, even at the time of framing the UDHR, the world actively turned away from the colonised territories and mandate lands.[27] The claims of rights went hand in hand with the denial of rights; the claims of equal and inherent humanity were never too removed from the denial of humanity for a vast number of people. Law generally, and human rights law in particular, may not always be able to depict these contestations, but it is important to note that they are never distant from the practice of law itself.

The question of prohibition of torture is an apt example in this regard. In the last two decades, mainly because of the 'War on Terror', the issues around legitimacy of incarceration and torture come up

---

23. Ishay, *The History of Human Rights*, 328.
24. For instance, one of the key acts conducted by Napoleon's army in the aftermath of the French Revolution was to invade Haiti in 1802 to control the slave rebellion.
25. See, for instance, Upendra Baxi, "Voices of Suffering and the Future of Human Rights," *Transnational Law & Contemporary Problems* 8 (1998).
26. Ishay writes that alongside the passage of the English Bill of Rights in 1689, the English Parliament also passed the Tolerant Act in the same year which 'though allowing some dissenters to practice their religion, continued to exclude Jewish and Catholic worship.' Ishay, *The History of Human Rights*, 78.
27. The Mandate system was instituted by the League of Nations in the aftermath of WWI and the fall of the Ottoman Empire, under which the victorious 'colonial powers… agreed to bring the mandate territories toward self-government' Ishay, *The History of Human Rights*, 188.

repeatedly within the general political discourse. There are those who hold the position that torture is prohibited by virtue of the Torture Convention and customary international law.[28] However, there are also those who hold the position that torture may be permissible for the protection of the wider society. These positions can also be traced to case law from different countries,[29] as well as to the jurisprudence of the European Court of Human Rights.[30] However, what gets left out of the picture is the political, conceptual, historical and sociological terrain of these approaches. It is important to acknowledge this key human rights issue goes back several centuries, and the arguments can find their roots within legal and political philosophy, especially in the ideas of deontology and utilitarianism. More importantly, we have to acknowledge how torture has been used as a technology of power, as an instrument to initiate and sustain the totalitarian ambitions of some states and political entities.[31] It is therefore necessary to appreciate that the right not to be tortured is inherently tied up with the history and politics of domination, power, and curbing of political dissent.

The Politics of Human Rights

As mentioned above, understanding the contested terrain of human rights becomes important when we acknowledge how conceptual, political and historical forces feed into the structures of human rights law. For instance, the demarcation between civil and political rights on the one hand and economic, social, and cultural rights on the other, may be historical accidents rooted in the Cold War, but they have become increasingly normalised within the field. They are either categorised as positive or negative rights or, along with a third set of rights (which includes solidarity rights such as the right to self-determination), are labelled as the three generations of rights. But while these labels are

---

28. Convention against Torture or Other Cruel, Inhuman or Degrading Treatment or Punishment (adopted 10 December 1984, entered into force 26 June 1987) 1465 UNTS 112.
29. See, for instance, Public Committee Against Torture in Israel v The State of Israel, Supreme Court of Israel, 1999, HC 5100/95, available at www.jewishvirtuallibrary.org/jsource/Politics/GSStext.html.
30. See, Ireland v United Kingdom, European Court of Human Rights, 1978 2 EHRR 25.
31. The Pinochet case being a prime example in this regard. *Regina v. Bartle and Commissioner of Police for the Metropolis and others, ex parte Pinochet* [1999] UKHL 17, [1999] 2 WLR 827.

often used within the mainstream human rights discourse, it is increasingly acknowledged that these delineations are unhelpful with regard to the overall cause of rights and justice.[32] For instance, positive and negative rights are said to correlate to positive and negative duties: security of person was historically considered to be a negative right, which meant that the only obligation on the state (and any other duty bearers) was to refrain from harming an individual. The rights to education and healthcare, on the other hand, were considered positive rights which required the state as the main duty bearer to take positive measures to enable education provision for the citizens. However, we now recognise that not only are healthcare, education, economic and social equality, and safety or security of persons interlinked (as the pandemic has made evident), but that ensuring the security of persons requires the state to take significant positive measures. The idea of generations of rights is equally problematic as it implies a progressive sequence within the rights regime, either with regards to importance or immediacy. The wider human rights discourse and the human rights instruments are increasingly moving away from this division between positive/negative rights or generations of rights, with the EU CFR, mentioned above, being a key example of a modified approach towards the indivisibility of rights.

Another key difficulty emerges from the practice of international law itself. As international law does not flow from and is not enforced by, an overarching authority, there is no one sovereign authority or a global state (yet) that could come up with human rights standards or impose it on all the actors. Human rights law therefore depends on the inter-relationship of states and the various domestic and international organisations. This is primarily where power disparities between states (the power of the permanent five members of the UN Security Council, for instance), and between states and other institutions (such as multinational corporations or multilateral institutions) also creep in. This also means that situations in which sovereign authorities prove unable or unwilling to safeguard their citizens or other individuals, the protection of human rights falls victim to political, ideological and nationalistic considerations.

Regardless of the claims of inviolability and universality of human rights, the enforcement and protection of rights depends on societies, actors, and particularly the states. When states prove unable or unwilling to protect rights, or societies and individual actors refuse

---

32. Upendra Baxi, *The Future of Human Rights* (Oxford University Press, 2006), 124.

to accept their duties, then the foundational ideas of human rights have to be reconsidered. It is all the more necessary today as forces of populism, exclusion and regression gain momentum. The accountability of powerful actors, search for socio-economic equality, notions of social justice, the regulation and accountability of transnational actors and corporations—these issues are inherently linked with the assumption of duties to fulfil and protect human rights. Many of these are taken as political rather than purely legal or conceptual issues, but a refusal to engage with them means that the human rights paradigm begins to lose its legitimacy and its moral authority. It is precisely because of this that Baxi calls for a turn to the 'politics for human rights' rather than a politics of human rights, which means re-evaluating the whole paradigm, its role, and the interests of its actors, with a view to bringing marginalised and excluded voices to the centre of the human rights discourse and interpret the world from their perspective.[33]

Conclusion

This brief and critical introduction to human rights law attempted to introduce the reader to two facets. One aspect is the international, regional, and domestic human rights regimes and to highlight how they exist as different spatial and temporal layers within the wider legal framework. The second aspect was to show that any critical and contextual understanding has to step outside the bounds of human rights law in order to return to it in a more informed fashion. Human rights law lies in the middle of a terrain of contestation laid out by societal, conceptual, historical and political issues, and it takes root from divergent strands and trends. The notion of human rights, therefore, is one of constant struggle, and to understand human rights law contextually and critically requires first an understanding of that which moves it.

---

33. Baxi, *The Future of Human Rights*. Baxi, *The Future of Human Rights*, 80-81.

Erratum: This chapter is an early draft that was printed in error. Please refer to the ebook (ISBN: 978-1-910761-08-3) for the correct and updated version of this chapter.

34

Thinking Rights as Relations

HUMAN RIGHTS, LEGAL THEORY

Bal Sokhi-Bulley

Can we be friends? This is an unusual question with which to begin talking about rights. You might start with more obvious questions, like 'what are human rights' and 'do rights *work*'? I am starting from a critical position that rights are technologies of governmentality. 'Governmentality' is a term and mode of thinking I take from the poststructural philosopher Michel Foucault and means the 'conduct of conducts'.[1] In other words, the regulation of behaviour. Applied to rights, governmentality reveals rights as a governing discourse, not only an emancipatory one. Once we know this, the question of whether they work or not is not the interesting or important question. Instead, we should ask: how might we perform critique to imagine possibilities for freedom outside of rights?[2] The value of this question is to prompt resistance to the regulatory dimension of rights so that we might find ways to be governed less and to live better together in friendship rather than in rights. I illustrate the value of a critique of rights as *friendship*, or what unfolds below as a relational ethics for rights, by looking at the denial of citizenship in the UK's hostile environment. I concentrate on two examples: the Windrush Scandal and, in particular, the case of Shamima Begum.

---

1. Michel Foucault, 'The Subject and Power' in *Power: Volume 3: Essential Works of Foucault 1954-1984*, ed. James D Faubion, trans. Robert Hurley (Penguin, 2002), 326, 341.
2. Ratna Kapur, *Gender, Alterity and Human Rights: Freedom in a Fishbowl* (Edward Elgar Publishing, 2018).

Rights as Governmentality

Suggesting that rights are technologies of governmentality is to say that rights, at the same time as they emancipate, regulate identities, and produce the dominant narrative of events. Governmentality, as a way to interpret the functioning of power relations within modern society, applies to pretty much everything; we are governed, and govern ourselves, for instance through the institution of the university to become employable, model students of law and reputable academics who produce good, highly-rated research. In terms of rights, a governmentality lens magnifies the power relations that operate to produce good, virtuous, and humanitarian actors (e.g. INGOs like Human Rights Watch) and good, desirable, and active citizens (e.g. the active citizen of Britain's Community and Society policy). The point is not to show that this is good or bad. A governmentality lens is useful in highlighting how this might be *problematic*. How does Human Rights Watch regulate what rights *are*, how we ought to protect them and where resources should be focused? Whilst it is not *bad* that 15 year olds in the UK are encouraged to take part in National Citizen Service and become the best version of themselves, is it dangerous that the resultant active citizen becomes a docile and compliant participant in government? Can she resist if she rejects the *right* way to be an active citizen; or, does the criminalization of racialized youth during the 2011 London Riots reveal how active citizenship became a condition for claiming rights as a desirable, deserving citizen?[3]

You may not remember the riots. But you will remember the hostile environment. Or environment_s_, plural. In 2020, universities became hostile environments. Academic staff and students went on strike for an unprecedented fourteen days to counter the neoliberal governmentality of an institution that was turning us into businesses and consumers. Did we have a right to do so? The strike was not illegal but in contrast to exercising our right to strike we were instead, I'd suggest, making a claim to relating to each other differently (the picket lines saw no hierarchies), to doing education differently (the teach outs were interdisciplinary and without structure) and practicing a right not to work.[4] This right, as I have argued in the context of migrant rights

---

3. Bal Sokhi-Bulley, *Governing (Through) Rights* (Hart, 2016), Chapters 4 and 5.
4. Bal Sokhi-Bulley, 'Reflections on a Strike: Friendship As/And the Future of Rights', *Critical Legal Thinking*, 13 September 2018, accessed 31 July 2020, https://criticallegalthinking.com/2018/09/13/reflections-on-a-strike-friendship-and-as-the-future-of-rights/.

for non-economically active migrants and in the context of persons with disabilities,[5] does not exist as a juridical right. It is, I suggest, a relational right.

I take the idea of relational right also from Foucault. Relational rights are not juridical rights. They are not justiciable. A relational right has to exist in a culture that invents ways of relating, types of values, and exchanges between individuals that are new and not recognized by the institution.[6] Such rights are based in our relations, not associations, with each other and are a way in which we can respond, with responsibility (or what Haraway calls 'response-ability'[7]),to hostile environments.

In 2020 we also experience a different kind of hostility we have not known before; a virus that threatens our lives, our practices of living, our social behaviour. Can we respond to COVID-19 with rights? The state has obligations to protect;[8] there are arguments for dying with loved ones by your side being a fundamental part of the right to private and family life (Article 8 of the European Convention on Human Rights, ECHR).[9] But will the response to the coronavirus be in enacting *more rights*? Or is this more about understanding the importance of how we *relate* to each other? About how our lives are interdependent, how we should care despite being estranged from each other (we cannot all feel each other's pain or circumstance). These are ethical and not juridical questions.

---

5. Bal Sokhi-Bulley, 'A Postmodern Approach to Elizabeta Dano v Jobcenter Leipzig' in *Research Methods for International Human Rights Law: Beyond the Traditional Paradigm*, eds. Damien Gonzalez-Salzberg and Loveday Hodson (Routledge, 2019), 69-97; Ivanka Antova and Bal Sokhi-Bulley, 'Disability Counter-Communities: Resisting Precarity with Friendship' in *Precarity and IR*, eds. Ritu Vij, Elisa Wynne-Hughes and Tahzeen Kazi (Palgrave, 2020).
6. Michel Foucault, 'The Social Triumph of the Sexual Will' in *Ethics: Volume 1: Subjectivity and Truth: Essential Works of Foucault 1954-1984*, ed. Paul Rabinow, trans. Robert Hurley (Penguin 2000), 157, 159-60.
7. Donna Haraway, *Staying with the Trouble: Making Kin in the Chthulucene* (Duke University Press, 2016), 2.
8. Natasa Mavronicola, 'Positive Obligations in Crisis,' *Strasbourg Observers*, 7 April 2020, accessed 31 July 2020, https://strasbourgobservers.com/2020/04/07/positive-obligations-in-crisis/.
9. Owen Boycott, 'Dying Surrounded by Family "a Fundamental Right" Says UK Judge,' *The Guardian*, 5 May 2020, accessed 31 July 2020, https://www.theguardian.com/law/2020/may/05/dying-surrounded-by-family-a-fundamental-right-says-uk-judge.

After Governmentality/ After Rights

Ethics is that 'missing something that can help cure what ails democratic life' and the practice of freedom.[10] In my current work, I come at this from my Foucauldian intellectual position to interpret ethics as a care of the self. Typically, ethics is about care for others;[11] yet Foucault suggests that the care of oneself, conducted as practices of freedom that do not necessarily adhere to the processes of freedom articulated in a moral code (e.g. rights), can create a new culture. This culture, or mode of life, is *friendship*. Now, Foucault argues for friendship as a way of life for the subject he was interested in, the homosexual, and making gay practices of living desirable. I think we can stretch our critical imaginations and apply this concept to how we treat the abandoned 'other' of the hostile environment, who has been abandoned by rights.

'The hostile environment', announced in 2012 by Theresa May as Home Secretary, was intended to 'create a really hostile environment for illegal immigrants'.[12] Yet this hostility has come to erode citizenship. Two examples illustrate this. The first is the Windrush Scandal, where Commonwealth citizens (the Windrush generation) were forcibly removed, detained, denied healthcare, dismissed from work, and even lost their lives under the justification that they do not have 'leave to remain'. What if this were a 'right to remain'?[13] Would it make a difference? Of course, it would create an institutional framework to appeal wrongful removal. But would it recognise *belonging*—the fact that people like Paulette Wilson, Anthony Bryan, and Sylvester Marshall lived fulfilled lives and practiced being with others here, in this country that they knew as home?[14] My second example is even more stark and the example I want to concentrate on for a moment: a case of revoking citizenship in the interests of 'public good' and national security (BNA

---

10. Ella Myers, *Worldly Ethics: Democratic Politics and Care for the World* (Durham and London: Duke University Press, 2013), 1.
11. Or, care for the Other as per Emmanual Levinas. See Ella Myers, *Worldly Ethics: Democratic Politics and Care for the World* (Duke Universiy Press, 2013), 21-84 for a comparison between Foucauldian and Levinasian ethics.
12. James Kirkup and Robert Winnett, 'Theresa May Interview: "We're going to give illegal migrants a really hostile reception,' *The Telegraph*, 25 May 2012, accessed 11 September 2020, https://www.telegraph.co.uk/news/uknews/immigration/9291483/Theresa-May-interview-Were-going-to-give-illegal-migrants-a-really-hostile-reception.html.
13. See 'Right to Remain', accessed 31 July 2020, https://righttoremain.org.uk/
14. Amelia Gentleman, *The Windrush Betrayal: Exposing the Hostile Environment* (Guardian Faber, 2019).

1981, section 40(2)); the treatment of Shamima Begum.

British-born Begum left her home in Bethnal Green in 2015 to join ISIS in Syria. In February 2019, then Home Secretary Sajid Javid revoked Begum's citizenship, defending his order as 'stripping dangerous dual nationals of their British citizenship' under the new laws provided for by the 2019 Counter-Terrorism and Border Security Act.[15] Begum's family have appealed the decision under Articles 2, 3, and 8 ECHR (right to life, freedom from torture, and right to private and family life). The appeal will be heard in the mysterious world of the Special Immigration Appeals Commission (SIAC), which means there is no trial. Meanwhile Begum remains in a refugee camp in Northern Syria. Begum states she 'made a mistake' and wants to come home.[16] Her story, narrated as above, with reference to the institutional framework and language of rights, is one where she is undesirable (she is not the active, volunteering, compliant young citizen of Britain's Community and Society) and, in effect, abandoned. The juridical culture of rights has produced this abandonment. What if we narrated the story differently, focusing on Begum as an ethical subject with relational bonds with her community, who deserves right treatment by virtue of citizenship?

In this version of the story, Begum is a child who was groomed online to join a cult.[17] She made a 'mistake' (in her own words) and wants to come home. She married and had three children—maybe forcibly, we don't know, but we do know that they all died of preventable malnutrition and disease. Does she deserve mercy, generosity, forgiveness? There is no 'right' to these things—just as there is no right to make mistakes, no right to come home, and no right to right treatment.[18] These are not juridical rights but they are relational rights—rights that can be performed even though they do not exist in a legal document; rights that rely on one's coexistence within a community.

---

15. 'Sajid Javid on Shamima Begum,' 18 February 2019, accessed 11 September 2020 https://www.youtube.com/watch?v=QGAsE-TpTKg.
16. Quentin Somerville, 'Shamima Begum: What Was Life like for the IS Couple in Syria?' *BBC News*, 3 March 2019, accessed 31 July 2020, https://www.bbc.co.uk/news/world-middle-east-47435039.
17. Katherine E Brown, 'Bethnal Green Girls Need to Know There Is A Way Out of Islamic State Cult,' *The Conversation*, 26 February 2019, accessed 31 July 2020, https://theconversation.com/bethnal-green-girls-need-to-know-there-is-a-way-out-of-islamic-state-cult-38004.
18. Bal Sokhi-Bulley, 'Rights as a Distraction from "Belonging": A Response to the Shamima Begum Ruling,' *Critical Legal Thinking*, 28 May 2019, accessed 31 July 2020,, https://criticallegalthinking.com/2019/05/28/rights-as-a-distraction-from-belonging-a-response-to-the-shamima-begum-ruling/.

The Begum case illustrates both the reality that rights do not work *and* the possibility of imagining something else, *after* rights. A *culture* in which we respond to Begum with *friendship*. That means, to practice a mode of behaviour that employs generosity—featured as *examining our conscience*, engaging in *silence*, and *listening* to others.[19] It means understanding that rights can be more than juridical concepts; that they need to acknowledge an ethical dimension where we care for ourselves by caring about how we exist in a community *with* others. The feminist ethics of care is instructive here. The 'feminist critique of liberal autonomy', writes Hunter, favours 'a more plausible account of individuals as relational, always connected and dependent upon others'. In feminist ethics, care is therefore necessarily relational and, moreover, is the practice of what we actually *do* rather than simple adherence to (legal) norms; it is 'a range of *doings* needed to create, hold together and sustain life and continue its diverseness'.[20] But to the feminist ethics of care I would add that we need to acknowledge estrangement and betrayal.[21] We cannot know Begum or see her in ourselves. Her so-called betrayal is the reason we should extend care, generosity, and right treatment to her—indeed, we have betrayed her by not protecting her from being groomed online, by our unproblematic and acceptable form of citizenship that makes us desirable and so able to claim rights. To see Begum, we must adopt an intersectional lens that highlights and respects the key features of her subjectivity—she is brown, female, and Muslim.[22] She is the abandoned racialized citizen of the hostile environment, where whiteness equates to desirability and it is the black and brown 'other' who must do the labour of proving they are desirable.

This is perhaps a lot to take in for the student of human rights. We know that rights are that which we 'cannot not want';[23] 'the magic

---

19. Michel Foucault, 'On the Genealogy of Ethics: An Overview of Work in Progress' in *Ethics*, 253, 273-77.
20. Maria Puig de la Bellacasa, *Matters of Care: Speculative Ethics in More Than Human Worlds* (University of Minnesota Press, 2017), 70. See further Joan C Tronto, *Moral Boundaries: A Political Argument for an Ethic of Care* (Routledge, 1993), 103.
21. Maurice Blanchot, *Friendship* (Stanford University Press, 1997), 291; Tom Roach, *Friendship as a Way of Life: Foucault, AIDS and the Politics of Shared Estrangement* (State University of New York Press, 2012).
22. Kimberlé Crenshaw, 'Mapping the Margins: Intersectionality, Identity Politics and Violence Against Women of Color,' *Stanford Law Review* 43 (1993),1241; Kimberley Brayson, 'Of Bodies and Burkinis: Institutional Islamophobia, Islamic Dress and the Colonial Condition,' *Journal of Law and Society* 46(1) (2019),55-82.
23. Gayatri Chakravorty Spivak, *Outside in the Teaching Machine* (Psychology Press,

wand of visibility and invisibility, of inclusion and exclusion, of power and no power'.[24] But what happens when they don't work? I'm not saying that we must become friends with the abandoned; that a critique of rights as a relational ethics of friendship makes us the friend of our striking lecturers,[25] of Paulette Wilson, of Shamima Begum. What I am saying is that to respect the practice of freedom we need to invent modes of behaviour that surpass the code of rights. We need to do friendship—as a practice of care and shared estrangement that not only sees our complex identities but magnifies them, so we are no longer disadvantaged because we resist, or we made a mistake and/or because we are brown, female, and Muslim.

1993), 279.
24. Patricia Williams, *The Alchemy of Race and Rights* (Harvard University Press, 1991), 164.
25. Bal Sokhi-Bulley and Sara Jane Bailes, 'Are We "Friends"? Doing Friendship in Hostile Environment(s),' *Sussex Strike Collective*, 14 March 2020, accessed 31 July 2020, https://ucusussex.wixsite.com/strike2020/post/are-we-friends-doing-friendship-in-hostile-environment-s.

Concept: Space

Andreas Philippopoulos-Mihalopoulos

Despite advances in legal geography, it is still conceptually hard to see how space and law also go together. We are used to thinking of space as something material, grounded, the stuff around us; and of law as textual, abstract, immaterial. But we should try and think differently about both.

Space is of course the ground underneath our feet and the distance between us and another person or object. But it is more than that. Space is not just feet and inches—these are human-centred conventions and indeed of a specific Western variety. Space is not just a container in which we emerge, but the stuff that runs through everything. Our bodies are not just *in* space but are made *of* space (famously, an average human entrail is about 15 ft long). Space is also the immaterial understanding of psychological distance, or the phenomenological conception of how far the next village is. Finally, space is the connections and relations between the various bodies, human and nonhuman, the encounters and the conflicts, the future possibilities and even the utopian impossibilities.[1]

Similarly, we need to change our view of law. Law is not just textual, abstract and immaterial. We carry the law in our bodies, in our gestures, in our dreams: the law is embodied. We speak and read the law, but we also touch and hear the law (think of what happens when you

---

1. Doreen Massey, *For Space* (Sage, 2005)

touch someone inappropriately or when you hear a police siren right behind you). We think of the law as something that is produced in the parliament (at best) but we forget that we all produce different kinds of law everyday of our lives. We live law.[2]

Putting together space and law means that there can be no law that is aspatial, that takes place in geographical abstraction, that does not emerge from the ground. And likewise, that there is no space without law, actually or potentially. My personal contribution to the literature is the notion of the *lawscape* which suggests that law and space are coextensive. So, next time you walk down the street, think of how many laws and norms you obey (from not carrying firearms to crossing on the green light) and how many new laws and norms you create (while on a scooter, or when you always take the same route to college

---

2. Margaret Davies, *Law Unlimited* (Routledge, 2017)

Concept: Strategy

Stacy Douglas

Defund the police. Abolish prisons. Land back. These are radical slogans for contemporary social justice movements. Proponents of these campaigns do not want to see one more dollar spent on policing that serves a privileged minority, not one more cage built to advance the prison-industrial complex, and not one more argument in favour of a purportedly benevolent settler-colonialism, over and above indigenous sovereignty. Such advocates see a firm line between supporting vs. destroying systems and institutions of injustice. These slogans communicate that there is no good in working with the legal system for reform; their sentiments echo the words of Audre Lorde: 'the master's tools will never dismantle the master's house.'[1] On the other hand, there are those that argue for engagement with the systems and institutions that repress. These advocates argue that transformation can happen from within and that there is a moral and civic obligation to try and effect such change. Activists from camp A argue that those from camp B are 'liberals', blinded by a faith in false justice that is unable to account for the uneven playing field upon which our lives play out. Activists from camp B argue that those from camp A are purists and, therefore, unrealistic in their goals. Further, they contend, radical purist claims mean absolving oneself from civic action and criticizing from

---

1. Audre Lorde, "The Master's Tools Will Never Dismantle the Master's House." 1984. *Sister Outsider: Essays and Speeches.* Ed. Berkeley, CA: Crossing Press. 112

an armchair unaffected by the day-to-day realities of living under state-sanctioned oppression.

Such oppositional conceptions are intimately tied to the logic of the state. As Zygmunt Bauman and others have argued, the move to absolute classification and uniformity came hand in hand with the emergence of the modern state.[2] A requirement for governing at such a large scale, the modern state instituted systems that introduced 'territorial and functional separation,'[3] law being the preeminent mode of communicating and deciding on such matters. This drive to assimilation led to the ousting of difference, debate, and ambivalence. And yet, of course, it is part and parcel of the mythology of law to falsely narrate itself as objective and decisive.[4] While the state attempted and attempts to govern through homogenization, its logics are constantly undermined and undone; its project is always incomplete. And one way to engage both camps outlined above, is to expose this truth.

Critical legal strategy can rebuff demands to reprise oppositional thinking. Critical legal strategy can both engage with 'black letter' legal campaigns and show how such a focus is limited. For example, contemporary land claim cases in Canada demand that settler colonial law be contested so as to afford indigenous nations control over their land and lives. However, legal negotiating with the settler colonial state will not do away with its fraudulent claim to sovereignty; its foundational claim to lawful authority can and must also be challenged. Holding two positions—one of immanent legal engagement and one of transcendent critique of the law—is not a problem, but an asset. Understanding and embracing this ambivalence is also part of a critical legal strategy that refuses to fetishize the binary logic of the state. The fragility of absolute separations must be exposed in governance, as well as in the strategies we employ to confront it.

---

2. Zygmunt Bauman, "Modernity and Ambivalence." *Theory, Culture & Society* 7.2–3 (1990) 158
3. Ibid. 145
4. Peter Fitzpatrick, *The Mythology of Modern Law*. (Routledge, 1992)

37

Trusts and Kleptocracy

EQUITY AND TRUSTS LAW

Adam Gearey

A critical approach to equity and trusts strips away doctrinal obfuscation to reveal the real concerns of the subject: the ongoing transformation of a body of norms suited to the distribution of wealth.[1] The critical question: to what extent—if at all—it is possible to use trust law to make wealth visible and (at very least) tax it for the public good? Of course, the inequitable distribution of wealth is a political problem. The taxation of wealth by a capitalist state is always going to have limits. There may, however, be areas of intervention that could—at a practical level—make some differences. For instance a register of beneficial interests held in trust might allow some public record of private holdings of wealth.[2] The main objective of this essay, though, is not to

---

1. Wealth can be understood (in part) as the capture of surplus value (see fn. 15 below) produced by labour and other holdings of 'material substances' - 'material and intellectual wealth-meat as well as books' (Marx 1951 170). In defining wealth in this way, Marx is working in and against the contemporary sense of the term in political economy. Wealth may take the 'durable' form of gold and silver but it is not just a store of 'material substances.' Wealth includes the 'the whole boundless mass of immaterial values, daughters of the moral capital of civilised nations, etc.' Jérôme-Adolphe Blanqui, *Histoire de l'Economie Politique* (Brussels, 1842 152). The link with 'values' and 'moral capital' is important. In this sense, the control of wealth is the command over resources of 'civilisation': the terms of living well- both materially, and immaterially. Wealth is thus inseparable from a more general problematic political community. How can forms of political community be developed where wealth is 'shared'- to sustain decent ways of living well for all citizens?

2. See Richard Murphy, *Dirty Secrets: How Tax Havens Destroy the Economy* (Verso, 2017). The Tax Justice Network has advocated strongly for a register of beneficial interests. See www.taxjustice.net

recommend reforms. Rather, it is to encourage critical thinking about equity and trusts. If we can elaborate a Marxist approach to equity, that gives onto an understanding of the trust as a way of capturing surplus value, a node in the state-finance network, then we have made progress. We will be able to see what the subject can tell us about how the rich hide their wealth- and what we can do about it.

The conventional study of trusts is characterized by two main approaches. The text book approach presents trust law as a more or less unproblematic collection of 'black letter' rules and principles that can be learnt to achieve legal knowledge and pass exams. Whilst some books are better than others, there are few books that step outside of this paradigm. There are, though, more sophisticated scholarly engagements with trust law. These can be roughly divided into two camps. A no nonsense positivistic reconstruction of the subject as a coherent body of rules and a 'school' that argues for the distinctive ethical qualities of equity.[3] The most minimal claim put forward by this essay is that an approach that draws on Marx's ideas has more explanatory power than its rivals.[4] The more extended claim is that a Marxist approach to the subject immunises the critical lawyer from the boredom and political disconnect of black letter law. Rather than the neat articulation of rules and principles, ethical or not, we can see the subject as characterized by profound tensions; tensions that critical lawyers might be able to exploit.

But to what end?

In order to set up the argument it is necessary to examine some key concerns. A brief consideration of the history of the trust will be followed by an engagement with ideas of conscience and fiduciary office. We will then turn our attention to the law of tracing and the

---

3. For representative pieces from these two 'camps'- see James Penner, 'An Untheory of the Law of Trusts, or Some Notes Towards Understanding the Structure of Trusts Law Doctrine,' *Current Legal Problems* 63 (2010), 653-675 and Irit Samet 'What Conscience Can Do for Equity' *Jurisprudence* 3(1) (2012), 13-35.

4. This has been sketched out in the following publication: 'Equity and the Social Reproduction of Capital', *Polemos* 2017, 11 (1), 55-72; 'We Want to Live': Metaphor and Ethical Life in F.W. Maitland's Jurisprudence of the Trust' *The Journal of Law and Society*, 43 (1) (2016) and 'Equity in a Severe Style: The Phenomenology of Spirit, Conscience and Critical Legal Thinking' *Australian Journal of Feminist Legal Studies*, 2015 41 (1). See also 'The More He Argued the More Technical He Became' Surplus Value in the Law of Trusts, in Nick Piska and Hayley Gibson, *Critical Trust Law* (Counterpress, forthcoming) and 'Rereading Capital: Notes Towards an Investigation of Politics, Law and Pensions' in *Althusser and the Law* Laurent De Sutter ed., (Routledge, 2013), 111-119.

development of trust law in offshore financial centres. In order to grasp the centrality of the trust to capitalism, we will also think about how Marx's notion of surplus value can help us unlock the secrets of the trust as a legal form embedded in class relationships.

Conventional historical accounts present the trust as a technical, apolitical device that enabled the 'private law of Henry III's day' to transform itself into the 'land law of the England...of the twentieth century.'[5] Other mainstream approaches are narrowly focused on institutional change, in particular that of the court of equity and the role of the Lord Chancellor.[6] Such histories do, of course, identify important themes about the social and economic background of the law. They have also taken seriously the idea that the trust is 'inexplicable' without some understanding of the 'social environment in which it developed.' However, for the most part legal historians have fastidiously avoided any reference to class or capitalism. The story of the trust merely recounts the 'natural human desire[..]' to 'preserve and transmit family wealth.'[7] In place of such assumptions, it is necessary to open the study of the trust to a critical understanding of the role played by legal doctrine in the justification and legitimization of capitalist power.

The origins of the trust can be located in the medieval context and

---

5. Frederick Pollock and Frederic Maitland, *The History of English Law*, Volume II (Cambridge University Press, 1968), 1. Equity as a jurisdiction grew up in the early medieval period. The common law courts had developed a writ system to provide remedies in certain disputes. If a common law court could not issue a writ, a remedy would not be available. However, it was possible to petition the Crown. The work of dealing with the petitions was passed to the Lord Chancellor. The Court of Chancery, presided over by the Lord Chancellor, developed a body of rules and principles that ran in parallel to the common law and defined the jurisdiction of equity. Equity was seen to be flexible and discretionary, but, over time, equitable principles became as formalised as those of the common law. The trust was an institution invented by the courts of equity. As well as creating the trust, Chancery also developed remedies like specific performance. The Judicature Acts 1873 and 1875 'fused' the jurisdictions of common law and equity. Maitland's commentary on the Judicature Acts produced the celebrated metaphor that equity is a 'gloss or supplement' on the common law; and as such, the two bodies of law form a coherent whole. See F. W. Maitland, *Equity: A Course of Lectures* (Cambridge University Press, 1902).
6. William Rodolph Cornish and Geoffrey Clark, *Law and Society in England 1750-1950* (Sweet and Maxwell, 1989), 26-7, 71-4,126-7. Cornish and Clark do address the 'stirrings of socialism' within British political thought, but this theme is not central and remains somewhat disconnected from this discussion of equity and trusts.
7. Chantal Stebbings, *The Private Trustee in Victorian England* (Cambridge: CUP, 2002), 8. A statement that echoes Maitland's claim that the trust was 'almost essential to civilization.' See Frederic Maitland, *Equity: A Course of Lectures* (Cambridge University Press, 1949) 23.

social struggle over the distribution of landed wealth.[8] With the passing of the medieval period and the eclipse of the feudal nobility, the rising bourgeoisie reinvented the trust, but landed aristocrats were still able to use trusts to preserve their estates. Despite tensions between these class factions, there was a surprising amount of agreement over the transmission of familial wealth. Trusts of realty and personalty provided nodes around which forms of hegemony could develop. Economic changes occasioned by the interaction of mercantile, industrial and commercial capital refocused the trust around transformed land and capital markets. The trust was refined as a legal vehicle for investment, as well as developing its role as a vehicle for the preservation of dynastic wealth. In the second phase of the industrial revolution, the trust assumed its contemporary form, spurred on by the development of banking and capital markets.

In the later part of the nineteenth century, increasing prosperity encouraged a growing middle class to make use of trusts in the same way that the aristocratic elite and the *haute bourgeoisie* had done in the past. Whilst scholarship is needed to properly establish the point, it would certainly be possible to argue that the trust became adapted as a vehicle for the capture and storage of resources extracted from the colonies; indeed, the use of trusts by different social classes can be linked to the broad social commitment to a colonial order, and the growth of the financial and banking sectors of the economy. The colonial legacy of trust law can also be traced into the development of the offshore industry. The trust is now itself a commodity- a legal vehicle that can be purchased and employed by a global elite making use of offshore financial centres. Offshore trust law effectively purges the trust of its pre-modern remainders, and creates a legal superstructure suitable for the global tribute economy of late capitalism.

We want to turn from these historical themes, and examine the structure of the trust as a legal relationship. Our focus will be on the concept of conscience and the development of the fiduciary office of trustee. The genius of capitalism seizes upon institutional forms and adapts them to its own ends. Certain 'gifts' of culture are re-purposed to provide for the needs of capital (but not entirely without remainder).[9]

---

8. What historians have dubbed the 'slow moving history of the agricultural sector.' See R.S. Neale 'The Bourgeoisie has historically played a Most Revolutionary Part' in, *Feudalism, Capitalism and Beyond* ed. Eugene Kamenka and R.S. Neale (Australian National University Press, 1975), 84-104, at 94.
9. Marx speaks of the 'gifts of nature' to Capital; and this idea has been adapted to suggest that certain cultural 'gifts' are also appropriated by capital. See *Capital, Volume*

The capitalist form of the trust would be unimaginable without the centuries of development of equity.[10] Pre-capitalist legal institutions and principles cannot be seamlessly transformed. The work of transformation is the task of contemporary trust law- a form of exorcism; or at least, the negotiation of terms for the (more or less peaceful) accommodation of feudal spirits.

Conscience is fundamental to the form of the trust. Conscience can be seen as an understanding of the affective relationships between people and things. Emotional relationships between people and things are problematic, as capitalist markets require all things to be exchanged for money. From the bona fide purchaser rule to the maxims that justify the suspension of formalities in certain exceptional cases, it would seem that equity carries forward different ideas and practices. Market relationships are not just about exchange, and legal rules must do more than preserve title and the terms of its exchange. For instance, equity asserts that if a purchaser of a legal interest does not act in good faith, s/he is bound by those interests that a person acting in good faith should have taken into account. Moreover, there are compelling arguments that the letter of the law can be suspended in certain compelling situations, when fairness or justice demands. The key insight is that property relationships are never completely or properly commoditised or formalized. Our argument is that an account of equity—conventional or critical— needs to take the plasticity of the trust and equity seriously. Equity and trusts is a study in the imperfect adaptation of feudal institutions to the demands of the market.

We could elaborate this argument and suggest that an aura of ownership (even in a somewhat attenuated sense) continues to define the office of the trustee.[11] Feudal law articulated relationships in terms

---

III, Part 6, Chapter 44.

10. In this sense, trust law is a hauntology. Hauntology can be traced to Jacques Derrida, *Spectres of Marx* (Routledge, 2004). The term is used in this essay to describe the sense in which there are elements of trust law, that are disturbing for positivist understandings of the subject. The hauntological presence of 'remainders' of medieval relationships, such as the aura of ownership, are also harder to integrate into the modern law of the market than the champions of ethical equity would allow. For a hauntological approach to equity that bears some relationship to the argument presented in this essay, but cuts its own path, see Piyel Haldar, 'Equity as a Question of Decorum and Manners: Conscience as Vision' *Pólemos* (2016) 10 (2), 311-327.

11. The aura of ownership can be understood as a person-thing relationship. Notions of loyalty and hierarchy defined these relationships in the pre-modern period. The historical transition from the pre-modern to the modern could be understood as the slow dissipation of the aura of ownership. A thing, or a commodity produced for sale

of obligations of conscience, loyalty and fealty. Take, for example, the medieval law of stewardship. A steward was employed by a land owner to look after and manage agricultural resources. The proprietary remedy against the steward reflects the fact that the steward was promise bound to look after things; and if necessary to return the thing that had been lost. The aura of property was thus protected.[12]

These principles influenced equity's approach to the fiduciary office of trustee. Over the centuries the office of trustee changed as capitalism developed. The aura dimmed as the trustee was gradually subsumed under the real relationships of market capitalism and became a functionary offering services for a wage. Target Holdings v Redferns [1995] 3 W.L.R. 352 shows the courts reframing liability for contemporary managers of capital. The aura has not, however, completely dissipated. The courts commit themselves to preserving onerous duties of loyalty, and then carefully distinguish them from duties with less exacting forms of liability that are applied to trustees in breach of trust.[13]

The tangled case law around matters of third party liability for

---

on 'anonymous' markets is not 'imprinted' with relations of fealty. However, property relations still develop auras. The relation (should you be fortunate enough to have one), for example, with one's family home. One has the sense that it is somehow more than a commodity that can be sold. These peculiar relationships with things appear most markedly in intimate (or non-commercial context). Feminist work in equity has understandings of the domestic work that- although invisible to law- has both an emotional relationship with property (and even a possible legal claim). However, feminists have not made use of the notion of the aura. Developing critical thinking in equity might require working between Marxist and feminist registers to further this kind of analysis. Ernest Gellner's work on disenchantment may be essential for such projects. On the aura, see Ernest Gellner, *Reason and Culture: The Historic Role of Rationality and Rationalism* (Cambridge University Press, 1992). See Lisa Sarmas, 'The Gendered Nature of Trusts Law'. *Precedent*, vol.144, (2018), 14-17; and see also Anne Bottomley 'Women and Trust(s):Portraying the Family in the Gallery of Law' in *Land Law: Themes and Perspectives* Bright, S. and Dewar, John, ed. (Oxford University Press, 1998).

12. The aura of ownership could also be linked to the way in which the trust was used to conceal wealth and to frustrate feudal taxation. Notions of loyalty and fealty were thus themselves transformed, and opened onto notions of ownership divorced from a feudal context. Thinking this problem through also requires an engagement with the hauntological aspect of the trust. In a feudal context it anticipated the post feudal; in the modern, capitalist context, it preserves fragments of the pre-modern. The trust haunts itself. In other words, strict ideas of tautology and linear models of historical change that can be found in certain traditions of Marxist scholarship are inappropriate to the study of equity and trusts. The Derridean provenance of hauntology suggests that a different spirit of Marx may be more helpful in understanding the tricks of the trust.

13. For an elaboration of these themes from a slightly different perspective, see Robert Herian 'The Castrated Trustee: Jouissance and Breach of Trust', *Pólemos*, 11 (1) (2017), 97–115.

breach of trust reveal a similarly perturbed normative landscape. We could link the aura of ownership to tensions caused by persistent residues of ethical or moral norms in the law. Is third party liability fault based or strict? Is a restitutionary analysis more appropriate to the traditional equitable approach? Akindele v BCCI [2000] 3 W.L.R. 1423 is exemplary of these problems. Unconscionability appears to have replaced earlier attempts to divide up knowledge, as the courts flip-flop between different conceptualizations of liability. The interminable arguments over liability for dishonest assistance also seesaw between different interpretations of a concept that bears stubborn traces of affective relationships that cannot be easily expunged from commercial dealings.

Tracing can be understood against this backdrop. The doctrines of tracing deal with a fundamental problem of capitalism. Money, that great enabler and store of exchange value, can destroy title and ownership. Many of the key tracing cases concern sharp or fraudulent financial practices, but this should not distract us from inherent problems in the normal functioning of the system. How is it possible to protect the aura of ownership? It is not surprising that one of the major authorities, Re Diplock [1948] Ch 465, contains an extended mediation on the role of the spiritual courts and the control of property. Reading between the lines, one can hear echoes of the medieval fear and hatred of money. Indeed, the denunciation of the international banking clearing system by one of the foremost legal scholars is reminiscent of the encyclicals of a medieval Pope, or of the criticisms of wealth by the Venetian monk Ortes who Marx found so 'original and clever.'[14] The system 'threatens to obstruct [legal claims] as soon as transfers are made'—offering 'comfort to all launderers.'[15]

The structural problem tracing confronts is the transformation of one thing into another. What remains? What can be traced? It is indeed surprising that the most recent and inventive analyses of tracing make use of the transformations of value. However, despite the protests of its apologists, the notion of value remains problematic. Indeed, to understand value, we need to resort to the opening chapters of *Capital*. An account of value remains compromised if we cannot see through to the source of value in the exploitation of labour. Behind the commodity is socially necessary labour time predicated on class power and the

---

14. Karl Marx, *Capital Volume 1* (Lawrence and Wishart, 1977), 578.
15. Peter Birks, Overview: Tracing, Claiming and Defences in *Laundering and Tracing* ed. Peter Birks (Clarendon, 1995), 289-399, at 310.

private ownership of the means of production. Value, is not of course, surplus value, but our point is that the law of tracing does provide a partial glimpse into the realities of capitalism.

How might the concept of surplus value allow us to see more clearly what is at stake?

Behind the concept of surplus value is the idea that profits derived in the productive economy can be separated or detached from productive activity.[16] The process that produces and distributes surplus value is thus obscured. A beneficial interest—whether under a trust or a sub trust- is the legal form taken by surplus value.[17] Beneficial interests are valuable because they represent forms of surplus value- captured by public or private interests and held in trust- that can be invested or traded to capture more surplus value. Thus, Justice Hildyard's understanding of a beneficial interest as a 'right to a right' is correct.

---

16. Surplus value is a key term in Marx's thinking. The most basic way into the term is to think, at least first of all, of the idea of profit. However, profit is only one aspect of a much broader problematic. The starting point for a sophisticated understanding of surplus value is to think about an economy structured around production, distribution and exchange. Surplus value is generated in the sphere of production. Commodities are produced by the exploitation of labour power and exchanged on markets for money. Profit, if it arises, does so at point of sale. Surplus value takes a money *form*, but, this is a representation–money is not surplus value. Capitalism is driven by the ongoing search for markets and profits- its own valorisation of itself. Surplus value is produced by the exploitation of labour power in production, but it is distributed through various claims made by 'factions' of capital. As such, surplus value can take a quantitative, money form- but- the crucial point is that if one thinks only in terms of money and quantities, one loses the sense in which it is fundamentally a class relationship. Surplus value is class relationship in two senses: it is created in and through the relationship between productive capital and labour; but, there is also class struggle within capitalism over shares of surplus value. For example, if a bank has lent money to enable production to take place, then that bank will make a claim on surplus value. Likewise, surplus value may be claimed by landlords through rent. In recent years, finance capital has structured itself around the capture of value in productive economy. Property law in general- and equity in particular effectively make the sphere of production disappear. It would seem, from this perspective that 'money' (or property) is the source of value. Quite the contrary. Money conceals both the source of surplus value, and struggles over its distribution.

17. This is one form that surplus value could take. It would also be possible, for example, to see dividends as forms of surplus value. A more extended analysis could focus attention on the diverse forms that surplus value takes in law. Property itself could be analysed as 'frozen' form of surplus value; likewise (for example) the trade in uncertificated securities could be seen as another way of articulating surplus value and creating a market for its exchange. The point, of course, would be to understand the different ways in which law both articulates and conceals wealth and power.

[18] It is hardly a surprise that the 'right to a right' is the right to be a commodity—something that can be bought and sold.

It is now possible to appreciate the importance of the trust to capitalism. The trust is a way of effectively storing, exchanging and growing surplus value. In Piyel Haldar's metaphor, the trust is a greenhouse; an incubator of wealth. A beneficial interest is a form taken by surplus value once it has been *removed* from direct production and made available for investment or market exchange. The fundamental link with productive activity may come in and out of focus, but without the production of surplus value a beneficial interest would be worthless.

Against the libertarians, who see the trust as an organic form that grew out of the genius of civil society, we need to realize that the state is essential to an economic system based on the distribution of surplus value. We are concerned with particular articulations of the state-finance network where the court mediates between claims to surplus value made by different factions of capital and the state's own share of surplus value. The state's role as the guarantor of market norms also needs to be supported by the courts. The state finance network is not without its own implicit tensions. For instance, private ownership of capital is not *threatened* by the revenue raising powers of the state as it is dedicated to the preservation of market society. The court is part of this network. In other words, the court must articulate those norms that 'balance' the demands of the state for taxation, the oversight of economic systems, and the 'private right' to wealth.

These tensions play themselves out in the development of offshore trust jurisdictions. Offshore trusts are about 'business and commercial enterprise.' [19] To sustain this vision, offshore has to present itself as a 'bastion of capitalism' and 'free enterprise' bravely holding out against the tax hungry state. However, this libertarian freedom song cannot be too strident. The rebels actually require the legitimacy that a legal order can give- even if this position requires some compromise with nation state and its powers of taxation. The advocates of offshore have been particularly successful in this endeavour: 'offshore law cannot be effectively challenged if onshore states are now redefining their own legal systems so as to incorporate so-called offshore type.'[20]

---

18. *SL Claimants v Tesco* [2019] 10 WLUK 405.
19. Rose-Marie Antoine, *Trusts and Related Tax Issues in Offshore Finance Law* (Oxford University Press, 2007), 265.
20. Antoine, *Trusts and Related Tax Issues*, 266.

Thus, the offshore world defines itself in and against a growing international regulatory structure that uses various mechanisms to ensure something like compliance with international standards. Working with international agencies, and making the necessary legal changes, various offshore jurisdictions seek to show to the world that they are 'clean.' Alongside this commitment to reform, though, powerful forces seek to exploit loopholes, and push the law in directions that benefit rich clients. Thus, recent developments such as STAR or VISTA trusts refine the form of the trust, ridding it of inconvenient medieval remainders- and producing ways in which wealth can be both controlled and hidden. Critical trusts scholarship could perhaps plot these tensions–especially to the extent that they are revealed by litigation-- and shed some light on the darkness of these Augean stables.

Conclusion: Aux Armes, Citoyens ?

Maitland's famous metaphor of equity as a gloss or supplement to the common law must in turn be supplemented. Equity is sometimes disruptive, other times incorporated into the capitalist architecture like a priest hole in a renovated Tudor mansion.[21] Neither quite capitalist, nor properly pre-capitalist, neither formalized nor a field of wild discretion, equity remains a work in progress. As such it can be opened to critical interventions.

Working critically within the law of trusts is not easy. It is a technical and complex area of law. The first step is perhaps to realize the subject's plasticity. We can read trust law as the 'story' of the imperfect—and ongoing- adaptation of a medieval legal concept to the requirements of capitalism. There are tensions in the case law that emanate from this process of transformation---and the question posed by this essay is the extent to which these tensions can be exploited. But how can tensions be exploited along the lines traditionally understood by anti-capitalists? This is a difficult question to answer. Whilst it may be possible to find—for example in the law of pension trusts- fields of intervention where the interests of working people could be furthered and protected-- the argument above is more tentative. A starting point is to see the subject as organized around a thematic of wealth and its concealment. Is there a disruptive presence of ethical or moral norms within equity? Do they allow us to trace- even in a shadowy form- radical possibilities for

---

21. Acquired by a hedge fund manager and within easy commuting distance of London.

shaping markets for the common good? For the moment, the mission for the critical student of trusts (should s/he/they choose to accept) is to work on those legal strategies that might frustrate the kleptocratic global 'elite.' And make them pay.

Further Readings

- Anne Bottomley, 'Women and Trust(s):Portraying the Family in the Gallery of Law,' in Bright, S. and Dewar, John (eds) *Land Law: Themes and Perspectives* (Oxford University Press, 1998)
- Brenna Bhandar, 'Critical Legal Studies and the Politics of Property,' *Property Law Review* (3) (2014), 186-194.
- R.B.M. Cotterrell 'Power, Property and the Law of Trusts,' *Journal of Law and Society* 14 (1987), 77-90.
- Adam Gearey, 'The More He Argued the More Technical He Became' Surplus Value in the Law of Trusts, in Nick Piska and Hayley Gibson (eds), *Critical Trust Law* (Counterpress, forthcoming)
- Piyel Haldar, 'Equity as a Question of Decorum and Manners: Conscience as Vision,' *Pólemos* 10 (2) (2016), 311-327.
- Brooke Harrington, *Capital Without Borders: Wealth Managers and the One Percent* (Harvard University Press, 2017).
- Robert Herian, *Capitalism and the Equity Fetish: Desire, Property, Justice* (Palgrave Macmillan, 2021).
- Andres Knobel, Trusts, *Weapons of Mass Injustice, Tax Justice Network*, at http://www.taxjustice.net/wp-content/uploads/2017/02/Trusts-Weapons-of-Mass-Injustice-Final-12-FEB-2017.pdf
- Richard Murphy, *Dirty Secrets: How Tax Havens Destroy the Economy* (Verso, 2017)
- Lisa Sarmas, 'The Gendered Nature of Trusts Law,' *Precedent* 144 (2018), 14-17.
- Carla Spivack, 'Beware the Asset Protection Trust,' *European Journal of Property Law* 5(2) (2016), 1-26.
- Carla Spivack. 'Due Process, State Taxation of Trusts and the Myth of the Powerless Beneficiary: A Response to Bridget Crawford and Michelle Simon,' *UCLA Law Review* Vol. 67 (2019) 2.

38

Intellectual Property

INTELLECTUAL PROPERTY LAW

Ben Farrand

As a field of study, intellectual property (IP) law is mountainous. Concerned with 'the protection of the expression of ideas', which many standard textbooks will tell you,[1] any attempt to teach across the range of different subjects and issues of IP will barely scratch the surface. IP comprises copyright, the protection of creative works such as books, movies, and music; patent, the protection of inventions such as chemicals, medicines, and computer components; trademarks, the images, words, and sounds associated with undertakings and their brands; as well as a range of 'associated' or 'tangential' rights such as the protection of designs, geographical indications, trade secrets, and circuit topography. Then, there are the issues: how do we protect creative works on the Internet, where anything can be copied and shared at little cost? Should the patenting of methods of isolating genes be permitted? What about the patenting of weapons? Should geographical indications of origin be used to give a territorial monopoly over the use of a word associated with a region, such as 'Champagne' or 'Feta'? Assuming ten weeks of teaching, with two hours of lectures per week, covering all these in as much detail as it deserves is a Herculean task, if not a Sisyphean one. It stands to reason then, that the study of intellectual property law, even at undergraduate level, needs to be selective.

---

1. For example, Lionel Bently, Brad Sherman, Dev Gangjee, and Phillip Johnson, *Intellectual Property Law* 5th ed. (Oxford University Press, 2018); Abbe Brown, Smita Kheria, Jane Cornwell, and Marta Iljadica, *Contemporary Intellectual Property: Law and Policy* 5th ed. (Oxford University Press, 2019).

Narrative and Counter-narratives

There are three broader narratives about IP in which teaching about the subject can fall.[2] The first is perhaps the most typical and forms the basis of many textbooks — this is the IP mainstream. In this, the time-limited monopoly afforded to the right-holder (which including when considering journal articles or other academic writings, often is *not* the creator of the work) is a necessary trade-off for the incentivisation of new works when considered from an Anglo-American economic approach,[3] in which a 'consequentionalist' rationale based in economic incentives to produce more works, or a reward for the creation of the work by the author under a Continental European *droit d'auteur approach*[4], in which protection is afforded on the basis that it is 'right' to recognise the effort of the author. Origins and justifications for the existence of this right will often point towards theorists such as Locke (even though Locke never discussed the idea of *intellectual* as opposed to physical property),[5] Bentham,[6] and Hegel.[7] However, in much mainstream teaching of IP, these theories will largely be something touched upon in a first lecture or two, before being largely forgotten as lectures get into 'the substance'.

Another narrative that may be apparent in IP teaching is the somewhat more 'libertarian' approach that is heavily influenced by one branch of Chicago-school economics. It is an approach that is heavily critical of copyright and patent as systems of monopoly, and much of the discussion of these subjects may focus on IP's anti-competitive effects. Referenced works may include texts such as 'Against Intellectual

---

2. Given the subject matter of this textbook, this is an admittedly unnuanced approach—even within mainstream IP teaching, for example, it is possible to take a 'legal history' approach, which may critique certain developments. This approach does not tend to question the inherent worth, value, or rationale of IP however, unlike the other narratives to be discussed.
3. Robert P Merges, *Justifying Intellectual Property* (Harvard University Press, 2011).
4. Willem Grosheide, 'Moral Rights,' in *Research Handbook on the Future of EU Copyright* ed. Estelle Derclaye (Edward Elgar 2009).
5. One example and critique, can be found in Roland Spitzlinger, 'On the Idea of Owning Ideas: Applying Locke's Labor Appropriation Theory to Intellectual Goods,' *Masaryk University Journal of Law & Technology* 5/2 (2011).
6. William M Landes and Richard A Posner, *The Economic Structure of Intellectual Property Law* (Harvard University Press, 2003).
7. Kanu Priya, 'Intellectual Property and Hegelian Justification,' NUJS Law Review 1/2 (2008).

Monopoly' by Boldrin and Levine,[8] which goes into abusive uses of patents in order to prevent competition from new market entrants in arguing for the abolition of an inherently anti-competitive pseudo-property right. Kinsella would similarly argue that IP is incompatible with libertarian beliefs, and from a libertarian perspective, should be abolished.[9] Running through this narrative is a certain state-scepticism, hostility to regulation as encroaching upon liberty, and the idea that a self-correcting market for products and services are hindered as the result of corporate monopolies over culture or invention.

A final narrative is that which best fits this collection, namely the critical approaches to IP. Often drawing from other subjects, such as social justice, it critiques IP not on its compatibility or not with the thoughts of (predominantly, if not exclusively) white male thinkers from the 17th and 18th centuries, but on its merits as a system for achieving socially desirable ends. Insights here may draw from social justice theories applied to regulation in order to determine the extent to which IP brings about the benefits it purports to achieve, such as the betterment of society through making readily available literary, artistic, and health-enriching works.[10] Some work, such as that by Chander and Sunder, operates within a liberal law as justice paradigm, but insights also come from Critical Legal Studies-originating perspectives, such as Third World Approaches to International Law (or TWAIL)[11]-informed critiques of the impact of pharmaceutical or agricultural patents held by large multinational corporations on the health, well-being, and economic security of developing countries, be they in sub-Saharan Africa or South America.[12] Another critique concerns how geographical indications of origin used to protect regional territorial associations to

---

8. Michele Boldrin and David K Levine, *Against Intellectual Monopoly* (Cambridge University Press 2008).
9. Stephan Kinsella, 'Intellectual Property and Libertarianism' [2009] Liberty 27.
10. Anupam Chander and Madhavi Sunder, 'Is Nozick Kicking Rawls' Ass? Intellectual Property and Social Justice,' University of California Davis Law Review 40/3 (2007).
11. TWAIL constitutes a form of legal analysis that seeks to interrogate the colonial legacies of international law as a system, and indeed a system of thought, reorienting the study of international issues away from a 'Western liberal' perspective that often appears to deprioritise the interests and experiences of peoples and nations in Africa, South America and Asia.
12. See for example Titilayo Adebola, 'Examining Plant Variety Protection in Nigeria: Realities, Obligations and Prospects,' *The Journal of World Intellectual Property* 22/1 (2019); Ruth L Okediji, 'The International Relations of Intellectual Property: Narratives of Developing Country Participation in the Global Intellectual Property System,' *Singapore Journal of International & Comparative Law* 7/2 (2003).

food products can be used to 'protect' markets for agricultural goods in the EU against larger-scale producers in Africa.[13] Ideologically, many of these approaches can trace their arguments to Marx's writings seeking to better understand the liberal underpinnings of the IP system,[14] with insights from critical theorists such as Foucault, as well as from critical race and feminist theory.[15] These accounts place IP within the sphere of neoliberal legal activities, creating regulations that seek to commodify, individualize and economize.[16] The key divergence between these narratives and those of the 'libertarian right' on IP, however, lies in the tendency of this work to consider how the IP system can be used to benefit those who have historically suffered under it, recognising that unconstrained corporate power in the absence of regulation is likely to make a bad position worse. Or, to put it another way, in the State of Nature, rather than peaceful co-existence with large market players, the individual artist is likely to starve as the multinational entertainment conglomerate uses their work without attribution. Where critical perspectives on IP and mainstream accounts agree is that a complete absence of any protections lead to parasitic behaviours and unjust outcomes; where they differ is in what the purpose of the various forms of IP are, who they benefit, and who they *ought* to benefit.

Thinking Critically About IP? The Example of Pharmaceutical Patents and COVID-19

This divergence in narratives could not be made clearer, nor could the implications be revealed more starkly, than in considering the question of the role of patents in securing access to vaccinations to combat the spread of COVID-19. At the time of writing, COVID-19 has had catastrophic effects on human health throughout the world. By June 2021 in the UK, more than 152,000 people have died from

---

13. Justin Hughes, 'The Limited Promise of Geographical Indications for Farmers in Developing Countries,' in -*Geographical Indications at the Crossroads of Trade, Development, and Culture: A Focus on Asia-Pacific*, ed. Irene Calboli and Ng-Loy Wee Loon (Cambridge University Press, 2017).
14. Peter Drahos, *A Philosophy of Intellectual Property* (Routledge, 1996).
15. Gordon Hull, *The Biopolitics of Intellectual Property: Regulating Innovation and Personhood in the Information Age* (Cambridge University Press, 2020); Carys J Craig, 'Critical Copyright Law and the Politics of "IP",' in *Research Handbook on Critical Legal Theory*, ed. Emilios Christodoulidis, Ruth Dukes, and Marco Goldoni (Edward Elgar, 2019).
16. See, for example, Steven C Ward, *Neoliberalism and the Global Restructuring of Knowledge and Education* (Routledge, 2012).

the disease; in the US, this number is over 594,000. Vaccine efforts in these countries have progressed at an impressive rate, however, to the extent that in the UK, more than 60% of the population have received at least one vaccine dose. This has meant that despite the infection rate increasing in June resulting from the spread of the Delta variant, the NHS Providers chief executive has stated that this has helped to break the link between hospitalisations and deaths.[17] Nevertheless, this success story is not reflected in developing countries and the Global South. Brazil, for example, has seen more than 477,000 deaths from the disease, and vaccination efforts have been hampered by a lack of supply. Similarly, India has had more than 353,000 deaths, and due to the high transmissibility of the Delta variant, has seen official figures of above 400,000 daily infections in May 2021. While Indian vaccination efforts have been more successful than Brazil's, the limited supply of vaccines has hampered efforts to gain control of the situation. The entirety of Africa represents only 1% of the globally administered vaccines.

For mainstream IP narratives, the efforts to develop new vaccines against the coronavirus are a huge success. Whereas the average drug takes several years to be developed, tested, approved and disseminated, this entire process took just 362 days for the Astrazeneca and Pfizer vaccines to receive emergency use validations from the World Health Organization. The speed of the creation of these vaccines was the result of unparalleled data sharing between researchers allowing for multiple vaccines to be developed in tandem, hugely significant amounts of money being dedicated to that research, and agreements quickly being formed with pharmaceutical companies to facilitate speedy manufacturing. This, an IP-mainstream argument runs, could not have happened in the absence of strong patent protections.[18] Patents, this line of reasoning goes, allows for parties to be confident in sharing data and information in the knowledge that they can recoup their investments and ensure future profits. IP laws have therefore facilitated a quick and effective response to the pandemic as public and private sectors have cooperated in developing and disseminating a vaccine that will benefit society, in the knowledge that their financial positions are secure. This

---

17. Sarah Marsh, 'Link between Covid cases and deaths has been broken, says senior NHS boss', (*The Guardian*, 9 June 2021) https://www.theguardian.com/world/2021/jun/09/link-between-covid-cases-and-deaths-has-been-broken-says-senior-nhs-boss Accessed 9 June 2021.
18. Institut Stanislas de Boufflers, *The waiving of intellectual property: a poor response to a real problem*, Position Paper of the Stanislas de Boufflers Institute (19 May 2021)

ties in closely with the traditional philosophical justifications for intellectual property protection based in the incentivisation of invention; by incentivising new works through granting a time-limited monopoly over an invention, society ultimately benefits through the production and distribution of that invention. So ingrained is this understanding of the interaction between patents and invention that many IP textbooks will take this as an unquestioned starting point in its discussion for the rationale for granting IP rights, indicating a certain hegemonic position that this discourse possesses in this field of law. This rationale does not need to be justified, instead it *is* the justification from which all further analysis begins. However, the story of access to medicines is one that suggests that the situation is not nearly so clear cut. While there may be benefits derived from those inventions, it is necessary to interrogate whether those inventions exist and are produced purely because of that patent. For Hyo Yoon Kang, in contemporary capitalist societies, patents are less 'right' and 'incentive' and more a form of speculative form of economic security, a commodity to be bought, sold or exchanged as necessary.[19] Furthermore, they are inventions that can contribute to the perpetuation of global inequalities, particularly in the field of health. Examples abound: inabilities to secure HIV antiretrovirals in the case of South Africa due to the cost of the patented medicines; the historic lack of significant investment in treatments of diseases such as Malaria and other 'third world diseases' that are not perceived as being profitable; and now, of course, global disparities in access to COVID-19 vaccines. Academic critics of the mainstream narrative regarding the importance of strong patent protections for ensuring global access have recommended the approval of South Africa and India's request that a waiver of the international IP rules under the Agreement on Trade Related Aspects of Intellectual Property Rights (TRIPS) be granted, allowing for manufacturers to scale up production and distribution of the vaccine absent threats of litigation for breach of patent.[20] These academics point out the high levels of public subsidy provided for the production of these vaccines, and efforts to promote voluntary agreements to supply vaccines to developing nations such as COVAX and C-TAP have not been supported by patent holders.

---

19. Hyo Yoon Kang, 'Patent as credit: When intellectual property becomes speculative', *Radical Philosophy* 194 (2015).
20. Siva Thambissety, Aisling McMahon, Luke McDonagh, Hyo Yoon Kang, Graham Dutfield, *The TRIPS Intellectual Property Waiver: Creating the Right Incentives in Patent Law and Politics to end the COVID-19 Pandemic*, LSE Working Paper (2021)

While a form of flexibility exists in TRIPS to allow for the compulsory licensing of medicines under Articles 31 and 31*bis*, the historic successes of compulsory licensing have been limited, and countries seeking to use them to secure access to essential medicines have been subject to both legal and extra-legal pressures as a result. Therefore, waiving the patents for a limited time in order to facilitate the production of vaccines to benefit the Global South (and indeed, the world, by reducing the chances of new variants that are more vaccine-resistant developing) would ultimately result in a greater benefit than these medicines being protected by patents. Responses to this by mainstream IP academics have been at times withering,[21] arguing that any vaccine shortfall is not the result of the patent system, but for other reasons such as less developed supply lines of production capacity, while largely reproducing patent orthodoxy in their narrative concerning the importance of patents for innovation (suggesting that future pandemics would be worse if there was a risk that companies could not financially benefit from the medicines produced to combat that epidemic). A critical analysis would then ask, if the majority of funding for these vaccines came from the public sector, shielding the pharmaceutical companies from the economic risks, that these problems of access exist in spite of the supposed benefits of the patent system, and that the production capacity does not exist to produce them even if the right was waived, then why is a waiver so objectionable?

FURTHER READINGS

- Boldrin M and Levine DK, *Against Intellectual Monopoly* (Cambridge University Press 2008)
- Chander A and Sunder M, 'Is Nozick Kicking Rawls' Ass? Intellectual Property and Social Justice' (2007) 40 *University of California Davis Law Review* 563
- Craig CJ, 'Critical Copyright Law and the Politics of "IP"', *Research Handbook on Critical Legal Theory* (Edward Elgar 2019)

---

21. In addition to the Institut Stanislas de Boufflers paper cited at (n 18), see Reto M. Hilty, Pedro Henriques D. Batista, Suelen Carls, Daria Kim, Matthias Maping, Peter R. Slowinski, *Covid-19 and the role of intellectual property: Position Statement of the Max Planck Institute for Innovation and Competition* (7 May 2021)

- Drahos P, *A Philosophy of Intellectual Property* (Routledge 1996)
- Hull G, *The Biopolitics of Intellectual Property: Regulating Innovation and Personhood in the Information Age* (Cambridge University Press 2020)
- Kang, H.Y, 'Patent Capital in the Covid-19 Pandemic: Critical Intellectual Property Law', (*Critical Legal Thinking* 9 February 2021) https://criticallegalthinking.com/2021/02/09/patent-capi- tal-in-the-covid-19-pandemic-critical-intellectual-property-law/ Accessed 9 June 2021
- Kinsella S, 'Intellectual Property and Libertarianism' [2009] *Liberty* 27
- Merges RP, *Justifying Intellectual Property* (Harvard University Press 2011)
- Ward SC, *Neoliberalism and the Global Restructuring of Knowledge and Education* (Routledge 2012)

39

Money

BANKING AND FINANCE LAW, LAW & ECONOMICS

*Stephen Connelly**

It is common in legal studies that money be taken for granted. Students will discuss the rules of contract law using examples in which a monetary value is deemed consideration for the delivery of commodities, yet this money will be treated as just another widget to be exchanged. Damages for torts and breach of contract will be assessed in monetary terms, but the values discussed will not be critiqued. The capital invested in and employed by a corporation will be regarded formalistically in company. The situation becomes particularly troublesome for students subjected to 'law & economics' approaches, where they are invited for example to calculate when someone should accept the risk and cost of breaching a contract using monetary values that are as immutable as the numbers used to represent them. To use money uncritically in this way (and for that matter mathematics) is to deprive oneself and others of a great deal of understanding.

What is the relationship between law and money? To explore this question in an introductory manner, I suggest it is useful to explore three classes of theory about what money is: the realist or credit theory; the nominalist theory; and the conceptualist theory.

A naïve version of *realism* is this: that there is a correspondence between the material entities of the world and the ideas the mind has of them, and that universal ideas such as 'cat' or 'value' correspond to universal aspects of the material object under consideration (and its relationship to the cat species). In particular, a realist might argue that a table is made up of legs and a top, and bits of wood and nails. All these components are things, but in addition their relationship as a table is something as well. Once you see that, you notice that all things can be broken down into relationships of constituent parts which are themselves relations, and so on. Identifying what a thing is now reduces to understanding relations. In monetary terms the realist might notice that people are economically related by contracts, property rights, debts and credits, and argues that these relations are 'real'. Money is just such a real relation.

Nominalism holds that ideas have no such import; the *only* entities are the material things 'out there' and our ideas are mere fictions–the names we define for the matter we encounter. In money terms, money's significance is a fiction created by humans, and monetary value is what is agreed (or commanded) by humans. Why though should we believe one fiction rather than another? Why should some stamped metal be money and not, say, a seashell? Nominalists tend to supplement their doctrine with a theory of command: the determinant of what is true/good/money from amongst the fictions is the command that it be so by someone with authority (God/state). In simple terms: if a king says sticks are money, then they are money because the king said it.

Conceptualism holds that the universal ideas are entities but that they do not need our minds to be–concepts are also entities that subsist independently of individual minds. An idealist might say that a square table expresses the idea of a square which subsists somewhere, even when there are no squares in existence. We are more interested in various materialist accounts, which for example might argue that a human symbol expresses some complex social structure or process. Indeed, the social structure or process may well have generated the symbol. Money is a classic example of this: conceptualists (as I call them) regard money as a symbolic expression of a complex social structure (the actually existing state) or process (capitalism).

This threefold classification may be usefully compared to the Michel Aglietta's *Régulation Approach* to money.[1] 'Régulation' here does not mean technical rules issued by an authority, such as 'financial regulation'. Rather it means the way an economic system is ordered, drawing on the sense of 'regular'. The Régulation Approach is interested in the way an economic system is ordered during particular historical periods, and particularly how it manages to sustain itself in the face of crises. Over the last 40 years Aglietta has developed this classification of monetary systems:

    a. *Centralized*: this corresponds to my 'nominalism'. Under a centralized system the only money that is issued by the central

---

1. Michel Aglietta, *Money* (London: Verso, 2018).

authority, and it amounts to a debt owed by that authority. In its pure form individuals cannot incur debts; they can either only transfer goods, services, or the centralized form of money
   i. This system is very stable, but it means that a person can only buy an asset if they have assets or money of equivalent value *now* to exchange. No one can buy 'on credit'.
   ii. The only debtor is the central authority, and if it cannot pay then the whole system collapses very quickly.

b. *Système fractionné* (fractionated system): corresponds to realism and is the opposite of the centralized system. Here anyone can be debtor and creditor, and while central money may exist, the primary means of exchange are 'money equivalents' which are nothing other than debt obligations, i.e I pay you by transferring to you a debt owed by a third party..
   i. Individuals can buy on credit, both because they can owe a particular seller and because that seller can 'sell' the credit to a third party.
   ii. This system is intrinsically unstable because (a) the value of the debt varies with the particular debtor and the speculative beliefs of any transferee; (b) debts fall due at particular times–a debt owner may be required to pay others now, but only hold debt no one wants and which is due only in the future.

c. *Système hierarchisé* (hierarchical system): is not conceptualist, but a mixture of the above and corresponds most closely to today's financial systems. Here the centralized authority issues money, but also (i) permits the creation of private, negotiable debts; and (ii) operates a 'mesoeconomic' system that mediates between the two, usually through a set of banks which have a direct credit line with the central authority and which themselves 'create' money for their customers.

In what follows I discuss a nominalist, realist, and some conceptualist accounts of money. We will see that English law adopts a nominalist approach–an approach which has the effect of occluding money's deep relation both with debt and with the society in which it operates. I thus seek to place the narrow law of money within its political economic context.

English Law's Nominalism

Aristotle sought to define money by listing the functions which people have suggested it performs. Mann modernises this, suggesting that money is:
  i. a medium of exchange;
  ii. a measure of the value or as a standard for contractual obligations;
  iii. a store of wealth; and
  iv. a unit of account.

He argues that generally (i) is regarded as money's key feature, but I think it is not so difficult to run at least (i), (ii) and (iv) together in English law as aspects of the same function, namely that of being 'a fixed and unvarying "price" in terms of a unit of account that is generally accepted within a given society for payment of debt or for goods and services rendered'.[2]

For English law's view, here firstly is Dicey & Morris' definition of the nominalist theory of money:

> A debt expressed in the currency of another country involves an obligation to pay the nominal amount of the debt in whatever is the legal tender at the time of payment according to the law of the country in whose currency the debt is expressed (lex monetae) irrespective of any fluctuations which may have occurred in the value of that currency in terms of sterling or any other currency, of gold, or any commodities between the time the debt was incurred and the time of payment.[3]

This is nominalist because we do not look to the real meaning or value of £100 (in, say, gold, or even subjectively) to establish whether someone who pays £100 has satisfied their obligation so to do. Rather, £100 has been given a final, if fictional, definition by the state of issuance (the UK). £100 is a name. If £100 is stated (i.e. paid) its value is the value of its statement.[4] In this way the nominalist theory is closely linked to the command of the sovereign. A sovereign defines £100 as

---

2. (Mishkin, *The Economics of Money, Banking and Financial Markets* (New York: Addison Wesley: 1986) pp.8-9
3. Dicey & Morris, *Conflict of Laws* (2000) 13th ed., Rule 206).
4. See also *Davis Contractors Ltd v Fareham Urban District Council* [1956] UKHL 3, a contract is not frustrated just because it is a bad bargain or costs have increased; Nb. *WJ Alan & Co. v El Nasr* [1972] 2 WLR 800. Here a party accepted payment by means of letter of credit priced in an alternative currency (GBP not Kenyan shillings). The party was then estopped from demanding payment in Kenyan shilling.

100 units of 'money' and this definition is *objectively* true because its truth value is commanded by the state.

Von Mises captures the 'flatness' of legal nominalism when he distinguishes the legal from the economic definitions of money thus:

> The fact that the law regards money only as a means of cancelling outstanding obligations has important consequences for the legal definition of money. What the law understands by money is in fact not the common medium of exchange but the legal medium of payment. It does not come within the scope of the legislator or jurist to define the economic concept of money.[5]

It is interesting to compare this with Aglietta's classifications of money. The UK monetary system is not centralized but hierarchical, yet English law proceeds as if it were only centralized: there is only one kind of money, and it is what the state says is money.

When the English court has been asked to define money, rather than the obligation to pay, it discloses once again the need to refer to, but rule out, the role of debt in providing meaning:

> [money is] that which passes freely from hand to hand throughout the community in final discharge of debts and full payment of commodities, being accepted equally without reference to the character or credit of the person who offers it and without the intention of the person who receives it to consume it [6]

In searching for meaning it suggests, but dismisses, the idea that money is a kind of debt obligation. To understand these *dicta*, we must examine the conflicting proposal–that money has everything to do with creditworthiness and debt.

The Realist Account of Money

The nominalist theory regards money as a neutral factor in relations. We can imagine a sort of capitalist end-of-days scenario to grasp this, where all economic relations were wound up, and all the money in the world was 'cleared'. This would essentially mean that when all transactions are complete everyone holds some real value (a commodity) and no one holds money. The nominalist theory would see no difference when money drops from the relations. The credit theory of money, on

---

5. Von Mises, *The Theory of Money and Credit* (London: Jonathan Cape: 1953) p.69.
6. *Moss v Hancock* [1899] 2 QB 111, 116

the other hand, seeks to show that money is not neutral, but is itself a separate tradeable commodity with its own value. What is more, this value distorts '*true*' value when the commodity is priced in money. Mitchell-Innes has no link to the Régulation Approach but his account provides a very approachable illustration of one of Aglietta's *système fractionné*.

The value in question is *debt*. Money is defined as a [negotiable] debt obligation. In 1913 Mitchell-Innes proposed a thought experiment in which a simple economic grouping—a village—uses debt as a means of payment. Imagine that Desyn is a villager and a cobbler. He makes some shoes and offers them for sale to Angie, Bertie, and Charlie. Angie is a farmer; Bertie is a thatcher; and Charlie is a blacksmith; and they all want new shoes. Now in a non-monetary system it seems that they only way Desyn will part with his shoes is in exchange for goods he wants (this is called barter), and if he does not want Bertie's roofing expertise just now then Bertie will not obtain new shoes. The classical economic account would have it that at this point the village economy will fail unless money is invented. But the anthropological evidence supports Mitchell-Innes' argument that this non-fit of interests is no problem at all. At the very least Desyn will want thatching for his roof at some point in the future, and so he accepts from Bertie a promise to provide thatching when Desyn needs it. This promise is recorded, perhaps on paper, perhaps carved onto a stick, into clay, or some other medium. Desyn accepts similar promised from Angie and Charlie, and all receive their shoes.

Think about why Desyn accepted these promises. He must *believe* that Angie, Bertie and Charlie will perform their obligation when asked to do so, and it helps that he knows them personally, given that they all grew up in the same village, or at least are related to people who did. The Latin for believe is *credere* and 'he believes' is *credit*. Hence, we call Desyn's assessment that Bertie and the others will keep their promises in the future as credit, and the attribute of being so credible as *creditworthiness*.

Presently Desyn requires goods for his own purposes, and so he goes to Ephraim, Farhad and Gethin, who respectively produce chicken eggs, wine and hats. Again Desyn could exchange shoes for these commodities but if the sellers do not want shoes he now has two possible solutions: (a) he can promise to each of E, F and G that he will provide shoes when demanded; or (b) he could transfer to them the promises of A, B and C to provide goods or services. For example, if Farhad needs his roof fixing then he may accept Bertie's promise to Desyn that he fix a roof, that promise now being transferred to Farhad. In effect Desyn has paid for wine using a promise of a third party; in other words, Mitchell-Innes argues, the promise has become money.

We can make certain comments about what has happened here:
a. A legal point: that while the debt is a contractual obligation to deliver goods or services, we are not interested in the promise as an obligation but rather as some property capable of being transferred to someone else. Just observe that contract law and property law are two distinct methodologies or discourses for judging a state of affairs (and it matters not as between themselves that they be in contradiction).
b. A political economic point: that in this system money arises as the set of promissory relationships within the village. It arises from below, so to speak, and because money is said to originate in relations the credit theory of money could also be called a realist theory, in the sense that reality is defined as all the relationships between things.
c. A political theoretic point: that this model of promissory relations bears comparison with Hobbes' social contract theory.

Returning to the village, Mitchell-Innes now introduces the moneychanger into the equation such that all participants come to regard this new person's obligations to pay as most creditworthy, again by reference to moneychanger's ability to pay but also acceptability to any villager as a promisor. Why? Well, whereas the villagers all specialized in their various trades, the moneychanger specializes in this: the assessment of creditworthiness. If Desyn holds an Angie debt, he could loan this to moneychanger and moneychanger will promise to 'repay'. This is particularly useful if no one trusts Angie but the moneychanger. The moneychanger potentially accepts debt that no one else would. Now Desyn has moneychanger debt and he can buy goods in exchange for it. The moneychanger debt will be accepted if people regard moneychanger as creditworthy, and the fact that moneychanger now may hold significant amounts of other debts deposited him would suggest that he is capable of meeting his obligations.

So, for example, Desyn deposits Angie's debt with moneychanger, and in exchange Desyn now holds moneychanger debt. He purchases goods from Ephraim in exchange for a promise by Desyn to deliver some service. Ephraim then deposits this debt with moneychanger, who issues new moneychanger debt to Ephraim. At the close of the day, moneychanger looks at his table and sees that he owes Desyn, but that thanks to Ephraim's deposit he has a debt now owed to him by Desyn. So, what does he do? He simply 'sets off' the debt Desyn owes to him against the debt he owes to Desyn. If we assume that the two cancel each other out we are left with a debt owed by Angie to Moneychanger, and a debt owed by Moneychanger to Ephraim. The moneychanger will set off many such debts at the end of each business day in a process called *clearing*.

Observe now what the medieval moneychanger is doing. He acts as a kind of translator of credit worthiness between people who do not have enough information about each other or do not otherwise trust each other sufficiently. By acting in this way, the villagers need not stop at the bounds of their immediate community but may deposit with the moneychanger debts owed by persons from other villages, and even towns and cities far away. Medieval moneychangers developed networks of bankers to assess local creditworthiness and clear debts in distantly spread trade networks. Suddenly individual, highly specific communities of social indebtedness become bound together by these trans-community debt relations mediated through the language of early finance. And it was finance, for nothing required the moneychanger to wait for deposits in order to issue bank debt; the moneychanger could initiate the whole process by issuing the bank debt to someone like Desyn in exchange for a promise by Desyn to repay—the making of a loan.

As David Graeber has noted, the anthropological evidence for these practices are widespread and go back to Sumerian times. Furthermore, the things people used to record these debts were remarkably varied, from shells, to annotated wage slips, to tally sticks, to dried fish: all cases in which money in the legal, nominalist sense was simply not present. Yet law, or at least normativity, was present. Modern law regards these debts as obligations but refuses to regard them as money. So be it. But by doing so the law blinds itself to the functional equivalence of state-issued monies and the variety of real money relations constituted as between people, more often than not today via the mediation of private banks. That is why economists will speak of bank money. After all, that is what you pay with when you use your contactless debit card.

We should not, though, be so quick to jump from our ideal village to modern bank money. Of the greatest interest is the origin of the real money in the community of obligation; in a kind of morality of indebtedness linked to whether someone is credible. On the one hand, you might think that someone like Angie who does not repay would be morally condemned by everyone in her community for breaking her promise. Yet there is just as much evidence that in some communities, repayment of a debt is an insult: being bound to someone enhances community ties, whereas repayment is the clearest statement that one wishes to end a the communal relationship.[7] You should ask yourself: in the history of debt, what effect did the invention of bank money have on these communal relationships?

Some Conceptualist Theories

Broadly what unites conceptualist theories is an account of money which regards the money form as an expression or appearance of some underlying process. Of these theories, some could be said to tend to idealism in that they regard money not unlike a religious symbol that signifies an incommensurable ideal entity, be it ancestors, gods or *the* God, or the state or nation. Others tend to be materialistic, regarding money as an expression of concrete economic processes and our valuation of them.

The Violence of Money

By way of example, Aglietta & Orléans[8] use the theologico-literary theory of René Girard to argue that money arises from an originary violence to become the bearer of all our desires and indeed hates. In a mirror-image of Hobbes, Girard argues that where a person desires the other it is but a short series of steps from failing to obtain this object of desire to, firstly, seeking to emulate that person and, secondly, desiring those objects which the other desires. For Aglietta & Orléans this leads to a conflict over attainment of the desired object; to violence and possibly death. Simply agreeing not to fight as per a social contract will not do; rather, the monarch emerges to perform two functions: (a) as with Hobbes, the Leviathan-monarch is capable of a sovereign violence with which the individual cannot hope to contend; but more fundamentally (b) the Leviathan-monarch is the desirable other *par excellence*–a desirability accentuated by the excess of its incontestable power. Again, we find the individual seeking to emulate the desired other by seeking that which the other desires: wealth. Aglietta & Orléans argue that with the issuance of sovereign coin, and the demand of its return through taxation, money becomes the desired

---

7. See for example Graeber, *Debt* (New York: First Melville House, 2011) p.100.
8. Michel Aglietta & André Orléans, *La violence de la monnaie* (Paris: PUF, 1982).

object of all. This process has the advantage of deferring all particular struggles between persons away from individual objects and onto a generic object of desire which maintains this status precisely because sovereign violence is all but insurmountable.

In the third stage identified by Aglietta & Orléans, money escapes the control of the sovereign as mercantile trade develops across borders, and both coin and credit monies circulate. Money is abstracted from the body of the sovereign and now circulates as a symbolic bearer of an ideal sovereign power representative of the circulating 'wealth of nations' as a whole. Money in a sense becomes attainable; the original conflict between particular persons for an individual object is taken up as a generalized conflict between all persons for an object characterized as having no intrinsic value save that it be the object desired by everyone else. Speculation is now understood as a modern instantiation of originary violence in which financiers, seeking to imitate each other, battle for control of the object of desire, and its speculative 'value' reflects nothing other than this desirability.

Primordial Debts

Michel Aglietta has subsequently sought to play down the more poetic aspects of this theory of money's violence, but subsequently members of the *Régulationist School* finessed some of these findings into what is known as 'Primordial Debt Theory'. The core of the theory is that monetary policy and social policy are the same thing because money and society are linked through debt. This sounds similar then to the credit theory of money, but whereas a realist argues for the reality of common ideas as intrinsic parts of entities (a particular debt relation between persons is part of each unit of money), Primordial Debt Theory adopts the conceptualist stance that these debts become abstracted from real relations and are transferred to a notional creditor such as the ancestors, gods, or the community as a whole. Money then expresses this incommensurate debt relation that each person owes to this abstract entity. Bruno Théret qualifies this by claiming that that which is expressed is the state.[9]

Théret draws on the idea, due to Feuerbach, that humanity creates its own gods. He writes:

---

9. Bruno Théret, 'The Socio-Political Dimensions of the Currency: Implications for the Transition to the Euro,' *Journal of Consumer Policy*, 22 (1999) 51-79.

At the origin of money we have a 'relation of representation' of death as an invisible world, before and beyond life–a representation that is the product of the symbolic function proper to the human species and which envisages birth as an original debt incurred by all men, a debt owing to the cosmic powers from which humanity emerged.

Payment of this debt, which can however never be settled on Earth–because its full reimbursement is out of reach–takes the form of sacrifices which, by replenishing the credit of the living, make it possible to prolong life and even in certain cases to achieve eternity by joining the gods. But this initial belief-claim is also associated with the emergence of sovereign powers whose legitimacy resides in their ability to represent the entire original cosmos. And it is these powers that invented money as a means of settling debts–a means whose abstraction makes it possible to resolve the sacrificial paradox, by which putting to death becomes the permanent means of protecting life. Through this institution, belief is in turn transferred to a currency stamped with the effigy of the sovereign–a money put in circulation but whose return is organized by this other institution which is the tax/settlement of the life debt. So, money also takes on the function of a means of payment.

Théret draws on Auguste Comte and French revolutionary tradition to argue that the state is the secular God that occupies the place of the originary creditor, granting us security, health, learning. The state however is to be understood not as the sum of public institutions but the product of living social-economic relations. Théret envisages a currency like the euro both symbolically representing the European Union *and* actively fostering the further social communality of European citizens.

A number of arguments can be adduced against Primordial Debt Theory:

a. As with Hobbes' State of Nature, Primordial Debt Theory largely rests on a pseudo-historical fiction.
b. The concept of state debt is never fully identified and one might say that Primordial Debt Theory proponents are not describing a social datum but construing various sub-facts to fit their theory.
c. Credit theory identifies a relationship between persons. Primordial Debt Theory supposes a 'relationship' between each person and some ineffable which arguably includes that same person, being a taxpayer. Whether this structure is sound or not, it no longer describes a debt relationship (I cannot owe myself).
d. Théret places considerable weight on the role of the Euro as a unifying currency. It is questionable whether the Euro has had the predicted effect of uniting the EU socially.

Yet what Primordial Debt Theory allows us to do is appreciate the flatness and paucity of law's understanding of money. When we are invited to reduce matters of law, particularly contract law, to a comparative analysis of price, the appearance of arithmetic neutrality amounts to nothing more than a comfort blanket against the deep social issues at play behind the money form.

Imperialism

As a final example of a conceptualist theory, we might consider an account inspired by the speculative hypothesis of RM Cook[10] as to how the Athenians invented coinage. Athens pursued a policy of expansion, but the conquest of other city states generated a common problem for the Athenian military–overlong supply chains. A force that remained unfed due to delay in delivery of supplies, or broken supply chains, could become mutinous. The Athenians needed an efficient just-in-time way to feed troops, and the answer was involved the invention of money.

Consider a small Greek town, and for arguments sake it has three factors of production: a smith, a tanner and a farmer. The farmer acquires just enough leather clothes and shoes from the tanner, and just enough tools (like a plough) from the smith, and in exchange he provides the tanner with animal hides and food, and the smith with food. The smith (who we pretend is happy to repair and sharpen existing tools) supplies these to the farmer and the tanner, and he also receives clothes, an apron, and shoes from the tanner. The tanner, duly supplied by farmer and smith, gives them just what they need. The key here is that everything that is consumed in this town is produced by this town. It is *autarkic*—there is no additional demand that it produce more, nor any internal shortfall, and it does not produce a surplus.

On conquering such a town, a representative of Athens would proclaim this law: that every year each person must pay a tax. This was not original; people has had to pay tithes of corn or hides before. What was new was that this tax was to be paid in Athenian coin. All very well, but 'Where,' asked the new subjects, 'were they to find coin? It doesn't grow on trees.' The clever response was that the coin was to be found in the pockets of the soldiers, who were paid with it. Clearly the subjects could not rob the soldiers; to obtain the coin they had to trade for it–meet the demand of the soldiers (food, wine, 'entertainment'

---

10. I owe this reference to Graeber.

etc.). The result was twofold: not only did the soldiers receive their much-needed supplies at the point of need, but in order to meet the tax requirement the subjects re-configured their economic activity to meet the soldier's demand. An autarkic town (a town that could feed itself) suddenly had to feed an army and pay tax, in addition to feeding itself. Thus, newly conquered regions were integrated economically within the Greek military apparatus. Autarkic towns were now subjected to an external demand which could only be met by a reconfiguration of the mode of production in those towns. On the due date taxes were collected and the coin was taken back to Athens. For what purpose? To be sent out again as pay for conquering soldiers, thus reinitiating the whole military economic cycle and sustaining a new social reality we can call the state, or even a kind of imperialism.

Graeber gives a modern example of this from imperial colonialism. General Gallieni deployed a *taxe moralisateur* in Madagascar for precisely this purpose–the duty to pay tax would cause the Malagasy to move from subsistence farming to growing cash crops to feed metropolitan France. This was because only cash crops could be sold for Francs, delivery of which was a requirement of tax policy. The Malagasy resisted this for some time; even when they were made to harvest sugar cane there are reports that the cane would be burnt in great bonfires in village centres, depriving the French of the commodity. Ultimately the weight of war's economic force won through.

By relating nominal money and real debt relations to a third term–the singular power of a sovereign to impose a tax–I claim we have slightly better understanding of the conceptual nexus that drives money in the general sense. The concept is the process constituted by these three terms: the particularity of the money name, the general relations of indebtedness in the economy in question, and the specificity of the sovereign imposition.

Conclusion

We seem to have travelled far from law's judgement that money is just whatever the state declares it to be. Yet law has been with us all the way. The realist theory is not pure economics; as debt relations break away from personal knowledge of the debtor to abstract bank monies, law steps in to recognise that an obligation is itself properly capable of alienation and enforcement. The law does not call these obligations money, but these obligations serve a monetary function *and* law likewise serves that function in recognising the obligations as enforceable, even when alienated to third parties. At this stage, however, law feels subordinated to the real and is arguably a supplementary feature of the realist account. With conceptualist theories, however, law is reintegrated into the money form because particular debt obligations cease to be the signified of a given debt obligation or money token. Money now is the expression or, if you will, *appearing* of a god, state, or concrete economic relations as a whole. The abstract legal fiction (be it money, debt obligation, share, security), shorn of any particular relation, functions as a symbolic differentiator. On the one hand it reveals the incommensurable by signifying sovereign, state, god, economic system; on the other it draws a veil over the violence of money by distracting our attention towards that symbolic abstraction. We must appreciate therefore that 'rules and legal institutions…are not merely cover for pre-existing economic relations; they in fact enable their conception and development'.[11]

---

11. (Lyon-Caen, A. & Jeammaud, A., *Droit du travail, démocratie et crise*, (Arles: Actes Sud, 1986):p.9.

40

Technology with Legal Education

LEGAL EDUCATION, BLOCKCHAIN, LEGAL THEORY

Robert Herian

During this chapter I offer a brief account of technologies with legal education and present a case for the importance of studying technological effects on law. At the heart of that relationship is a tension between the latter (slowly) recognizing the unavoidability of the former in its future. The following discussion draws on aspects of my research on blockchains within Anglo-American common law jurisdictions, and my wider research on law, data, and technologies. Distributed ledger technologies (DLTs), of which blockchains are a species, are a form of ICT infrastructure used across commercial and civic sectors. The Bank of England explains the operation of DLTs as 'a database architecture which enables the keeping and sharing of records in a distributed and decentralized way, while ensuring its integrity through the use of consensus-based validation protocols and cryptographic signatures.'[1] In reality, the bulk of present DLT use-cases involve financial services. These 'ledgers' are cryptographically secure databases for storing and recording novel forms of digital property (e.g. tokenized securities[2]), relying on quasi-legal forms, chiefly 'smart contracts', to transact across networks without prejudice.[3] Here I am interested in

---

1. Bank of England (2017) The economics of distributed ledger technology for securities settlement. Staff Working Paper n.670. Available at: https://www.bankofengland.co.uk/-/media/boe/files/ working-paper/2017/the-economics-of-distributed-ledger-technology-for-securities-settlement. pdf?la=en&hash= 17895E1C1FEC86D37E12E4BE63BA9D9741577FE5 [Accessed: 10 February 2021]
2. See, for example: https://www.sygnum.com/ [Accessed: 10 February 2021]
3. Robert Herian, 'Smart contracts: a remedial analysis' (2020b) 30(1) *Information and Communications Technology Law* 17.

two aspects of DLTs. First, how DLTs and their stakeholders make use of and exert control over particular legal forms and vernacular (i.e. property, contracts, etc.). Second, how legal education, in providing the underpinnings for legal practice and helping to shape legal ideas, confronts and deals with technological phenomena such as DLTs to ensure the integrity of tomorrow's lawyers and legal thinkers.

The Language of the New

Like learning any new system of language, legal education has a significant role to play in the general reception and adoption of technologies by society. This may not seem obvious at first blush and, I argue, legal education in England and Wales does little to express the deep technological contexts in which legal subjects are embedded. This is a mistake. It is no longer workable for legal education, or the different legal environments it feeds, to pick whether technologies matter. Of course, some matter to the law more than others, or rather are of greater legal significance. I use the term 'technologies' generally here, but it is reasonable to argue that, for example, surveillance technologies (drones, CCTV, face-recognition algorithms, etc.,) ought to be of greater concern to law's social and political obligations than other technologies. Perhaps only because such technologies, and the law-and-order strategies that rely on them, arouse greater moral outrage?

Technology affects humanity, non-humanity, and the environment in many direct and indirect ways. Many technologies also shape the methods and purposes of other technologies in an onward chain of global techno-mobilization occurring machine to machine. This is so with aspects of artificial intelligence (AI), machine learning algorithms, and the distributed networks that encompass DLTs and blockchains. As a result, there are several factors we need to take into consideration when approaching the subject of technologies with law. A key one which does not concern the engineered tool or object we refer to as a *technology*, is the language and jargon of technologies. This includes what such language conceals, yet still contributes to the pervasive techno-morality we all find ourselves enmeshed in and from which laws develop.

Design, engineering, and implementation determine how technologies are spoken of by technologists, stakeholders, and acolytes. Adopters of technologies, whether early or late, savvy or ignorant, thus find themselves amongst a language barely understood. The language of our technologies commands us as much as the technologies themselves. We 'speak in tongues' in the Information Age of data, apps, bytes, bits, uploading, downloading, logging on, and so on. As users of ICTs and subscribers to online platforms, humanity is interpolated by powerful and growing ecosystems that create physiological and psychological change in the individual. Change that offers little or no time for acclimatization, yet renders identities anew as a priority in the historical march of informational societies.[4] Socialization through and by technology is symptomatic of our existence in the twenty-first century affecting all areas of life, including the law. Legal education, therefore, must confront these effects, which means understanding how they transform law itself.

There are always problems getting to grips with the language of the new. But it is perhaps comforting to recognize that this is a fundamental legal task, and that lawyers, therefore, are well-placed to understand and interpret these strange languages and alien concepts. I refer here to how technologists speak about technologies, but also to the code that technologies and software are themselves written in. 'Whenever something online appears to be simple, indeed 'whenever anything at all is done online', claim Ethan Katsh and Orna Rabinovich-Einy, 'there is a great deal of complexity hiding somewhere in the background [...] the magic of software *hides* complexity, thus providing the users of well-designed software with the illusion of simplicity. The interface may be simple to use but the infrastructure is anything but.'[5]

Melanie Swan makes a similar point: 'new technology application's pass into public use without much further consideration of the technical details as long as appropriate, usable, trustable, frontend applications are developed'.'[6] Terms such as 'spreadsheet' or 'ledger', therefore, conceal the fact that a DLT or blockchain is, to paraphrase Alexander Galloway, 'a decentralized network composed of many different data fragments.'[7] We cannot expect lawyers (leaving to one side patent attorneys) to understand the full complexity of technologies at the level of engineering. Of primary importance, therefore, is to understand what informs or lies beneath the language of technologies, including the contexts (social, cultural, economic, and political) in which they operate.

---

4. Manuel Castells, *The Rise of the Network Society* (Wiley-Blackwell, 2010), 22.
5. Ethan Katsh and Orna Rabinovich-Einy Orna. *Digital Justice: Technology and the Internet of Disputes* (Oxford University Press, 2017), 76.
6. Melanie Swan. *Blockchain: Blueprint for a New Economy.* (O'Reilly, 2015)
7. Alexander R. Galloway. *Protocol: How Control Exists After Decentralization.* (MIT Press, 2014), 64.

Blockchains are a good of example of this. Described in a convenient and recognizable form, 'a ledger', normalizes a blockchain by accessible comparison, but it also situates that blockchain within the *long durée* of double entry bookkeeping and thus technologies as central to performing capitalism. The plain language of 'the ledger' invokes important bureaucratic features, such as auditability, accountancy, and calculability. But it also aims to normalize and thus encourage adoption of a technology that, I argue, makes the line between consumer and citizen fainter.[8] The language of blockchain, we can say, is the primary symbolic system used to give the social reality of the technology an intelligible form. Hence in a RAND Europe and British Standards Association (BSI) 2017 report it was proposed that there was a need to focus on terminology and vocabulary as a short-term goal in determining standards to support the development of the technology).[9]

Smart contracts are another good example of how a new technological paradigm skews language, and in this case the specific legal terminology of 'contract' With smart contracts we find a rather confused mix of definitions. Some play-down the legal validity of smart contracts by claiming that 'contract' refers to a programming convention rather than a legal instrument. While others, such as the *Blockchain Technology Act* passed by the Illinois General Assembly (IL-HB553), invoke the authority of a smart contract as a record stored and verified on a blockchain. This is not the place to delve, in depth, into smart contracts—something I have covered at length elsewhere—but it is worth noting how smart contracts are an important example of technology changing laws directly and indirectly.[10] Not only do they transform our view of the law of contract, but also of the law of property and conceptions of obligation, all of which are longstanding conventions of private law placed into question by the forms and processes that smart contracts represent.

---

8. Robert Herian, 'Blockchain, GDPR, and fantasies of data sovereignty' 12(1) *Law, Innovation and Technology* (2020)156
9. Advait Deshpande, Katherine Stewart, Louise Lepetit, and Sali Gunashekar. *Understanding the landscape of Distributed Ledger Technologies/Blockchain: Challenges, opportunities, and the prospects for standards.* (RAND Corporation, 2017) xiii.
10. Robert Herian, 'Smart contracts: a remedial analysis' 30(1) *Information and Communications Technology Law* (2020) 17.

Something Happening Here

We do not have to look hard to see a refraction of legal conventions by different technologies. But technologies, in turn, offer us novel ideas and practices that may find their way into law. This is something that legal education must seize upon. For example, my first foray into legal analyses of blockchains looked at trust. An overlap (homology) between the 'post-trust' promised by blockchains to counter-parties transacting online who are unlikely to know and, therefore, trust one another (a key the rationale of Bitcoin, for instance), and the equitable concept of trusts involving separation of legal and beneficial ownership.[11] Whilst there are several things we can say about the philosophy, politics, and psychology of trust relating to blockchains, it was a fundamental question of technology redefining an ancient legal mechanism (trusts) that interested me. What begins with a simple slip from one definition to another, therefore, develops into an analysis that runs deep into the seams of laws that have held fast for centuries. Crucially, we see through these analyses the threat or potential for technology to unpick those legal seams.

This is a terrifying prospect for conservative legal thought and practice, not least because the speed of technological evolution pushes law to think faster than it is comfortable doing. 'Agility' has become a byword for neoliberal subjectivity in the forging of entrepreneurial subjectivity. To be agile is to bend and work with prevailing economic winds. Technological 'disruption' is key to agility, and, therefore, as a critique of neoliberalism—simply defined by Richard Wolff and Stephen Resnick as a 'renewal of private forms of capitalism'[12]—we can point to the slow flow of the law as an important brake on ever accelerating progress. The threat that technology might summarily overturn the steady and certain applecart of the law thus invites scepticism and restraint from legal quarters (and beyond). The correct response is not to bury one's head in the sand, however. As an opportunity to experiment with the law, legal education can confront the looming spectre of technological disruption head-on and, by extension, place checks on neoliberal strategies. Technologies or law are never ascendant or unassailable truths. They are ripe for challenge and change. Legal

---

11. Robert Herian, 'Blockchain and the (re)imagining of trusts jurisprudence' 26(5) *Strategic Change: Briefings in Entrepreneurial Finance* (2017) 453
12. Richard D. Wolff and Stephen A. Resnick. *Contending Economic Theories: Neoclassical, Keynesian, and Marxian*. (MIT Press, 2012), 336

education ought not to pick sides between the two so much as consider hermeneutics of technology with law (or *vice versa*). The two reveal much about one another and it would be wrong to use one as a stick to beat the other.

While a coherent discipline—or perhaps this is the root of the problem—law and technology has never been a core area of legal knowledge taught as part of the qualifying law degree (QLD) in the law schools of England and Wales. Even though the QLD, as the main contemporary form of legal education in England and Wales, emerged and developed in step with the rise and amid public fears of 'data bank societies' from the late 1960s, technology remains peripheral.[13] Few traditional areas of legal knowledge—contract, constitutional, tort, equity, etc.—address the role technologies play in shaping them. Technology, it would seem to me, in the estimations of conventional legal education, is something that happens in the background, not something that shapes the social contexts in which law operates.

Conclusion

Legal education involving computer coding is increasingly commonplace, especially in the North American system, enabling the lawyers of tomorrow to read, interpret, and draft the language of sophisticated self-executing, intelligent computer contracts (e.g. smart contracts run by AI) and not just the natural language of dusty old calligraphic deeds or boilerplate terms and conditions. But if there is any truth to the long-held belief that law's inherent conservatism leads it to trail too far behind innovation, legal education provides abundant examples to support this belief. Simply, it is not good enough for lawyers or legal academics to ignore the role technologies *expressly* play in shaping legal knowledge, understanding, and processes.

---

13. Malcom Warner and Michael Stone. *The Data Bank Society: Organizations, Computers, and Social Freedom.* (George Allen & Unwin Ltd, 1970)

www.ingramcontent.com/pod-product-compliance
Lightning Source LLC
Chambersburg PA
CBHW071727080526
44588CB00013B/1923